WELFARE: THE ELUSIVE CONSENSUS • Where We Are, How We Got There, and What's Ahead

WELFARE POLICY PROJECT
of the
Ford Foundation
and the
Institute of Policy Sciences
and Public Affairs of
Duke University

ADVISORY COMMITTEE

John Dempsey
Mitchell I. Ginsberg
Tom Joe
Stanford Kravitz
Juanita M. Kreps*
Joan Leiman

Leonard Lesser
Steven Minter
Richard Nathan
Bert Seidman
Jule Sugarman**
Alair Townsend

* Mrs. Kreps, now Secretary of Commerce, was Vice Chancellor at Duke University when she served as a member.

** Mr. Sugarman, now a member of the U.S. Civil Service Commission, was Administrator of the City of Atlanta when he served as a member.

WELFARE: THE ELUSIVE CONSENSUS • Where We Are, How We Got There, and What's Ahead

Lester M. Salamon

Foreword by McGeorge Bundy

An Analysis of President Carter's Program
by Harvey D. Shapiro

Summary of Public Opinion Surveys
by Natalie Jaffe

and Summaries of Papers by
Edward K. Hamilton and Francine F. Rabinovitz,
Sar A. Levitan, David W. Lyon, Abe Lavine,
Herman P. Miller and Roger A. Herriot,
and William Lee Miller

PRAEGER PUBLISHERS
Praeger Special Studies

New York   •   London   •   Sydney   •   Toronto

Library of Congress Cataloging in Publication Data

Salamon, Lester M
  Welfare, the elusive consensus.

   1. Public welfare--United States. 2. Income main-
tenance programs--United States. I. Shapiro, Harvey
D. II. Title.
HV95.S23   361.6'2'0973   78-12163
ISBN 0-03-045601-0

PRAEGER PUBLISHERS, PRAEGER SPECIAL STUDIES
383 Madison Avenue, New York, N.Y. 10017, U.S.A.

Published in the United States of America in 1978
by Praeger Publishers,
A Division of Holt, Rinehart and Winston, CBS, Inc.

89   038   987654321

Printed in the United States of America

FOREWORD
McGeorge Bundy

Efforts to reform the welfare system have become a staple of American political life. They stem from a widespread sense of unease, concern, and frustration over welfare. But success has eluded us because the political combination to enact basic reform could not be put together.

The political problem has its roots, at least in part, in the tension over different sets of values that Americans cherish and that collide when they try to deal with welfare policy. On one hand, our ethos demands, in the name of equity and compassion, that the fortunate assist the less fortunate. At the same time, we believe that everyone who is able to work should work and earn a living. This leads to a division in our minds and feelings about the deserving poor and those who we suspect do not merit public assistance because somehow they are irresponsible or do not try hard enough to work.

In addition there is a host of other issues—some administrative, others relating to federal-state-local responsibilities and relationships, and still others stemming from the heterogeneity of what is often called the welfare population. These issues make the development of an equitable and efficient welfare system one of the most knotty and resistant problems on the country's agenda.

Some two years ago, while the nation was in recess on welfare in the wake of the divisive debate over the Family Assistance Plan in the early seventies, the Ford Foundation received suggestions that it help get a new effort at reform underway. The thought was to bring together some of the best thinkers and the most experienced policymakers and administrators to develop new approaches and options. We did so, in cooperation with the Institute of Policy Sciences and Public Affairs of Duke University. After extensive discussions, the group decided that the most useful service the Foundation could render toward this objective would be to gather pertinent information and support some careful studies of where we stand in welfare, how and why we got where we are, and where we might go from here. It was hoped that such information and analysis could be of help to localities, states, and the new administration that would take office in January 1977.

What follows is a distillation of that effort. The full set of materials was completed and reproduced by the Foundation in the summer of 1977, and distributed widely to policymakers, administrators, academicians, journalists, public-interest groups, and others concerned with welfare policy. In an effort to make the material still more widely available, it was decided to publish a condensed version of the materials in this form. The present volume reproduces in full the overview of the problem that also leads the earlier set of documents. It was written by Lester M. Salamon, a political scientist at Duke University who is currently with the federal Office of Management and Budget. Also reproduced is an essay on President Carter's welfare program by Harvey Shapiro and a brief summary of public opinion surveys, by Natalie Jaffe.

The rest of the volume consists of summaries, prepared by the authors themselves, or approved by them, of their larger and more technical contributions to the project:

- An economic analysis of proposals for the federal government's absorption of welfare programs in order to provide fiscal relief for hard-pressed state and local governments (by Edward K. Hamilton and Francine F. Rabinovitz).

- An examination of efforts and programs to link work with welfare (by Sar A. Levitan).

- An examination of who is in the welfare population at any given time and how much movement there is into and out of this group (by David W. Lyon).

- A report on problems of welfare administration and techniques to improve the management of income security programs (by Abe Lavine).

- An analysis of microsimulation as a tool for estimating costs and participation rates under various income assistance programs (by Herman P. Miller and Roger A. Herriot).

- Condensation of an essay on American values that impinge on welfare policy (by William Lee Miller).

We are grateful to all these authors and also to the members of the advisory group that helped the project. We believe this work can help the public dialogue that lies ahead.

McGeorge Bundy

CONTENTS

LIST OF TABLES

WELFARE: THE ELUSIVE CONSENSUS • Where We Are, How We Got There, and What's Ahead

1

INTRODUCTION: THE DILEMMAS OF REFORM

> If we are to restore confidence in government, the first order of business must be action on welfare reform.
>
> —Elliot Richardson

> Whatever happened to all those welfare reform proposals—a whole litany of them. What happened to them?
>
> —Daniel Flood

> The most important unanimous conclusion is that the present welfare programs should be scrapped and a totally new system implemented.
>
> —Jimmy Carter

In fiscal year 1977, the federal government spent approximately $200 billion, or 48 percent of its total budget, on income assistance programs.[1] This total included $149 billion in so-called contributory programs like social security, unemployment compensation, and Medicare; plus an additional $51 billion in various public assistance programs like Aid to Families with Dependent Children (AFDC), food stamps, subsidized housing, and Medicaid. Taken together, these sums represent a staggering jump of more than 600 percent over what the federal government was spending for income assistance activities a decade ago, in fiscal year 1966, when these programs cost the federal government only $32 billion and accounted for 24 percent of the total budget.[2]

In the face of this rocketing growth, Senate Budget Committee Chairman Edmund Muskie felt obliged to authorize a special study in 1975 to assess whether this seemingly endless growth was destined to consume the remainder of the federal budget as well, by the end of the century. Although the resulting report concluded that nothing of the sort was in prospect, that further increases could be held to the rate of growth of the gross national product (GNP) so long as Congress exercised careful management and modest restraint,[3] public concern about the nation's costly income assistance programs continues to run deep. As a recent U.S. Chamber of Commerce publication pointed out, "Most people, if asked today, would probably agree that the welfare system needs 'reform.'"[4] In fact, welfare has ironically emerged as one of the great unifying issues in American politics. Almost everyone is against it.

The problem, however, is that everyone is against it for a different reason. Recipients complain about benefit adequacy, taxpayers about excessive costs, state officials about cumbersome red tape in Washington, federal administrators about noncompliance by the states, policy analysts about inequities, and congressmen about work disincentives. To make matters worse, many of these concerns are in conflict. Reforms aimed at reducing inequities, for example, will likely extend coverage. Relief for local taxpayers can spell reduced benefits for recipients. As a consequence, consensus on the need for reform has so far yielded only a stalemate on the direction such reform should take.

This situation is further complicated by four additional factors that have long been features of American welfare policy, but which have changed significantly in recent years in ways that impede reform. The first is the sheer complexity of the income assistance programs. Instead of a coherent system, what has evolved in this country over the past 40 years is a staggering array of separate programs and subprograms, each with its own target population, benefit levels, eligibility criteria, application requirements, and administrative structures. At last count, no fewer than 62 separate federal programs were providing social insurance and aid to the needy, and several of these must be multiplied by 50 to reflect the fact that they are run differently—in terms of eligibility provisions, benefit levels, administrative procedures—from state to state.[5] Since most recipients obtain benefits under more than one of these programs,[6] the task of reform is complicated by the need to evaluate proposed change in one program not only on its own merits but also for its effects on recipients in all the other programs. As former Department of Health, Education, and Welfare (HEW) official Tom Joe explained in a recent interview, "We simply cannot afford to think of welfare reform apart from the other sizable social institutions like social security and unemployment compensation and all the others that provide benefits to the needy."

Not only does this complex program structure pose a conceptual problem for reform; it also poses a political problem, since the complexity of the programs is institutionalized in the structure of the congressional committee system and the executive branch of the government. Jurisdiction over the 62 federal income assistance programs is split among no fewer than 11 House committees, ten Senate committees, and nine executive departments and agencies,[7] each of which operates according to its own agenda, in response to its own internal priorities and procedures, its own external environment, and its own vision of its mission. As a result, it is institutionally difficult to produce consistent policy and sensible program interactions even when the needed changes are accurately conceptualized.

The barriers this situation poses for reform were vividly portrayed in the "notch" charts that Senator John J. Williams (D, Del.) produced during the Senate Finance Committee hearings on the Nixon administration's proposed Family Assistance Plan (FAP) in 1970. What these charts revealed was that FAP would put many recipients in the position of losing hundreds of dollars in assistance benefits if they earned an additional dollar of income because of the way eligibility criteria for other programs were worded. Yet, ironically, even if FAP planners had recognized this, the Finance Committee would not have had the jurisdiction to address the problem by bringing the other programs into line.

A second factor that has made it increasingly difficult to translate the consensus on the need for welfare reform into action is the fear on the part of those representing the poor that a reformed system will be less generous. Recent welfare policy provides ample support for historian David Potter's observation that Americans, because of our affluence, consistently tend to "overleap problems—to bypass them—rather than to solve them."[8] The early federal income assistance programs, as we shall see more clearly below, rested on a set of overly optimistic assumptions about the ability of the private employment system to provide income security to the American public, and hence about the ability of the subsequent insurance and assistance programs created in 1935 to take up the slack. When political pressures in the 1960s made it imperative to face up to the resulting shortcomings, Congress and the executive branch responded not with comprehensive reform but with a massive patch-up campaign that did "overleap" the problem without solving it. The resulting flurry of legislative and administrative activity greatly expanded the coverage and benefits of the basic social insurance programs; extended the eligibility period for unemployment compensation; made public assistance available to some intact families headed by an unemployed parent; provided liberal work-expense disregards to welfare mothers who work; increased AFDC benefits; created a broad program of medical aid for the poor; provided a comprehensive floor for the income of every family through food stamps, and replaced the separate state-administered assistance programs for the blind, aged, and disabled with a single national program.[9] Despite gaps, inequities, and inconsistencies, these changes considerably improved the benefits available to a sizable proportion of the poor. In fact, a recent Michigan Department of Social Services study reported that, thanks to the combination of benefits now available, 83 percent of Michigan AFDC cases sampled had incomes sufficient to lift them above the official poverty lines by 1974.[10] Any move to reduce benefits to Michigan recipients in order to equalize benefits with recipients elsewhere is therefore likely to encounter resistance, and the same reaction can be anticipated from recipients in other high benefit states. By increasing benefits, the recent changes have created a set of implicit entitlements that inevitably complicate the task of reform. Such complications were already evident during the dispute over the FAP, when welfare mothers from the high-benefit states opposed reform on grounds that it would reduce—or fail to increase—their own benefits even though it would aid a far larger group of needy people elsewhere. Similarly, in 1972, a year after enactment of the new Supplemental Security Income (SSI) program for the aged, blind, and disabled, Congress was persuaded to add a proviso requiring a complicated double computation system to make sure no existing recipient received less under the new system than under the old. Obviously, as the scope and level of benefits increase, as they have in recent years, the difficulty of framing comprehensive reform proposals that leave everybody better off increases even faster. Faced with this dilemma, at least some reformers have given up the pursuit of comprehensive reform altogether. As a Brookings Institution publication put it in 1974, "The growth of income support programs in recent years has made the case for welfare reform less compelling than it used to be."[11] At the least, these changes have given rise to a respectable body of opinion cautioning against major reform on grounds that it would likely do more to undercut the gains that have been made than to add to them.

A third factor complicating the task of reform is the impact welfare is believed by many to have on the work ethic, and the resulting political necessity to adapt welfare programs to the needs of the larger economic order. In this, American welfare policy shows its adherence to the principles first articulated in the seventeenth century English Poor Laws, which sought to restrict benefits to the clearly unemployable, keep benefit levels below the lowest wages available in the private market (the principle of less eligibility), and cast a stigma on the recipients of welfare.[12] With the "meshes" of welfare policy thus "spread over the entire labor system"—to paraphrase two historians commenting on the English Poor Laws[13]—reform proposals are forced to measure up against two separate standards at once: How well do they relieve suffering? And how effectively do they protect the work system that welfare is thought to endanger? Not only are these two frequently in conflict, but also the latter frequently takes precedence over the former, with the result that policy ideas that might help the needy are rejected out of fear that they might undermine the values under-girding the economic order.

The fourth reason why the consensus on the need for welfare reform has so far yielded only political stalemate results, paradoxically enough, from the successful application of systematic policy analysis to the welfare problem during the past decade. While this analysis has doubtless contributed substantially to our understanding of the problems that necessitate reform, it has also so effectively identified and highlighted the very real policy dilemmas inherent in any major reform proposal that it has unintentionally immobilized many of the advocates of reform.[14] One of the most severe of these dilemmas is the "work incentive trap," the fact that any effort to create work incentives for public assistance recipients under a single comprehensive welfare system, by allowing recipients to keep a portion of what they earn without losing benefits, automatically raises the income level at which benefits are still available and hence increases the number of people eligible for assistance.* As a result, a cruel dilemma arises for designers of comprehensive welfare reform proposals. They cannot easily provide adequate benefits and an effective work requirement without extending coverage and expanding costs beyond what many consider acceptable politically. Forced to confront this dilemma, some reform advocates have held out for a simple, comprehensive approach despite the need for lower benefit levels to make such an approach feasible while others have launched a search for alternative approaches that might avert this painful trade-off, even at the cost of somewhat greater administrative complexity. In the process, however, the reform consensus has been significantly fractured, even if not yet fatally.

In view of these and other factors, it seems clear that a systematic reassessment of the case for welfare reform is in order. Important changes have taken place since welfare reform last attracted widespread national attention, between 1969 and 1971. Yet these changes have not yet been fully incorporated into the prevailing wisdom. As a result, much of the debate over welfare reform seems stale and outdated, as supporters and opponents alike struggle to bring their views into line with the new reality. With a new presidential reform proposal now on the nation's agenda, there is a great need therefore to clarify the current situation and identify as systematically as possible the various alternative routes to change.

It is the purpose of this study to help in this effort by providing a broad reassessment of where we are, how we got here, and where we are going in welfare policy. To do so, the discussion falls into three parts. In the first part, Chapter 2, we analyze the present welfare system in the United States and evaluate the chief criticisms that have been directed at it. Chapter 3 then examines the roots of the present system in the history of American relief policy as it has evolved down to the present, seeking there an understanding of some of the features that appear irrational to many observers today. In Chapter 4, attention turns to the basic issues that are involved in any reform of welfare and to the ways in which various reform proposals handle these issues.

In providing this reassessment, it is not my purpose to recommend one approach over another. The purpose, rather, is to lay a solid factual foundation for the national debate on welfare policy that is about to occur by presenting in

---

*To see this, assume a benefit level of $3,600 for a family of four under public assistance. If this family is permitted to keep $1.00 out of every $3.00 it earns without any reduction in benefits (that is, a marginal tax rate of 2/3 since benefits are reduced at the rate of 2/3 of all earnings), then anyone making up to $5,400 ($3,600 ÷ 2/3) is eligible for some benefits. This is because a person earning $5,400 would have his benefits reduced by 2/3 × $5,400, or $3,600, which is the total amount of the basic benefit. But if recipients were required to surrender only $1.50 in benefits for every $3.00 earned (a marginal tax rate of 50 percent), then the break-even point rises to $7,200 ($3,600 ÷ ½).

one place the full array of reform options currently under serious discussion, and analyzing each of them systematically against the backdrop of what we know about how the current system evolved and about how it actually works. If as a consequence the next round of debate over welfare reform is more informed and focused, this study will have amply served its purpose.

NOTES

1. *The Budget of the United States Government, Fiscal Year 1976* (Washington, D.C.: U.S. Government Printing Office, 1978).

2. *Budget of the United States Government for Fiscal Year 1968* (Washington, D.C.: U.S. Government Printing Office, 1967).

3. U.S. Congress, Senate, Committee on the Budget, *Growth of Government Spending for Income Assistance: A Matter of Choice* (prepared by John Korbel, Congressional Budget Office), 94th Cong., 1st sess., 1975.

4. Council on Trends and Perspective, *High Employment and Income Maintenance Policy: A Report of the Council on Trends and Perspective* (Washington: U.S. Chamber of Commerce, 1976), p. 50.

5. U.S. Congress, Joint Economic Committee, Subcommittee on Fiscal Policy, *Income Security for Americans: Recommendations of the Public Welfare Study*, 93rd Cong., 2d sess., 1974, p. 2.

6. The existence of multiple benefits has long been assumed but only recently documented. In 1973, the Joint Economic Committee's Subcommittee on Fiscal Policy estimated that the 119 million recipients reported for the 26 major federal income transfer programs really represent only 60 million different people. A General Accounting Office (GAO) survey published the same year by the subcommittee verified this estimate by showing that in six different low-income areas, 60–75 percent of all recipients participated in more than one program, and 33–50 percent participated in three or more. In a further study published in April 1976, the Michigan Department of Social Services has provided even more detailed substantiation, demonstrating that the average AFDC recipient in that state receives income from 2.6 sources. In the case of the elderly, an Urban Institute study suggests that over 50 percent of all recipients of aid receive benefits from two or more programs.

For these data, see U.S. Congress, Joint Economic Committee, Subcommittee on Fiscal Policy, *Public Income Transfer Programs: The Incidence of Multiple Benefits and the Issues Raised by their Receipt*, Studies in Public Welfare, Paper no. 1, 93d Cong., 1st sess., 1973, p. 63; Vernon K. Smith and Gary Howitt, *The Economic Status of Michigan AFDC Families: An Analysis of Income and Benefit Receipt*, Studies in Welfare Policy, no. 8 (Lansing: Michigan Department of Social Services, 1976), p. 5; Federal Council on the Aging, *The Interrelationships of Benefit Programs for the Elderly* (Washington, D.C.: U.S. Government Printing Office, 1975), app. 3, p. 69.

7. Subcommittee on Fiscal Policy, *Public Welfare Study*, p. 1.

8. David Potter, *People of Plenty: Economic Abundance and the American Character* (Chicago: University of Chicago Press, 1954), p. 122.

9. For summaries of these changes, see Sar Levitan and Robert Taggart, *The Promise of Greatness* (Cambridge: Harvard University Press, 1976), pp. 33–86; Lawrence Lynn, Jr., *A Decade of Policy Developments in the Income Maintenance System*, Working Paper (Cambridge: Harvard University, John F. Kennedy School of Government, 1976).

10. Smith and Howitt, *Economic Status*, p. vii.

11. Barry M. Blechman, Edward M. Gramlich, and Robert W. Hartman, *Setting National Priorities: The 1975 Budget* (Washington, D.C.: The Brookings Institution, 1974), p. 182.

12. On the poor-law traditions of U.S. public assistance arrangements, see Frances Fox Piven and Richard Cloward, *Regulating the Poor: The Functions of Public Welfare* (New York: Vintage Books, 1971), pp. 123–82; Bruno Stein, *On Relief: The Economics of Poverty and Public Welfare* (New York: Basic Books, 1971).

13. J. L. and Barbara Hammond, *The Village Labourer* (London: Conguraus, Green, and Company, 1948), p. 161, quoted in Piven and Cloward, *Regulating*, p. 31.

14. David Austin, "Some Current Issues–What the Future Holds for Social Security and Income Maintenance Programs," (Paper presented at the 1975 Symposium of the Florence Heller Alumni Association, Brandeis University).

2

DO WE STILL NEED
WELFARE REFORM?

"Take some more tea," the March Hare said to Alice earnestly.

"I've had nothing yet," Alice replied in an offended tone, "so I can't take more."

"You mean you can't take *less*," said the Hatter; "it's very easy to take *more* than nothing."

—Lewis Carroll, *Alice in Wonderland*

At the heart of the debate over welfare reform are some fundamental differences in perception concerning where we are in income support policies, and thus whether more of the same will be better or worse. Before we can talk meaningfully about alternative reform proposals, therefore, it is necessary to establish clearly what the basic contours of policy in this area look like and what the major criticisms are. Accordingly, this chapter outlines the main components of the American income support system and evaluates each of six major criticisms that have been leveled at this system in the past, in order to see what force they still have in light of the changes that have occurred during the last decade and a half. With this as background, we can then turn in subsequent chapters to the historical roots of the present situation and to the suggestions that have been made to improve it.

INCOME ASSISTANCE PROGRAMS: AN OVERVIEW

One of the stumbling blocks to serious discussion of welfare reform is the confusion that exists over the meaning of terms. "Welfare," "public assistance," "income assistance," "income maintenance," and several other terms are used interchangeably. Yet their meanings are rarely specified, or are interpreted differently depending on the purposes to be served.

Since almost every government activity could qualify as a welfare policy in the sense that it contributes to the public welfare, it is important to be clear at the outset about which programs are the focus of attention here. In particular, we will use the term income assistance to refer to programs that provide income, or services in lieu of income, only to certain groups of citizens who satisfy specified eligibility criteria. Within this group, two further distinctions must be made: first, between programs that establish eligibility on the basis of prior service or contributions (social insurance programs), and those that establish eligibility on the basis of need (public assistance or welfare programs); and second, between programs that deliver benefits in the form of cash (cash programs), and those that deliver them in the form of commodities or services (in-kind programs).

For the most part, the discussion here will follow common usage by focusing primarily on the needs-tested programs, both cash and in-kind, for which we have reserved the terms welfare or public assistance. Among the in-kind programs of this sort, moreover, we generally restrict our attention to those for which cash could be readily substituted, ignoring those programs, like employment training or counseling, that provide services not readily translated into cash.

In adopting this usage, there is no intention to imply that the social insurance programs do not aid the needy. To the contrary, as we will see, these programs turn out to be the most effective sources of relief, largely because they tend to provide more ample benefits than the needs-tested programs. In assessing the operations of the income assistance system, therefore, we will need to examine the impact of the social insurance programs as well. Nevertheless, it is the needs-based programs that must be the primary focus in our discussion of welfare reform options, since these are the major targets of change.

One other important difference among these programs has to do with the extent of their reliance on state and local administration and financing. By and large, the social insurance programs are federally administered, while the need-based programs are jointly run by federal, state, and local officials, usually with state financial support. However, this distinction is by no means absolute. For example, unemployment compensation, a social insurance program, is a joint state-federal program, while food stamps, a need-based public assistance program, is wholly federally financed. The extent of state-local financial involvement has important implications for the way a program operates.

Using this basic framework, Table 2.1 outlines the major income assistance programs in existence as of 1976, and details the amount spent on them by federal, state, and local governments. A glance at this table suggests several basic features of American income security policy.

- The vast majority of income assistance expenditures go not for needs-tested welfare programs but for social insurance programs. In fact, the social insurance programs outspend the needs-tested welfare programs by a factor of more than two to one ($151.2 billion to $73.0 billion).

- Of the social insurance programs, the largest by far is the basic Old Age,

TABLE 2.1

Federal, State, and Local Income Assistance Programs, 1976

Program	Amount (billions)			Percent of All Expenditures
	Federal	State-Local	Total	
Social insurance: cash	$118.9	$14.5	$133.4	59
Old Age, Survivors', and Disability Insurance	72.7	–	72.7	32
Public employee retirement	8.2	7.8	16.0	8
Unemployment insurance	19.5	–	19.5	8
Railroad retirement	3.5	–	3.5	2
Military retirement	7.3	–	7.3	3
Veterans' disability compensation	5.2	–	5.2	2
Workmen's compensation[a]	1.5	5.7	7.2	3
State temporary disability	–	1.0	1.0	1
Other[b]	1.0	–	1.0	
Social insurance: in-kind	17.8	–	17.8	8
Medicare	17.8	–	17.8	8
Need-tested: cash	14.1	7.7	21.8	10
AFDC	5.8	4.9	10.7	5
Supplemental Security Income	5.1	1.6	6.7	3
Veterans' pensions	2.9	–	2.9	1
General assistance	–	1.2	1.2	
Other[c]	0.3	–	0.3	1

Need-tested: in-kind	35.6	15.6	51.2	23
Medicaid	8.6	6.3	14.9	7
Other health[d]	3.5	7.7	11.2	5
Food stamps	5.6	0.3	5.9	3
Child nutrition and other food aid[e]	2.3	0.5	2.8	1
Public housing	1.6	—	1.6	2
Other housing assistance[f]	3.5	—	3.5	2
Comprehensive manpower training (CETA)	3.3	—	3.3	2
Work Incentive	0.3	—	0.3	1
Other jobs and training[g]	2.1	—	2.1	1
Education grants	0.9	—	0.9	—
Other education[h]	1.6	0.1	1.7	2
Other social services	2.3	0.7	3.0	—
Grand total	186.4	37.8	224.2	100

Note: Dashes indicate amounts less than $100 million.

a Includes federal benefits for black-lung sufferers.

b Includes trade adjustment allowance and $50 bonus for beneficiaries of certain social insurance programs.

c Includes indemnity compensation to parents of veterans, assistance to Cuban refugees, general assistance to Indians, emergency assistance to needy families, assistance to Indochinese refugees.

d Includes maternal and child health care, community health, health services for the aged, Indian health services, crippled children's services, and veterans' care for non-service-connected disability (estimated at 50 percent of total veterans' hospital and medical care). State-local figure also includes subsidized hospitals and other public health activities.

e Includes national school lunch program; nutrition program for the elderly; special milk program; special supplemental food program for women, infants, and children; school breakfast program; child care food programs; food distribution program.

f Includes Section 502 rural housing loans, Section 236 interest-reduction payments, rental housing, Section 101 rent supplements, and Section 235 homeownership assistance payments.

g Includes temporary employment program and Job Corps.

h Includes Head Start, college work-study, guaranteed student loans, and national direct student loans. Cost of local public schools is not included.

Sources: Federal figures are from *Budget of the United States Government, Fiscal Year 1977* (Washington, D.C.: U.S. Government Printing Office, 1977). State-local figures are from Alfred Skolnik and Sophie R. Dales, "Social Welfare Expenditures, 1950–1975," *Social Security Bulletin* 39, no. 1 (January 1976): 8; Vee Burke, *Federal and State-Local Expenditures for Income Transfers to Persons with Limited Income, Fiscal Years 1975 and 1976* (Washington, D.C.: Congressional Research Service, June 18, 1976).

Survivors', and Disability Insurance (OASDI) program that most people have in mind when they use the term social security. Under this program, which now covers 90 percent of the nation's employed labor force, workers contribute a portion of their wages (as this is written, 5.85 percent of the first $16,500) to a trust fund containing equal sums from their employers. Upon retirement, disability, or death, the worker and/or his family is entitled to a benefit computed as a fraction of prior earnings. Beginning in 1975, these benefits rise automatically as the cost of living rises, thus providing a hedge against inflation.

Although the social security program has all the features of an insurance program, it differs markedly from regular insurance. In the first place, current beneficiaries, even as a group, draw far more in benefits than they contributed. This is possible because current contributors make up the difference, undoubtedly on the assumption that the subsequent generation of contributors will do the same for them. In the second place, although all benefits are related to prior earnings, the formula varies inversely with the size of the prior earnings. In other words, the lower the earnings were prior to retirement, the higher the benefits will be as a percentage of those earnings. In fact, beginning in 1972, persons with an average monthly wage of $110.00 or less were entitled to benefits larger than their average wage had been while they worked. As a consequence, the social security system has a redistributive effect.

• Of the remaining social insurance programs, two deserve special mention. The first is Medicare, the only in-kind social insurance program. Created in 1965, Medicare provides two forms of health insurance for the aged and disabled: hospital and selected hospital-related medical care insurance financed by payroll deductions and employer contributions; and optional outpatient medical care insurance financed half by enrollees' premiums and half by federal general revenues. Some 24 million people are covered by the first of these programs and 23 million by the latter. Together, they provide a broad range of medical care coverage to the elderly and disabled.

The second additional social insurance program deserving special note is unemployment insurance, which provides cash payments to unemployed persons who were formerly employed for a specified period of time in covered jobs (about 85 percent of all wage and salary workers). The benefits are financed by a special payroll tax levied on employers, and are geared to prior earnings. Although the unemployment compensation trust funds are administered by federal authorities, the program is operated locally through state employment security agencies, and allows for extensive variations among the states in tax rates levied against employers, benefit levels, benefit periods, and interpretations of suitable work requirements. To be eligible for payments, potential recipients must establish that they lost their jobs through no fault of their own, and must make themselves available for any suitable replacement job that is offered. Although the basic benefit period for aid is 26 weeks, a number of triggering mechanisms and special extensions have been added that now extend aid to as much as 65 weeks in special circumstances. To finance these added benefits, extensive borrowing from the federal treasury has been necessary in view of the high rates of unemployment during the 1970s. In 1975, some 3.5 million persons were receiving benefits in the typical week, and another 4.2 million has exhausted their benefits.[1]

• Among the needs-tested income assistance programs, which together account for $73 billion in expenditures, or almost one-third of the total, the largest by far are the in-kind programs. These programs make up a web of specially targeted assistance activities providing a host of services and commodities, from special nutritional supplements for nursing mothers to various forms of housing subsidies. Beyond the in-kind assistance programs shown in Table 2.1, moreover, is a collection of others that provide need-based assistance not easily replaced by cash (such as employment training, social services, and counseling). These programs would add $8.4 billion to the $51.2 billion in needs-tested, in-kind programs already shown in Table 2.1.

About half of the in-kind expenditures now go for two sizable programs. The first of these is Medicaid, which provides free health care to participants in the needs-tested cash assistance programs. At the discretion of the states, it can also be extended to persons who, while not eligible for these cash programs, have incomes low enough to be eligible once their medical expenses are deducted (the so-called medically indigent). Under the program, the federal government shares the total costs of a specified range of health services with the states according to a formula based on state per capita income. Administration of the program rests ultimately with the states. What is more, the states have some discretion in adding services beyond those mandated in the federal law.

The second major in-kind program is food stamps, which provide financial assistance to eligible recipients for the purchase of food. The assistance takes the form of stamps purchased from the government at discounted prices and redeemable in grocery stores as legal tender for the purchase of food. Eligibility is based on participation in the cash welfare programs or on family size and net income, which is total gross income minus deductions for a variety of expenses, such as taxes, social security payments, medical costs, and child care costs. (See Table 2.2.) The bonus value of the stamps, the difference between what the family pays for the stamps and what they are worth in the grocery store, is also geared to family size and income. A family of four with a net monthly income of less than $30.00, for example, pays nothing and gets $182 worth of stamps. A family of four with a net monthly income of $170–189.99 pays $47 for its $182 worth of stamps. As of April 1978, slightly more than 16 million people were benefiting from food stamps.

• Of the $21.8 billion spent on needs-tested cash assistance programs in 1976, only about half went for the AFDC program, which most people have in mind when they think of welfare. Created by the Social Security Act of 1935, AFDC provides federal assistance to states for payments to families where the father is absent or disabled. Beginning in 1961, assistance was also made avail-

TABLE 2.2

Food Stamp Purchase Schedule for a Four-Person Family, July 1978

Monthly Net Income	Monthly Coupon Allotment	Monthly Purchase Cost
$0 to $29.99	$182	0
$70 to $79.99	$182	16
$100 to $109.99	$182	25
$170 to $189.99	$182	47
$250 to $269.99	$182	71
$330 to $359.99	$182	95
$450 to $479.99	$182	131
$540 to $569.99	$182	158
$600 to $629.99	$182	158

Source: Federal Register 43 F.R. 21304, May 16, 1978.

able to families where the father was present but unemployed, though only half of the states have availed themselves of this form of assistance.

Under AFDC, the states determine the eligibility requirements, set the benefit levels, and administer the payments. They also contribute anywhere from 22 percent to 50 percent of the costs. As of January 1977, 3.6 million families, comprising 11.2 million people, were receiving assistance under AFDC.[2]

• In addition to AFDC, the Social Security Act of 1935, and subsequent amendments, created a series of needs-tested cash assistance programs for the adult categories: the aged, the blind, and the partially and totally disabled. These programs, originally jointly financed by the states and the federal government, were consolidated and federalized in 1972 in a new Supplemental Security Income (SSI) Program. Under this new program, the federal government provides a uniform minimum cash income to aged, blind, and disabled persons who fall below a federally specified income eligibility line. In addition, states are permitted to supplement this federal minimum at their own discretion. However, in states where benefits under the old categorical programs were higher than the minimum income provided under SSI, states are required to supplement the federal payment to bring it up to the prior level. In fiscal year 1976, the federal government spent $5.1 billion on this program, and state supplements came to $1.6 billion.

MAJOR CRITICISMS: AN EVALUATION

If, as should be clear, the income assistance system is complex and varied, so too are the criticisms that have been levelled at this system. In fact, the indictment of the "welfare mess" that has been so prominent in American politics for the past decade and a half consists of at least six different counts, some of which are at odds with each other. In particular, the welfare system has been accused of being (1) too costly, (2) not sufficiently generous, (3) inequitable, (4) a source of perverse incentives, (5) excessively complex, and (6) punitive.

To what extent does this list of criticisms, which was formulated for the most part during the early 1960s, still apply today, given the changes that have occurred during the past decade? How have these changes affected the case for reform?

Not surprisingly, the answers to these questions differ widely among students of social welfare policy. Indeed, within three years of one another, one team of researchers concluded that by the 1970s the American income assistance system represented "a relatively generous, complete, and comprehensive social welfare system,"[3] while another team viewed it as a series of "uncoordinated programs, with gaps, overlaps, cross-purposes, inequities, administrative inefficiencies, work and family support disincentives, and a waste of taxpayers' money."[4]

Before we can evaluate the major welfare reform proposals seriously, it is necessary to determine which of these views comes closest to the truth. To do so, this section assesses each of the six major criticisms of welfare policy cited above, in the light of data that take account of the changes of the past decade and a half. On this basis, it should then be possible to evaluate the current case for reform without the stereotypes of earlier days.

Cost

In political terms, the cost issue is the best place to begin, since it is the fulcrum on which the debate over welfare reform ultimately turns. The heart of this issue is the seemingly endless rise of income maintenance costs, despite earlier expectations that at least the welfare portion of these costs would decline over time as the scope of the social insurance programs was extended. The upshot has been a widespread concern that welfare spending has gone out of control and that drastic corrective action is necessary. But concern about program costs focuses on two other issues: administrative costs, and the distribution of the financial burden for welfare between the federal government and state and local governments.

Growth in Costs: Is the System Out of Control?

As noted in Table 2.3, federal outlays on income assistance programs quadrupled between 1965 and 1975, rising from $35.2 billion to $156.1 billion. More importantly, federal spending on needs-tested programs increased almost fivefold during this period, while total federal budget outlays rose just slightly over two and one-half times. In other words, federal income assistance expendi-

TABLE 2.3

Growth in Government Spending on Income Assistance Programs, 1965-75

Item	1965 (billions)	1975 (billions)	Percent Change (1965–75)
All federal budget outlays	$122.4	$324.6	265
Federal income assistance programs	35.2	156.0	443
Federal needs-tested programs	8.4	40.9	487
All state general revenues*	30.6	96.8	316
State outlays on needs-tested programs*	2.3	11.4	496

*Includes only revenue and expenditures from own sources.

Sources: Budget of the United States Government, Fiscal Year 1967 and *Budget of the United States Government, Fiscal Year 1977* (Washington, D.C.: U.S. Government Printing Office, 1966, 76); U.S. Bureau of the Census, *State Government Finances in 1975, State Government Finances in 1965* (Washington, D.C.: U.S. Government Printing Office, 1965, 1976).

tures grew at a rate that was two-thirds higher than the rate of growth of the overall federal budget, and the needs-tested portion of assistance expenditures grew nearly twice as fast as the total budget. Something similar was happening at the state level, where expenditures on needs-tested assistance programs grew at a rate that was 60 percent higher than the rate of growth of all state-originated general revenues.

Since a substantial part of this rapid increase took place during a period of general economic growth, when income assistance expenditures are expected to decline, it generated fears that things had gone out of control. How valid are these fears? Why have welfare costs risen steeply year after year? And what does this portend about the future in the absence of reform?

Ultimately, the answers to these questions are rooted in the pattern of American social and economic life. For, what comes to be defined as a welfare problem is frequently just the other side of a malfunction in some other social institution or policy, like the job market, the educational system, the health care system, or the family. The welfare system, in short, is called upon to correct, or at least cope with, the difficulties created elsewhere in society. To understand the growth in welfare fully, therefore, it would be necessary to examine the operation of each of these other institutions as well, something that lies well beyond the scope of this study.

Nevertheless, it is possible to throw some light on the question of whether income assistance expenditures are out of control by looking carefully at the actual content and immediate causes of the rapid increases in these expenditures that have recently occurred. Table 2.4, which details the changes in federal income assistance costs over the past decade, provides a basis for such an analysis.

Inflation and Social Insurance Growth. The first point to emerge from this table is that by far the largest part of the cost increase between 1965 and 1975 had very little to do with the welfare programs. Twenty-one percent of the $121 billion increase in income assistance expenditures over the decade resulted from inflation. Of the remainder of the increase, 73 percent, or $70 billion, came from the social insurance programs. But very little of this latter increase was due to uncontrollable factors built into the structure of the existing programs. In fact, in only two cases were such uncontrollable factors primarily responsible: in the civil service retirement program, where the aging of the enlarged cadre of civil servants that entered government during World War II produced automatic cost increases; and in the unemployment compensation program, where a dramatic escalation in costs occurred as a result of the sharp jump in unemployment in the early 1970s.[5] For the rest of the social insurance programs, the major sources of cost escalation were conscious policy changes that significantly altered the programs. Among the more important of these were:

• A major increase in social security benefit levels that raised the average monthly benefit for retired workers from $83.92 in 1965 to $205.47 in 1975, an increase of 245 percent, compared to a cost-of-living increase of 171 percent. (The introduction of a number of special provisions in unemployment insurance extended the payment period from 26 to 52, and then to 55, weeks.)
• A significant series of eligibility extensions that brought a sizable crop of new beneficiaries into the social security system for the first time: between 1965 and 1975, the number of social security beneficiaries rose by 10 million, from 21 million persons to 31 million.[6]
• Creation of a wholly new medical insurance program, Medicare, which added $14.8 billion to costs.

Since these changes represented important departures from previous programs, the costs they contributed were in some sense exceptional. To project the past decade's rate of growth into the future is to assume that similar additions and changes will continue to be made at a similar rate, which is unlikely. This is not to suggest that expenditures on social insurance programs will decline in absolute terms, or fall as a percentage of the GNP. Demographic changes, medical breakthroughs, alterations in life styles, and the decision in 1972 to peg social security benefit levels to the cost of living will likely keep costs rising. But the rate of growth seems likely to decline.

AFDC Costs. The second point that emerges from Table 2.4 is that the costs of federal needs-tested cash programs grew much more slowly than all income assistance costs during the past decade, except for one program—AFDC, which tripled in real dollar costs. Since this AFDC growth was the change that provoked the first concern about a welfare crisis and that transformed welfare

TABLE 2.4

Federal Outlays on Income Assistance Programs, 1965 and 1975

Program	Amount (billions)			Percent Change (1965–75, in 1975 dollars)	Percent of Total	
	1965		1975		1965	1975
	Actual	In 1975 Dollars	Actual			
Social insurance: cash	$26.8	$45.6	$100.8	220.0	76.1	64.3
Old Age, Survivors', and Disability Insurance	17.5	29.8	63.6	213.4	49.7	40.8
Civil Service Retirement	1.4	2.4	7.0	291.7	4.0	4.5
Unemployment insurance	3.1	5.3	13.5	254.7	8.8	8.7
Railroad Retirement	1.2	2.0	3.1	155.0	3.4	2.0
Military Retirement	1.4	2.4	6.2	258.3	4.0	4.0
Veterans' Disability Compensation	2.2	3.7	4.2	113.5	6.3	2.6
Other[a]	–	–	3.2	–	–	1.7
Social insurance: in-kind	–	–	14.8	–	–	9.5
Medicare	–	–	14.8	–	–	9.5
Needs-tested: cash	5.1	8.7	12.7	146.0	14.5	8.1
AFDC	1.0	1.7	5.1	300.0	2.8	3.3
Supplemental Security Income	1.7[b]	2.9	4.7	162.1	4.8	3.0
Veterans' pensions	1.9	3.2	2.7	84.4	5.5	1.7
Other[c]	0.5	0.9	0.2	22.2	1.4	0.1

Needs-tested: in-kind	3.3	5.6	28.1	503.6	9.4	18.1
Medicaid	0.6	1.0	7.1	710.0		4.6
Other health[c]	0.8	1.4	2.3	164.3	2.2	1.5
Food stamps	—	—	4.7	583.3	—	3.0
Child nutrition and other Food[c]	0.7	1.2	2.3	433.3	2.0	1.5
Public housing	0.2	0.3	1.3	1350.0	0.6	0.8
Other housing[c]	0.1	0.2	2.7	411.1	0.3	1.7
Job and training programs[c]	0.5	0.9	3.7	666.7	1.4	2.4
Other social services	0.2	0.3	2.0	200.0	0.6	1.3
Educational grants	0.2	0.3	0.6	—	0.6	0.4
College work-study	—	—	0.2	—		0.1
Other education	—	—	1.3	—		0.8
Grand total, income support	35.2	59.9	156.4	260.4	100.0	100.0
Total U.S. budget outlays	122.4	208.1	324.6	155.9		100.0

[a] Includes special benefits for disabled coal miners, trade adjustment allowance, $50 bonus for beneficiaries of certain social insurance programs.
[b] Represents cost of aid to the blind, old age assistance (OAA), and aid to the partially and totally disabled (APTD)—programs that predated SSI.
[c] See Table 2.1 for note that applies to this program.

Sources: Budget of the United States Government, Fiscal Year 1977 and Budget of the United States Government, Fiscal Year 1967 (Washington, D.C.: U.S. Government Printing Office, 1966, 1976).

TABLE 2.5

Changes in AFDC Program, 1967-71

Item of Change	1967	1971	Percent Change
Eligible families (thousands)	2,183	3,011	38
Participating families (thousands)	1,385	2,837	105
Benefit levels*	55.85	72.41	30

*Benefit levels shown are average monthly benefits per person, and are for 1965 and 1975, in real dollar terms.

Sources: Barbara Boland, "Participation in the Aid to Families with Dependent Children Program (AFDC)," Working Paper 971-02 (Washington, D.C.: The Urban Institute, 1973), cited in Heather Ross and Isabel Sawhill, Time of Transition: The Growth of Families Headed by Women (Washington, D.C.: The Urban Institute, 1976), p. 102; Social Security Bulletin 39, no. 7 (July 1976).

into what Daniel Patrick Moynihan termed "perhaps the leading conundrum of American domestic policy" in the 1960s,[7] it is important to be clear about its sources.

Broadly speaking, three sources of AFDC cost increases are possible: increases in the number of persons eligible; increases in participation among those eligible; and increases in benefit levels for those participating. For much of the 1960s, it was assumed that the first of these was most important, and fears were rife about a structural transformation of inner-city, especially black, family life, which would fuel a continuous increase in AFDC-eligible households. But, as Table 2.5 indicates, the most important source of cost increases during the period of the most rapid AFDC expansion, from 1967 to 1971, was not an increase in the number eligible for AFDC, but an increase in the proportion of eligibles who chose to participate. In fact, almost two-thirds of the growth in AFDC rolls during this period resulted from an increase in participation rates, leaving only slightly more than one-third to be accounted for by a growth in the number of female-headed families eligible for aid.* But since the participation rate reached 94 percent by 1971, it is unlikely that the AFDC growth rate of the past decade will continue. This assessment finds support, moreover, in other recent data, including new anthropological research suggesting that inner-city

*This was computed as follows: In 1967, 63 percent of the 2.2 million eligible families, or 1.4 million, were enrolled in the program. Had this rate prevailed in 1971, 1.9 million families would have been enrolled (63 percent of 3.0 million). Instead, 2.8 million were enrolled. Thus, of the 1.4 million additional participants, 0.5 million resulted from increased numbers eligible, and 0.9 million from increased participation.

families have far more strength and durability than was previously believed;[8] and information on AFDC turnover, which indicates far more economic change among the poor than was assumed, thus challenging the view that the AFDC population is an ever-expanding pool of people trapped in dependence.[9] In light of these data, it is not surprising that the AFDC caseload was relatively steady between 1971 and 1975.[10]

This is not to say that further pressures for AFDC cost escalation do not exist. The inadequacy of benefits in many states is one continuing source of upward pressure, despite a 30 percent growth of benefits in real dollar terms between 1965 and 1975. In only 26 of the 50 states did the maximum benefit levels at the end of 1975 come within 90 percent of the state's need standard, the amount of income the state judged to be minimally ncessary to live decently. Pressures are likely to persist, therefore, to bring payment levels into line with need standards in the remaining 24 states.[11]

The fiscal relief expected from the employment of AFDC recipients has not been realized either, at least not to the extent that it was anticipated during the 1960s, when Congress declared its intention to make "taxpayers out of taxeaters"[12] through a series of rehabilitation-assistance, work-training, and work-incentive features incorporated into the basic social security law. The hope, as Senator Russell Long put it, was to "reduce the welfare burden by helping AFDC recipients to become self-sufficient."[13] These efforts were prompted by the realization that 52 percent of all separated women and 72 percent of all divorced women were in the labor force, while only 21 percent of all AFDC mothers were.[14]

But by the mid-1970s, it had become evident that these efforts were having only limited success, largely because AFDC mothers are not like all other divorced or separated women. In the first place, they are far more likely to have child-care responsibilities. For example, as of 1973, five out of eight welfare mothers had children under six to care for. Putting them to work would thus require child-care assistance. Of those without children under six, about half were either already working or seeking work. This leaves only about 15 percent of all welfare mothers who neither have small children nor are actively seeking work.[15] And many of these lack the education and work experience to secure jobs that allow them to escape welfare dependency. According to one study, in fact, over one-third of all case closings were reopened within a year and, except for those originally closed for administrative reasons, most of the reopenings resulted from insufficient income or subsequent loss of job.[16] In view of this, it is not surprising that a recent Michigan report concluded that the primary consequence of the work incentive provisions, which allow AFDC recipients to keep $30 per month plus one-third of the remainder of all earnings in excess of work expenses, has been to increase AFDC costs by allowing recipients to stay on the rolls even after finding a job.[17] In short, whatever it achieves, moving AFDC recipients from welfare to workfare," as proposed by Senator Long and others, is not likely to accomplish any substantial cost reduction, once the costs of day care, training, and work incentives themselves are deducted. The prospect, in short, is for a considerable slowing of recent rates of AFDC cost growth, but not "quick fixes."

The Mushrooming of In-Kind Assistance. Perhaps the most important point that emerges from Table 2.4 is the dramatic surge of in-kind program costs that occurred between 1965 and 1975. If the $26.5 billion increase in the real cost of needs-tested programs that occurred during this decade, 85 percent, or $22.5 billion, resulted from the growth of in-kind benefits. By comparison, the $3.7 billion added to the federal budget by AFDC was a small increase. What has taken place, in short, is a dramatic change in the structure of needs-tested assistance. In 1965, in-kind programs accounted for only 39 percent of the costs of this assistance. By 1975 they accounted for 69 percent. Even if we restrict our attention to those in-kind programs readily replaceable by cash, the jump is still from 32 percent to 62 percent.

Since most of this massive expansion of in-kind program costs resulted from the creation of wholly new programs or the substantial revision of old ones, there is no reason to expect that the rates of increase in these programs experienced over the past decade will continue automatically into the future. The cost of the food stamp program, for example, rose from less than $1 billion to close to $5 billion within four years, largely as the result of expanded coverage following enactment of food stamp reform legislation in 1971. After reaching a peak of 19 million participants in 1974, however, food stamp rolls seem to have stabilized. The burst in expenditures for Medicaid had a similar cause. Medicaid came into existence only in 1966, and was opened automatically to AFDC and SSI participants. As participation in these cash assistance programs surged during the 1960s, for reasons we have already noted, Medicaid costs followed suit. Far from being the automatic product of inflated medical charges, the rise in Medicaid costs is rather the automatic product of the rise in cash assistance rolls. As one recent study put it:

> The most important factor in the rise of Medicaid costs has been the increase in persons eligible. Under a continuation of the present Medicaid program, increases in the number of eligibles would be a much less important factor since public assistance caseloads are stabilizing, and all but one state is currently participating in Medicaid.[18]

While there is reason to be somewhat sanguine about the rate of further cost escalation in food stamps and Medicaid, no such confidence seems warranted with respect to the other in-kind programs. In numerous cases, these programs establish an eligible population far in excess of the number the available program resources can serve, creating pressure from those who are eligible but cannot get their share. In the subsidized housing programs, for example, between 15 and 16 million families were eligible as of 1972, yet assistance was available to only 1.8 million.[19] In such situations, demands for increased spending on grounds of equity can be compelling.

On the whole, the dire predictions about continuously accelerating growth in public assistance costs thus seem grossly exaggerated. Much of the recent rapid growth stems from the addition of new programs, substantial jumps in benefit levels, coverage extensions under existing programs, and substantial surges in program participation rates. This kind of growth is not uncontrollable, but rather the product of conscious policy choices or one-time changes.

Although it is thus unreasonable to assume the simple continuation of prior growth rates, it is also unreasonable to expect that costs will level off in absolute terms, or decline as a proportion of GNP. Some reduction can be anticipated in unemployment compensation, and perhaps in food stamp costs, as unemployment rates decline. But costs are not likely to drop in other program components, and, in the case of in-kind benefits, upward pressures continue. The case for reform on grounds of overall cost is thus considerably less compelling than has been widely assumed on the basis of previous trends, yet it is still significant.

Administrative Cost

Closely related to the concern about the rising level of expenditures for public assistance benefits has been a concern about the system's administrative costs. Because of their categorical nature and their use of needs tests to establish eligibility, public assistance programs have always incurred higher administrative costs than social insurance programs. The latter, not being based on need determination, can be run with fewer personnel than programs that must constantly check and recheck the numerous factors that determine eligibility.

As the complexity of need-based assistance systems has increased in recent years, administrative costs have therefore expanded substantially, outpacing even the rate of growth of benefits. For example, as noted in Table 2.6, administrative costs in the AFDC program increased from $88.45 per $1,000 in benefits in 1971 to $123.90 in 1975, and were projected to climb to $147.93 in fiscal year 1977. In 1971, one out of every 12 dollars of AFDC costs went for administration. By fiscal year 1977, one out of every eight dollars went for administration. In the opinion of many, that is too large a diversion of resources.

The Fiscal Strain on State and Local Governments

What is important about the costs of income assistance programs is not simply their size, but the way they are distributed among the different levels of government. Each of the major need-based assistance programs, except food stamps, places substantial financial responsibilities on the states, through a variety of different mechanisms. Under AFDC, for example, two funding formulas are available to states. Under one, the federal government pays five-sixths of the first $18 in average monthly benefits, and then a percentage—called the federal percentage—of any balance up to $32.00. The federal percentage varies, by law, from 50 percent to 65 percent depending on the ratio of the state's per capita

TABLE 2.6

Administrative Costs in Major Public Assistance Programs, Fiscal Years 1971, 1975, 1977

Program	Total (millions of dollars)			Per Participant			Per $1,000 of Benefits		
	1971	1975	1977[a]	1971	1975	1977[a]	1971	1975	1977[a]
AFDC	485	1,042	1,496	52.01	94.09	130.05	88.45	123.90	147.93
Food stamps	104	592	689	11.13	34.72	36.46	61.54	134.76	116.56
SSI[b]	—	460	592	—	—	—	—	56.17	77.53

[a]Projected.
[b]Includes federal costs only.
Source: Congressional Research Service, "Administrative Costs of Public Assistance Programs." Mimeographed, 1976, p. 2.

income to the national per capita income (the poorer the state, the higher the federal percentage, and the smaller the state share). Under the second formula, which is available to states that have an approved Medicaid plan, the federal government pays from 50 percent to 78.28 percent of total AFDC benefits, depending again on the ratio of the state's per capita income to the national per capita income.

Under Medicaid, the federal government pays a percentage—called the federal medical assistance percentage (FMAP)—of the amount that states pay to doctors and hospitals for health care for the needy. The FMAP varies from 50 percent to 83 percent, depending on the state's per capita income, and the federal government pays 50 percent of administrative costs and 75 percent of Medicaid personnel training costs. Even the 1972 SSI program, which established a national system of assistance for the so-called adult assistance categories (the aged, the blind, the disabled), maintains a financial role for the states in the form of mandatory and optional supplementary payments.

To complicate fiscal matters still further, states have the option of shifting some or all of these costs to their cities and counties, and they have exercised this option with the same bewildering array of variations that characterizes other features of the system. For example, in 11 states, local governments are required to help finance AFDC; in 12 they are required to help finance Medicaid. Moreover, the funding formulas differ among the states, among programs within states, and among categories of costs (benefits, administration, training) within each program.[20]

Finally, states fund a number of non-federally aided welfare activities, most notably general assistance. Unlike the federal programs, general assistance provides aid to anyone in need, rather than restricting it to narrowly defined categories of people (such as the aged, the blind, single-parent families with children). At last count, 33 states had general assistance programs, and in 16 of them, local governments were required to participate in some fashion or another.[21]

Through these intricate funding arrangements, therefore, state and local governments bear a substantial share of the costs of public assistance. What is more, as shown in Table 2.7, this involvement has grown sharply over the past decade, despite a general increase in the relative and absolute size of the federal contribution. Thus state and local spending on needs-tested public welfare programs* increased more than fourfold in actual dollars, and two and one-half times in constant dollars, over the past ten years. During the same period, federal

---

*The definition of public welfare spending used here is that of the Census Bureau, which includes cash payments to the needy under the federally aided categorical assistance programs (OAA, aid to the blind, aid to the partially and totally disabled, AFDC, SSI), Medicaid payments, state general assistance, and related administrative expenses. Health and hospital services provided by the state or local governments are not included, nor are educational costs.

TABLE 2.7

Spending on Public Welfare, by Level of Government, 1965 and 1975 (billions of dollars)

Government Level	1965		1975	Percent Change	
	Actual	1975 Prices	Actual	Actual	1975 Prices
State	$2.3	$3.9	$11.4	495.7	292.3
City and county	0.9	1.5	1.9	211.1	126.7
Total state and local	3.2	5.4	13.3	416.6	246.3
Federal*	3.1	5.3	18.9	609.7	356.6
Grand total	6.3	10.7	32.2	511.1	300.9

*Includes only federal aid to states for needs-tested programs. To assure comparability over time, however, direct federal payments under SSI in 1975 were added on to the reported federal aid figure because SSI replaced three categorical programs formerly funded through federal aid to the states and therefore included in the 1965 federal aid figure.

Note: Data include only needs-tested programs—AFDC, OAA, aid to the blind, aid to the partially and totally disabled, Medicaid, SSI, and state general assistance.

Source: U.S. Bureau of the Census, State Government Finances in 1975; City Government Finances in 1974-75; County Government Finances in 1974-75; Governmental Finances in 1964-65 (Washington, D.C.: U.S. Government Printing Office, 1966, 1975, 1976, 1977).

TABLE 2.8

State Spending for Public Welfare as a Proportion of All State
Spending, 1965 and 1975, Selected States
(percentage)

State	All Sources		State Sources Only	
	1965	1975	1965	1975
California	17.3	24.3	10.9	17.4
Connecticut	14.8	19.9	10.7	12.3
Georgia	13.6	18.2	5.7	8.0
Louisiana	19.4	12.4	8.0	5.6
Michigan	9.5	27.1	5.6	20.2
Mississippi	14.4	12.5	6.9	5.7
New York	14.2	23.7	7.6	10.2
Oregon	10.2	15.5	8.7	11.8
Texas	12.1	13.9	4.2	5.2
All	13.2	18.5	7.5	11.8

Source: U.S. Bureau of the Census, *State Government Finances in 1975; Governmental Finances in 1964-65* (Washington, D.C.: U.S. Government Printing Office, 1966, 1975).

assistance for these same programs increased sixfold in actual dollars, and three and one-half times in constant dollars.

The reason for this sharp escalation of state and local costs, despite a more-than-proportionate increase in the federal share, has been the three-pronged impact of expanded AFDC participation, increased AFDC benefit levels, and the commencement of the Medicaid program, with its automatic coverage of the expanded AFDC caseload. The result has been to enlarge the bite that public assistance takes out of state and local budgets. As Table 2.8 shows, public welfare consumed 18.5 percent of all state spending in 1975, up from 13.2 percent in 1965. In other words, welfare spending is increasing at a rate that is 40 percent faster than the rate of growth of overall state spending. The same pattern holds when we deduct federal aid, and look at state welfare spending supported by state sources alone as a proportion of all state spending from state sources. For all states, welfare spending from state sources rose from 7.5 percent to almost 12 percent of state outlays between 1965 and 1975. In some states, like Michigan, these figures are even higher. Welfare consumed 27 percent of that state's general expenditure budget, and 20 percent of the expenditures funded by local sources, in 1975. The comparable figures for 1965 were 9.5 percent and 5.6 percent.

Similar figures could be provided for those cities and counties involved in the welfare business. For example, in Los Angeles County, welfare consumed 38 percent of the general expenditure budget in 1975; in New York City it consumed 25 percent.[22]

In all probability, public assistance expenditures would be far less problematic politically were it not for this intimate tie to state and local budgets. As we have seen, the aggregate costs of needs-tested cash programs, even including Medicaid, are small in comparison to overall income maintenance costs. It is the pattern of distribution of these costs that causes the problems, since state and local budgets are ill-equipped to accommodate them. For one thing, welfare needs are greatest in a time of economic downturn, but this is also the time when public revenues are low, and states and municipalities, unable to engage in deficit financing, are forced to reduce spending. In the second place, tying assistance payments to state and local expenditures has the effect of keeping benefits low precisely where higher benefits are needed: in the poorest states and localities, or those suffering from economic dislocations. In the process, the financing system contributes to wide variations in public assistance payments from state to state, a subject to which we will return when we consider the equity of the existing system. Finally, the current financing system produces a situation in which taxpayers in states with high numbers of poor immigrants end up paying to relieve problems that have their roots in other states. The financing arrangements thus fail to acknowledge that poverty is a national problem, resulting from broad interregional and national economic and social factors over which states and localities have only limited control. The states can neither limit the massive migration that has concentrated a substantial portion of the welfare population in the urban areas of the Northeast and West, nor alter the economic policies that help determine the size of that population or the degree of its need. Yet the states and localities are called upon to foot a substantial share of the bill.

Because of these fiscal pressures, the drive to relieve state and local treasuries has become one of the most politically potent elements supporting welfare reform. The U.S. Conference of Mayors, the National Governors' Conference, the League of Cities, the National Association of County Officials, and the Committee for Economic Development have all endorsed reforms designed to achieve fiscal relief for states and localities through federal government assumption of welfare costs. More than any other problem, therefore, the cost distribution problem stands at the center of political concern.

Adequacy

While concern about the level, rate of growth, and distribution of costs have dominated one side of the welfare reform debate, complaints about the inadequacy of the benefits provided by public assistance have dominated another. "For years," Gilbert Steiner wrote in 1971, "the missing ingredient in public relief has been a combination of federal, state and local support adequate to provide clients with minimum standards of health and decency.[23] In recent years, however, it has become increasingly difficult to evaluate the adequacy

TABLE 2.9

Incidence of Poverty in the United States as Reported in Census Bureau Data, Selected Years

Year	Persons (in millions)	As Percent of All Persons
1962	38.3	21.0
1966	28.5	14.7
1969	24.1	12.1
1971	25.6	12.5
1973	23.0	11.1
1975	25.9	12.3
1976	25.0	11.8

Source: U.S. Bureau of the Census, *Current Population Reports*, Series P-60, no. 103, "Money Income and Poverty States of Families and Persons in the U.S.: 1976, Advance Report" (Washington, D.C.: U.S. Government Printing Office, 1977), p. 34.

argument, for two reasons: first, there is still no agreement on how to define adequacy; and second, the proliferation of in-kind programs has greatly complicated the task of measurement.

So far as the definitional issue is concerned, debate still rages over whether an absolute or a relative definition of adequacy is appropriate. The absolute definition treats adequacy as that level of income required to provide an individual or family the bare minimum food, clothing, shelter, and related services necessary to avoid severe want. In practice, this level has been officially defined as three times the cost of the U.S. Department of Agriculture's "economy diet," on the assumption that the typical poor family spends one-third of its income on food.* The relative definition views poverty in terms of a comparison between the income available to the less well off and that available to others in the society. In this view, people feel poor when their income drops too far below the median, even though it may still be above the absolute poverty level. By convention, 50 percent of the median income is taken as the cutoff point in the relative definition of poverty.

Officially, the absolute standard has gained widest acceptance and is the one that will be used here. However, its shortcomings should be kept in mind. Aside from the failure to acknowledge the relative character of poverty, these shortcomings arise from the difficulty of applying a single standard to the variety of human experience. For example, a family with a chronically ill person may wind up with spendable income well below the poverty line, even though it

*For smaller families, a larger multiplier is used because of the fixed cost of household operation.

has gross income somewhat above it. Should that family be classified as poor or nonpoor? Under the official definition of poverty it would be nonpoor. However, in those states that have a program for the medically indigent under Medicaid, it could be classified as poor since such states deduct medical expenses from income in calculating eligibility.

Even when one has arrived at a definition, there is still a formidable measurement problem because the available income statistics fail to record the benefits provided by many of the government social welfare programs now in existence. In addition, different statistical series utilize different time periods, sampling frames, and populations. Even the charting of participation in multiple programs has only recently begun in earnest. Under the circumstances, the evidence on program adequacy must be analyzed with care.

The best starting point for such an analysis is the Census Bureau's yearly analysis of the poverty population in the United States, a report which provides the most comprehensive assessment available of the distribution of income in the country. As shown in Table 2.9, these census data strongly support the view that benefits currently provided by the welfare system are inadequate. After declining significantly between 1962 and 1966, and at a slower rate between 1966 and 1969, the number of poor persons (that is, the number with incomes below the poverty line) actually increased by 1971, declined again in 1973, and then began to grow again, both absolutely and as a proportion of the total population, after 1973.

Within these aggregate figures significant changes can be discerned in the composition of the poverty population. As noted in Table 2.10, as of 1975 the largest single sector of the poor still consisted of white families headed by a man under 65. This group accounted for 32.5 percent of all poor people, compared to 35.0 percent a decade earlier. Between 1965 and 1975, however, the proportion of the poor in black families headed by men dropped sharply, while those living in white and in black households headed by women rose, from 11.9 percent to 17.3 percent for the former, and from 10.7 to 15.7 percent for the latter. During this same period, the proportion of the aged among the poor declined substantially. What do these data suggest about the adequacy of public assistance benefits? Why do 26 million people remain poor at the end of a decade that witnessed dramatic expansions in income maintenance expenditures? And what is the meaning of the changes in the composition of the poverty-stricken population? To answer these questions, we must look at four key points.

Social and Economic Changes. The first point is that the extent of poverty is a function not just of the extent of the public income transfer system, but also of the character of broader social and economic conditions.[24] Between 1966 and 1975, significant changes took place in these conditions. In the first place, the number of female-headed households in the population climbed, and since such households have a higher incidence of poverty than male-headed households (34.6 percent versus 7.8 percent in 1975),[25] this translated into an even faster

TABLE 2.10

Distribution of the Poverty Population, 1966–75

Group	Number of Persons (in thousands) 1966	1975	Percent of Total 1966	1975
Under 65				
Male-headed families—white	9,986	8,414	35.0	32.5
Male-headed families—black	4,603	2,176	16.1	8.4
Female-headed families—white	3,394	4,487	11.9	17.3
Female-headed families—black	3,051	4,071	10.7	15.7
Unrelated individuals	2,094	2,963	7.4	11.5
Over 65				
In families	2,507	1,192	8.8	4.6
Unrelated individuals	2,607	2,125	9.2	8.3
Other	268	459	0.9	1.6
Total	28,510	25,877	100.0	100.0

Source: U.S. Bureau of the Census, *Current Population Reports*, Series P-60, no. 103 (Washington, D.C.: Government Printing Office, 1976).

rise in their share of the poverty population. In the second place, the economy took a tailspin during this period, producing widespread unemployment and a significant slowing of real economic growth. The results are reflected in Table 2.11, which shows the increase in the incidence of poverty that occurred between 1973 and 1975 among families headed by males under 65, which are normally the families with lowest poverty rates. In a word, many of the gains achieved by 1973 in reducing the incidence of poverty among these groups were wiped out by recession and unemployment, which apparently reduced pre-income transfer incomes by an amount greater than what the income transfer, or public assistance, system provided. On the other hand, it must be recognized that the impact of the recession would have been much harsher without the income transfer system.

Benefit Levels. A second explanation for the apparent persistence of poverty has to do with the benefit levels in the assistance programs. As we have noted, expenditures on these programs increased dramatically between 1965 and 1970. But expenditure figures reflect changes in eligibility and participation rates as well as in benefit levels. When we isolate the latter, significant variations appear, both among programs and over time, as shown in Table 2.12. In the first place, the only program in which average benefit levels rose consistently throughout this ten-year span was social security. By contrast, in AFDC and unemployment insurance, average benefit levels increased significantly between 1965 and 1970 and then leveled off or declined in constant dollar terms between 1970 and

TABLE 2.11

Incidence of Poverty among Families Headed by
Males under 65, 1971–75

Family Class	Poverty Rate*			Percent Change, 1973–75
	1971	1973	1975	
White	6.2	4.9	6.1	+24.4
Black	20.3	17.7	16.9	− 4.5
All	7.5	6.0	7.1	+18.3

*The poverty rate is the proportion of all persons in the designated class who are in poverty.

Source: U.S. Bureau of the Census, Current Population Reports, P-60, no. 103 (Washington, D.C.: U.S. Government Printing Office), pp. 33–34.

1975. These data help explain why the proportion of the aged in the poverty population declined between 1965 and 1975, and why the female-headed-family segment grew despite the availability of a cash assistance program (AFDC) specially designed for this group.*

Program Gaps and Leaks. A third part of the explanation of the apparent persistence of poverty despite welfare program growth results from the gaps and leaks in the programs. Except for food stamps (and Medicaid to a lesser extent), none of the major income assistance programs provides benefits solely on the basis of need. The social insurance programs, for example, condition benefits on age and prior employment in a covered job. The needs-tested programs require that recipients not only be needy but also be in a particular demographic category (aged, disabled, blind, or in a family with dependent children headed by a woman or, in some states, an unemployed male). The problem is that the categories exclude more people than they include, creating massive gaps in coverage. Most notably, no cash assistance, and only limited in-kind assistance, is available to male-headed families earning less than poverty-level wages (the working poor), or to poor families without children, or to unrelated individuals under 65. The results are reflected in surveys, conducted in 1971 by the University of Michigan's Survey Research Center, which show how the categorical character of the

*One further explanation for the difficulties experienced by female-headed families in the 1970s is the apparent tightening of application procedures and the resulting decline in acceptance rates that occurred, as states responded to growing welfare rolls with administrative procedures calculated to deter applicants.

TABLE 2.12

Average Monthly Benefit Levels in Major Cash Assistance Programs, 1965–75

Program	Constant 1975 Dollars			Percent Change	
	1965	1970	1975	1965-70	1970-75
Social security	$151.64	$173.35	$205.87	+14.3	+18.8
Black-lung	n.a.	254.66	247.70	n.a.	− 2.7
Unemployment insurance	252.88	302.52	281.48	+19.6	− 7.0
AFDC (per person)	55.85	69.51	72.41	+24.4	+ 4.2
SSI (and prececessors)	107.27	108.71	114.39	+ 1.3	+ 5.2

n.a. = not applicable.
Source: Social Security Bulletin 39, no. 7 (July 1976).

TABLE 2.13

Availability of Income Maintenance Assistance to Different Segments of the Poor, 1971

Segment of the Poor	Number of Pretransfer Poor Families (thousands)	Pretransfer Poor Families Not Receiving Transfers	
		Number (thousands)	Percent
Families with aged or disabled head	9,018	422	4.7
Families with nonaged head, without children	2,356	1,347	57.2
Families with children headed by a male under 65	1,659	844	50.9
Families with children headed by a female under 65	2,027	351	17.3
All families	15,059	2,964	19.7

Note: Income maintenance assistance includes cash assistance programs, food stamps, and General Assistance.

Source: Adapted from Michael Barth, George Carcagno, and John Palmer, *Toward an Effective Income Support System: Problems, Prospects, and Choices* (Madison: Institute for Research on Poverty, 1974), p. 25.

TABLE 2.14

Leakage of Social Welfare Expenditures to the Nonpoor, 1972

Program	Total Expenditures (billions)	Benefits to Pretransfer Nonpoor (billions)	Percent Spent on Pretransfer Nonpoor
Social security and railroad retirement	$80.1	$37.4	47
Public employment retirement	11.7	7.2	62
Unemployment insurance	6.8	5.3	78
Public assistance	10.8	1.3	12
Veterans' benefits	6.2	3.6	58
Other cash	7.4	5.9	80
Food stamps	1.9	0.3	16
Child nutrition	1.8	0.8	44
Housing	1.8	0.8	44
Medicare	7.0	3.7	53
Medicaid	7.5	1.9	27
Other health	10.0	5.2	52
Office of Economic Opportunity and other social services	2.2	0.4	18
Employment and manpower	3.9	1.1	28
Education (excluding local)	20.1	15.7	78
Total	142.7	71.4	50

Source: Adapted from Robert D. Plotnick and Felicity Skidmore, *Progress Against Poverty* (Madison: University of Wisconsin, Institute for Research on Poverty, 1975), pp. 56–57.

public programs limits the aid available to sizable segments of the poor, especially families headed by males under 65. (See Table 2.13.) The fact that this population group still comprises the largest single segment of the post-income transfer poverty population can probably be attributed substantially to this fact.

In addition to these gaps in the coverage of those who need assistance, the current assistance mechanisms also suffer from leaks through which money flows to the nonneedy. As Table 2.14 shows, these leaks are not confined to the insurance programs, which are not needs-tested. A study of the distribution of the 1972 social welfare expenditures, reported in Table 2.14, shows not only that about half of all assistance went to the nonpoor, but also that 15–25 percent of the assistance from the needs-tested programs went to the nonpoor, probably because of the possibilities for participation in multiple programs and the array of exemptions provided in calculating benefits and eligibility.

TABLE 2.15

Extent of Poverty Alleviation Achieved by Public Income Assistance Programs for Different Categories of the Poor, 1972 (thousands of households)

Household Type	Pretransfer Poor Households	Number and Percent of Pretransfer Poor Households Made Nonpoor by Each Program							
		Social Security		Other Social Insurance[a]		Public Assistance[b]		All	
		Number	Percent	Number	Percent	Number	Percent	Number	Percent
Aged head	8,643	4,450	51	630	7	381	4	5,461	63
Nonaged male heads with children[c]	2,011	138	7	211	10	115	6	464	23
Nonaged female heads with children	2,210	197	9	45	2	261	12	503	23
Nonaged head, no children[d]	4,776	581	12	461	10	212	4	1,254	26
Total	17,640	5,362	30	1,345	8	968	5	7,682	44

[a]Includes unemployment insurance, workmen's compensation, veterans' benefits, and government employee pensions.
[b]Includes old age assistance, aid to the blind, aid to the partially and totally disabled, and AFDC.
[c]Includes unrelated individuals.
[d]Most are unrelated individuals, but childless couples are included.

Source: Robert D. Plotnick and Felicity Skidmore, *Progress Against Poverty* (Madison: University of Wisconsin, Institute for Research on Poverty, 1976), p. 147.

The consequence of these gaps, leaks, and variations in benefits is to reduce considerably the effectiveness of the income maintenance system. According to one recently published study based on census data, only 44 percent of all pretransfer poor families managed to escape poverty thanks to the major income transfer programs. And as noted in Table 2.15, most of this help was provided by the social security program, which accounted for 30 percent of the total 44 percent. By contrast, the public assistance categories helped only 5 percent of the poor get out of poverty. This is consistent with what was noted earlier about the growth of social security benefit levels relative to those of the needs-tested programs, and helps explain the continued incidence of poverty among the nonaged.

Data Problems. Before we accept this overall conclusion about the inadequacy of the benefits provided by the income assistance system, however, it is necessary to take account of the severe gaps in the data upon which this conclusion rests. Two such gaps are most important. First, the census data underreport the amount of cash transfers paid out. In fact, about 20 percent more money is paid out in benefits than is ultimately reported on the census forms. Consequently, the extent of posttransfer poverty even in terms of cash income is probably not as great as the census reports suggest.

More serious than this, however, is the total failure of the census takers to record in-kind income. In all the census reports on poverty, only cash income, or cash transfers, are recorded. This means that social security payments, unemployment insurance, SSI, AFDC, and the like are treated as income; but food stamps, Medicaid, free school lunches, housing subsidies, and other noncash assistance are not. Since much of the dramatic change in income assistance expenditures over the past decade has taken the form of in-kind transfers, this introduces a massive error into the estimates of program adequacy, and an error that has grown over time.

One way to see this is to compare expenditures on in-kind transfers to the size of the census report's "poverty gap," the difference between the cash income actually received by the poor and what they would have had to receive to escape poverty. As Table 2.16 shows, federally financed in-kind transfers were more than sufficient by 1975 to eliminate the poverty gap that still remained after receipt of cash transfers. Based on this line of reasoning, one study has concluded that when in-kind transfers are counted, those considered poor in the official census figures as of 1973 really have incomes 30 percent above the average poverty line.[26]

The problem with this conclusion is that gaps and leaks plague in-kind transfers as much as cash assistance, and perhaps more so. As a consequence, it is not reasonable to assume that in-kind benefits are really distributed in a way that maximizes the relief from poverty. The design of these programs is far too cumbersome, and the goals far too numerous, to expect such efficiency in the pursuit of the single goal of relieving poverty. Yet, data to assess the actual impact of the in-kind transfers are still scarce. Analysts must therefore estimate

TABLE 2.16

The Poverty Gap and In-Kind Transfers, 1965, 1970, and 1975

Poverty Situation	Billions of 1975 Dollars		
	1965	1970	1975
Poverty gap before cash transfers	37.7	40.3	n.a.
Poverty gap after cash transfers	17.8	16.0	14.6
Amount of total in-kind assistance	5.6	13.0	28.2

Source: Robert D. Plotnick and Felicity Skidmore, *Progress Against Poverty* (Madison: University of Wisconsin, Institute for Research on Poverty, 1976), p. 140; U.S. Bureau of the Census, *Current Population Reports*, Series P–60, no. 103 (Washington, D.C.: U.S. Government Printing Office, 1976); *Budget of the United States Government*, 1967, 1972, 1977.

the distribution of in-kind program benefits. One such study, completed in 1975 and utilizing 1972 data, indicates that almost three-quarters of the pretransfer poor were actually helped out of poverty by the welfare system, when the value of in-kind benefits is included, compared to only 44 percent shown in the census reports, which include only the cash benefits. (See Table 2.17.) According to this study, 83 percent of the poverty gap is closed by the welfare system when in-kind transfers are included, compared to only 64 percent without them.

A recent Congressional Budget Office (CBO) study comes to a similar conclusion. Based on an elaborate computer model for estimating the impact of in-kind programs, this study concludes that while 25 percent of U.S. families were poor in 1976 prior to public transfers (including in-kind transfers), only 7 percent were after receipt of these income transfers. By contrast, the comparable Census Bureau figure was 12 percent.[27]

Taken together, therefore, these various studies of the impact of in-kind assistance suggest that the longstanding complaints about the inadequacy of benefits under the various income assistance programs must be seriously revised, at least to the extent that adequacy is defined in absolute terms. To be sure, the analyses to date rely on imperfect estimates about the distribution of in-kind benefits. In addition, they generally assume that in-kind benefits are worth as much to the recipients as they cost the government, which is probably untrue since these benefits force families to purchase more of a particular commodity than they may want, given their other needs. In the case of Medicaid, moreover, valuing benefits at their cost to the government leads to the curious situation in which families with extensive illnesses are credited with higher incomes even though the families themselves never see the money. Nevertheless, it is clear that the census data traditionally used to gauge the nation's success in eliminating poverty understate the progress that has been made, as the data fail to include

TABLE 2.17

Antipoverty Potency of the Public Income Transfer System with and without In-Kind Transfers, 1968, 1970, 1972

Year	Percent of Pretransfer Poor Households Helped over the Poverty Line by Transfers		Percent of Pretransfer Poverty Gap Closed	
	Cash Transfers Only	In-Kind Benefits Included	Cash Transfers Only	In-Kind Benefits Included
1968	35	52	57	69
1970	37	55	60	73
1972	44	72	64	83

Source: Timothy M. Smeeding, "Measuring the Economic Welfare of Low-Income Households and the Anti-Poverty Effectiveness of Cash and Non-Cash Transfer Programs" (Ph.D. diss., University of Wisconsin–Madison, 1975), cited in Robert D. Plotnick and Felicity Skidmore, *Progress Against Poverty* (Madison: University of Wisconsin, Institute for Research on Poverty, 1976), p. 144.

in-kind aid. If coverage and benefit levels are still not adequate to eliminate poverty altogether, they are clearly approaching it, especially when we reflect that some portion of those who show up below the poverty line in the official figures are young workers and students whose low income is temporary and a product of their just having begun working.[28] The case for reform on grounds of adequacy, therefore, is considerably weaker than it used to be.

Inequity

In pursuing adequacy by adding incrementally to the existing welfare structure, instead of reshaping it more fundamentally, however, the changes of the past decade have not addressed, or have actually worsened, some of the other dimensions of effectiveness, like equity and efficiency. Much of the current debate over welfare reform now turns on the question of how these other dimensions can be addressed.

The equity issue, the question of the basic fairness of the system, is probably the most intractable. Involved here are two interrelated issues: the disparities that the welfare system leaves among different segments of the poor (horizontal inequity); and the even more controversial advantages the system sometimes provides for the poor compared to the nonpoor (vertical inequity).

Horizontal Inequity

Two major features of the income assistance system are primarily responsible for horizontal inequities: the categorical character of the assistance programs, and the extensive discretion many of the programs leave to the states. The first of these refers to the way in which the needs-tested cash programs in particular define eligibility. Under these programs, eligibility is restricted not only to the needy, but also to certain categories of the needy, defined in terms of age, family structure, physical condition, as well as previous place of employment. As a result, sizable segments of the poor—especially households headed by males employed full time (the working poor)—have long been excluded from federally supported cash assistance. And while many states have general assistance programs to cover such families, coverage and benefits in these state programs are limited. The upshot is to deny assistance to children whose parents have stayed together.

Because AFDC and Medicaid leave decisions on eligibility, benefit levels, and other program matters up to the states, what a family receives also depends on where it lives. In Louisiana, for example, AFDC provides coverage for children up to age 21 but no coverage for families headed by unemployed fathers; requires no deduction for the value of a home in computing eligibility; and places a maximum ceiling of $122 on monthly benefits for a family of four, even though this is only 60 percent of what the state judges to be the need standard. In Connecticut, aid is available under AFDC only for children up to age 18;

TABLE 2.18

Extent of Inequities Produced by Public Assistance
before and after Payment of In-Kind Benefits

| | Equity Ratio* | | |
Income	Cash Only	Cash and Food	Cash, Food, and Housing
$0	58.6	70.6	87.1
$1,600	69.7	78.1	83.4
$3,200	63.5	69.9	74.5
$4,000	70.0	72.4	75.6

*The equity ratio is the ratio of the benefits available to a four-person male-headed family compared to those available to a four-person female-headed family. The higher the ratio, the greater the equity. When the ratio equals 100.0, benefits for the male-headed family equal those for the comparable female-headed family.

Source: Computed from data provided in U.S. Congress, Joint Economic Committee, Subcommittee on Public Welfare, *Studies in Public Welfare*, "Welfare in the 70's: A National Study of Benefits Available in 100 Local Areas," 93d Cong., 2d sess., 1974, pp. 36–37.

homes are included at their equity value in computing eligibility; the need standard is 64 percent higher than in Louisiana, and the maximum payment is $332, almost three times the Louisiana level. Such differences cannot be explained on grounds of income disparities or cost-of-living differences between the two states. While Louisiana paid a maximum of $122 to an AFDC family in 1974, for example, neighboring Mississippi, with per capita income three-fourths as high, was paying only half as much; and nearby Oklahoma, with per capita income only 10 percent higher, provided two times more.[29]

These horizontal inequities have been significantly reduced over the past decade by the expansion of some of the in-kind programs. The food stamp program in particular now functions as a kind of income floor available to all in need, regardless of family situation. It has thus helped relieve the inequities created by the AFDC program between female-headed families in need and all others. Data collected by the Joint Economic Committee's Subcommittee on Fiscal Policy in 1974 show that, without food stamps, a two-parent family of four with no income in 1972 would have been entitled to an average of only 58.6 percent as much assistance as a female-headed family of four ($1,419 versus $2,420). When food stamps were added, the two-parent family could count on 70.6 percent as much ($2,431 versus $3,442). As noted in Table 2.18, this relationship holds no matter what the level of earned income. With food stamps added, the non-AFDC family never falls below 70 percent of the benefits avail-

TABLE 2.19

Geographical Disparities in Public Assistance Payments
before and after Distribution of Food Stamps, 1972

	Ratio of Standard Deviation to Average Benefit Level	
Family Type	Cash Only	Cash and Food
Single individual	143.7	89.5
Couple	139.0	79.8
Mother and child	44.5	29.5
Mother and two children	41.7	25.7
Mother and three children	40.4	24.5
Father, mother, and child	117.5	65.6
Father, mother, and two children	116.6	62.5

Note: Data apply to cases with no private income.

Source: Computed from data provided in U.S. Congress, Joint Economic Committee, *Welfare in the 70's*, Studies in Public Welfare, no. 15, 93d Cong., 2d sess., p. 38.

able to the AFDC family. The inclusion of housing assistance, moreover, improves the equity picture further. And since food stamp benefits have increased since 1972, the current inequities are probably still smaller than those shown here.

The food stamp program has also reduced the inequities resulting from state variations in AFDC benefit levels. An unemployed mother with two children in high-benefit San Francisco, for example, would have received five times the AFDC assistance available to a comparable family in low-benefit Bolivar County, Mississippi, prior to obtaining food stamps. Because food stamp benefits are higher where other income is lower, however, when food stamps are added this disparity is reduced to two to one, considerably closer to the real disparity in living costs.[30] That this outcome is not an isolated instance is illustrated by Table 2.19, which compared the size of the standard deviation in benefit levels among states to the average benefit level, for different family types, using data assembled by the Joint Economic Committee's Subcommittee on Fiscal Policy. What becomes quite clear is that the relative size of that deviation is markedly lower when food stamps are added in, and this result holds for every family tupe.

Horizontal inequities in the public assistance system have been reduced by two other recent innovations as well. The first was the extension of AFDC benefits in 1961 to families where the father is present but unemployed, or employed less than 100 hours per month. While only half the states have adopted this program, and eligibility requirements are rigid, 4 percent of all AFDC families, or 676,110 persons, benefited from it as of 1976.[31]

The working poor have also benefited from a series of changes in the unemployment insurance laws during the past several years, most notably the benefit extensions first enacted on a contingency basis in 1970, made permanent in December 1974, and extended in March 1975. As a result of these changes, the basic benefit period for unemployment insurance recipients rose from 26 to 39 weeks, with provision for extension up to 65 weeks. In the process, according to a recent study, a significant segment of the working poor managed to avoid poverty, at least for a time. Extension of unemployment insurance benefits reduced the proportion of the poor among all whites who had exhausted their unemployment insurance benefits from 40 percent to 10 percent. For poor blacks, the reduction was from 55 to 21 percent.[32] In other words, the unemployment insurance program seems to have picked up some of the burden not addressed by the existing welfare system.

While some facets of the shift to in-kind benefits thus seem to have reduced horizontal inequities significantly, however, others have worked in the opposite direction. One of these is the tendency to make participation in the categorical cash programs the admission ticket to many of the in-kind programs. For example, only AFDC recipients and those who were receiving aid under programs for the blind, aged, and disabled as of 1972 are automatically eligible for Medicaid. Although federal law allows states to extend aid to the medically indigent—that is, those who are not receiving assistance under the categorical programs but whose income falls below a state-determined limit when medical costs are deducted and other exemptions excluded—only 25 states have exercised that option. As a result, most of the Medicaid funds flow to persons already receiving aid under the categorical cash programs, intensifying, rather than relieving, preexisting inequities. Eligibility for food stamps is more general, but this program produces similar results because of the automatic eligibility of AFDC recipients, regardless of their other posttransfer income. Thus AFDC recipients with incomes above the poverty level, thanks to AFDC payments and Medicaid, can receive food stamps in addition, whereas those with similar incomes, but not on AFDC, cannot.

The in-kind programs also generate inequities by incorporating directly many of the same kinds of frustrating state-by-state variations in program content and coverage that have long been the bane of reformers of the cash assistance programs. Under Medicaid, for example, the federal government specifies a mandatory list of services every state must provide to recipients of AFDC and other federal cash assistance programs, but then leaves it up to the states to decide whether to provide additional medical benefits and whether to aid other needy people beyond those enrolled in the federal cash assistance programs. As a result, a father who is employed on a low-paying job in Colorado and has a sick daughter would be wise to move to Montana, where he would qualify for Medicaid to cover her medical expenses. If her ailment required physical treatment, he would be better advised to move on to California, because in Montana such services are covered only for people receiving federally supported cash assistance.

Finally, inequities are built into the in-kind programs by virtue of funding limitations and disparities in participation. Benefits under in-kind programs are rarely available to all who are eligible. For example, only a relatively small percentage of the families eligible for housing assistance actually receive it, because of the limited funds made available. In other cases, funds are available but outreach is limited so that only those receiving cash assistance hear about the programs or learn about their own eligibility. Thus, one recent study of food stamp recipients found five times as many AFDC and SSI eligible participating as non-cash assistance eligibles.[33] Even more striking were the results of a 1976 study of persons who had left the AFDC rolls. Although almost all these people had participated in the food stamp program as AFDC recipients, and most remained eligible after leaving AFDC, only 11 percent reported that they continued to receive food stamps. Most of the remainder of the families did not realize they were still eligible.[34] In short, while we can demonstrate that the expansion of food stamps and other in-kind aid should have relieved some of the earlier horizontal inequities, it is harder to demonstrate that they actually have because of the peculiarities that exist in participation rates. Until participation and eligibility coincide, the inequities will persist, albeit less severely than earlier.

Vertical Inequity

Perhaps even more politically damaging than the horizontal inequities in the welfare system are the so-called vertical ones, those that result in a higher income after welfare for those who start off poor than is ultimately available to those who start off nonpoor. This is the problem that former Congresswoman Martha Griffiths said prompted her to undertake an exhaustive inquiry into welfare policy as chairwoman of the Subcommittee on Fiscal Policy, of the Joint Economic Committee, in 1972–74. It is a problem that is illustrated by the story Mrs. Griffiths tells, in the foreword to the subcommittee's report, about a woman in her district who earned $5,300 per year, yet ended up, after taxes and expenses, with less than another woman in the same district who had access to a federally subsidized home and drew $750 per month ($9,000 per year) in untaxed AFDC payments.[35]

This concern that recent changes in welfare benefits have left welfare recipients better off than the working poor echoes a longstanding principle of relief policy in both Britain and the United States: the principle of "less eligibility," which holds, in the words of the British Poor Law Commission of 1834:

> The first and most essential of all conditions, a principle which we find universally admitted . . . is that his [the welfare recipient's] situation on the whole shall not be made really or apparently so eligible [that is, desirable] as the situation of the independent laborer of the lowest class.[36]

Since this principle grew out of a desire to avoid any interference by the relief system in the workings of the labor market by making it disadvantageous for workers to go on relief, there is a certain irony in the fact that its most egregious violation in the American context resulted from an effort to stimulate welfare recipients to work. The provisions in question were the amendments to the basic AFDC law enacted in 1962 and 1967 to give AFDC recipients an incentive to find jobs by permitting them to deduct their work expenses from their income and keep a portion of anything they earned over this. This was achieved by requiring the states to deduct all work-related expenses, and additional flat $30 per month, plus one-third of all remaining earnings from the income of any AFDC recipient prior to computing benefits. Benefits are then computed on the remainder, as if this other income did not exist. If Mrs. Griffiths's $5,300-per-year constituent had a coworker on AFDC, for example, and if this coworker claimed $1,000 in work-related expenses (taxes, child care, transportation), then she could end up with gross income of $7,473 per year, or $2,173 more than the non-AFDC recipient on the same job. The $2,173 bonus is the amount of AFDC benefits to which the recipient is entitled after work expenses and the "$30 plus one-third" are subtracted from earnings and the remainder is applied against the need standard.* Since the AFDC recipient is also eligible for Medicaid, the real disparity may be even greater than this cash difference implies. In fact, an AFDC recipient, even without working, could easily be receiving more than the working woman, when food stamps and Medicaid are included.

What this demonstrates is the trade-off that exists between benefit adequacy and equity, between improving the lot of current program recipients and improving the degree of equity between program recipients and low-wage workers who are not on welfare. Because of this trade-off, concern about the vertical inequities in the welfare system provides another argument to counter pressures for improved benefits. Congresswoman Griffiths has stated the argument forcefully: "The theory of comparing what is given in welfare with what is needed is foolish. 'What is needed' is a phony standard set up by a paternalistic middle class. The real standard is what similar people earn, and how they are treated."[37]

By focusing on the inequities between the poor and the nonpoor, however, this argument ignores the far more substantial inequalities that separate the poor and the nearpoor alike from the rest of the population. To the extent that welfare benefits are limited to avoid invidious comparisons between the poor and the nearpoor, less progress can be made in reducing overall income inequality. In

---

*This example assumes that the recipient would be entitled, without the job, to the full $400 per month available to an AFDC recipient with a family of four in Michigan. The calculations are as follows:

Countable earnings = $5,300 − $1,000 (work expenses) − $360 ($30-per-month disregard) − $1,343 (33 percent exemption) = $2,627
AFDC benefits = $4,800 (needs standard) − $2,627 (countable income) = $2,173
Total income = $5,300 + $2,173 = $7,473

other words, the pursuit of equity ironically can end up increasing the degree of overall inequality.[38]

One solution to this dilemma is, in Nathan Glazer's phrase, to "reform work, not welfare."[39] As Glazer sees it, the heart of the inequity problem is that the welfare system now offers advantages—in the form of medical coverage, security, stability, and benefits—far in excess of those available from most of the jobs open to the inner-city poor. Rather than taking these benefits away from the welfare population, Glazer asserts, we should make them available to those in the low-wage and seasonal labor market. As Glazer puts it: "Let us leave welfare where it is, and try to make work—the kind of work that people on welfare, or the fathers of children on welfare, might take—more attractive."

Whatever the solution, it should be clear that the inequity issue is one of the most sensitive and politically explosive in the debate on welfare reform. Viewed as a whole, the changes of the past decade seem to have reduced the inequities between those who get nothing and those who get something, while increasing the disparities between those who get something and those who get much more. Although the equity of the system as a whole has doubtless improved, the political salience of the vertical inequities has overshadowed this improvement in the public mind. But it should not be ignored.

Disincentives

Concern about the degree of equity in public assistance is closely related to that about possible incentives or disincentives built into the system. Three types of hypothesized incentive effects in particular are of concern: those that discourage work, those that discourage family stability, and those that encourage migration. In each case, what is important is not just whether the incentive is present, but also whether it is strong enough to affect behavior.

Work Disincentives

As discussed more fully in Chapter 3, the structure of public assistance in the United States was designed to avoid any adverse impact on the incentive to work. The categorical approach that characterizes the whole pattern of public assistance in this country reflects this goal. Public aid was made available only to those considered nonemployable: the aged, the blind, and the disabled; dependent children and their caretakers. Employables were offered no assistance except when they were thrown out of work through no fault of their own, or when they retired. Since employables were not entitled to relief and relief recipients were not expected to work, it seemed logical to deduct anything a relief recipient earned from the amount of benefits made available. This constituted a marginal tax rate of 100 percent on earnings (that is, the full amount of earnings was deducted from the public benefits provided, so that unless the recipient got a job paying in excess of prevailing AFDC benefits, it did not pay to work.

Two important changes shattered this logic. First was the transformation in attitudes toward working women that occurred during the 30 years following the passage of the Social Security Act in 1935. By 1970, 43 percent of all women were in the labor force. Among separated and divorced women, this figure reached 52 and 72 percent respectively.[40] Simultaneously, a change was taking place in the composition of the AFDC caseload. For one thing, the widow caring for her children after the death of her husband was replaced, as the typical AFDC recipient, by the never-married or separated mother of a child whose father had apparently abandoned the family. And for another, the welfare rolls were opened in 1961 to families with unemployed fathers, at least in half the states.

Taken together, these changes significantly altered earlier public attitudes about the nonemployability of AFDC recipients and increased concern that AFDC was harboring numerous employable persons who were shirking their responsibilities. In response to these concerns Congress moved in 1962 and 1967 to provide work incentives in the AFDC program by permitting states to deduct work expenses and $30 plus one-third of remaining income when computing benefits.

Many of these work incentives have been cancelled out by the operation of other programs. Each of the in-kind programs supplementing AFDC had its own marginal tax rate, so that the combined loss in benefits from an additional dollar of earnings could, theoretically at least, be greater than one dollar. As one example, while AFDC taxes net earnings at a 67 percent rate (benefits decline $2 for every $3 in earnings in excess of expenses and $30 per month), the food stamp program taxes participants an additional 30 percent. Based on program operations in 100 areas, the Joint Economic Committee concluded that this can mean in practice that the income left, after work expenses and benefit reductions for employed AFDC and food stamp recipients can average as little as 20 cents per dollar earned.[41]

Beyond these marginal-tax-rate problems is a whole series of so-called notch problems. A notch is a point in the public assistance benefit scale where an additional dollar of earnings makes a recipient ineligible for other public programs. Readers of Ann Landers's column will recognize this as the problem posed recently by a group of St. Paul welfare mothers who wrote to complain:

> Not one of us would be on welfare if there was a decent alternative. It's the last resort this side of begging on the street, staying with some creep for the sake of a meal ticket, or committing suicide.

> It's bad enough to be on welfare, but getting OFF is even worse. When we do find work, our food stamps, medical insurance and other benefits are reduced to the point where we are worse off than when we were on welfare. So—we stay on.[42]

Perhaps the most severe of these notches occurs in eligibility for Medicaid. AFDC and food stamp benefits decline somewhat gradually as earnings increase, but Medicaid benefits click off suddenly at the point where the family ceases to be eligible for AFDC, or passes beyond the cutoff point for coverage for the medically indigent. An additional dollar of income can thus spell financial disaster for a recipient family, denying it access to $500–$1,000 in medical care. Similarly, in states with AFDC coverage for families with unemployed fathers, moving from part-time to full-time work automatically means the loss of all benefits.

These work disincentive features apply not only to AFDC recipients. As in-kind benefits have been extended to wider segments of the population in the interest of greater equity, they have exposed millions of families not on cash assistance to complicated marginal tax rates.[43] Social security and unemployment compensation raise similar questions.

The more adequate the benefits and the more comprehensive the coverage of the public assistance system, therefore, the more significant the potential work disincentives. Concern about work incentives thus constitutes a restraint on pressures for expanded benefits.

But the key question is the real impact these incentives have on work behavior. To what extent do work disincentives actually reduce work?

Although considerable work has been done on this question, the results are far from definitive. Most analysts conclude that, while work disincentives do affect work behavior in the direction hypothesized, the force of these effects is not very great for working-age males, though it is somewhat stronger for married women, female family heads, and older men.[44] The New Jersey income maintenance experiment, for example, showed that the work effort of employed males was only marginally affected by the availability of an income guarantee, almost regardless of the tax rate. The percentage change in the work effort of women was greater, but this was largely a product of the low level of employment at which they started.[45]

The force of the work incentive argument is also affected by the fact that most welfare mothers have responsibilities that make them unavailable for work, and by the fact that most of the jobs available to them do not pay well enough to make a work incentive feature in the welfare system cost effective.

For example, one recent study, after demonstrating a significant statistical relationship between work incentives and work among AFDC mothers, conceded that what is "of much greater importance" is the fact that "even very large percentage changes in the policy parameters (i.e., marginal tax rates, flat exemptions and deductions for work expenses) result in very small absolute changes in the employment rate of AFDC mothers."[46] A similar study of experience under the 1967 AFDC work-incentive amendments in Michigan came to the same conclusion: despite the clear positive relationship between improved work incentives and increased work among AFDC recipients, the size of the work increases was so small in absolute terms as to suggest that "those factors which constrained employment prior to the exemption's implementation continued to do so after its implementation." Primary among these were the demographic characteristics of the AFDC population and the limited job opportunities available to them in the labor market. According to this study, in fact, the wages earned by those who went to work in response to the 1967 work incentives were so far below the new break-even point for AFDC that the costs of the work incentives exceeded the benefits (reduced AFDC payments resulting from increased employment and earnings) by a factor of ten to one.[47]

These results are consistent with the generally disappointing results of the WIN (Work Incentive) program, which sought to channel a higher proportion of welfare mothers into jobs via special training efforts, and with research on the work orientation of the poor. Both of these demonstrate an eagerness to work on the part of welfare mothers that is dampened less by the high marginal tax rates of welfare than by the limited jobs available at sufficient rates of pay.[48]

Family Stability Disincentives

Related to criticisms of welfare's work disincentives are criticisms of AFDC's impact on family stability. Because federal cash assistance is unavailable to low-income households headed by a full-time employed male, it may be financially advantageous to the family if the male leaves. At the very least, the financial loss from his departure can be minimal.

These disincentives to family stability were reduced somewhat by the extension of AFDC eligibility to families headed by an unemployed parent (the AFDC-U program) in 1961, and by the provision of food stamps and, in some states, General Assistance and Medicaid for two-parent working families. However, only 24 states have adopted AFDC-U programs, and eligibility criteria in these states are so strict that less than 160,000 families are enrolled.* Food stamp and Medicaid extensions have only slightly reduced the financial advantages of the AFDC family over the two-parent family with low wages,[49] and recent efforts to locate the fathers of AFDC children and force them to make child support payments can paradoxically produce additional family disruption if the father has formed another family.

However, it is easier to identify financial disincentives to family stability than to establish that such disincentives actually affect behavior and, if so, how much. One of the problems is that the behavior in question is really a series of actions involving decisions to have a child, to separate, to establish a separate household, to remarry, and so on. Although some research has established that

---

*To be eligible for AFDC-U, the father must have been unemployed for 30 days prior to receipt of benefits, not refused a bona fide offer of employment or training, have six or more quarters of work in any 13-calendar-quarter period ending within one year prior to the application for benefits, register with the state employment office, and not be receiving any unemployment compensation.

higher AFDC benefits are associated with higher proportions of families headed by women,[50] it is not at all clear that this results from AFDC's impact on the separation part of the equation. When welfare mothers have been asked what prompted their separation from a husband or boyfriend, few have noted the AFDC-family-disincentive argument, pointing instead to such factors as mistreatment, other relationships, and incompatibility.[51] In addition, a substantial portion of the apparent rise in female-headed households resulted not from a rise in female-headed families, but rather from decisions by existing female heads of families to set up their own households apart from those of parents or relatives.[52] Finally, noting the lower remarriage rates for nonwhite female heads of households, Heather Ross and Isabel Sawhill conclude that "the more important welfare contribution to female-headedness—at least for black families—is through incentives to continue in female-headed status rather than to enter that status initially."[53] To the extent that disincentives have an effect, in other words, it is to reduce pressures to remarry rather than to cause separation in the first place. Some of the latter disincentives are likely to be relieved by recent court decisions that allow AFDC recipients to continue receiving benefits after they remarry, as long as the new father is not shown to be contributing financially to the children.[54]

Even those studies that establish a link between female-headed families and welfare find an even stronger link with wage rates. One study found a 10 percent increase in AFDC benefits associated with only a 2 percent increase in the proportion of female-headed families in an area. By contrast, a 10 percent increase in female wage rates was accompanied by a 7 percent increase in female family heads, and a 10 percent increase in male wage rates by an 8 percent decline in female family heads. In short, the lack of economic opportunities for males and the presence of jobs at decent wages for women are two or three times more potent than welfare benefits in accounting for high proportions of families headed by females.[55]

It seems doubtful, therefore, that much of the growth in female-headed households, even among the poor, can be attributed to the family stability disincentives built into categorical aid programs.[56] This is not to say that such disincentives ought not to be eliminated on grounds of equity. The case for reform on these grounds is quite strong, especially in view of the Supreme Court's opinion in *Lewis v. Martin*, which allows children to receive AFDC payments while living with a stepfather, but not while living with their natural father. But to promote such reform on grounds that the existing system is stimulating family dissolutions, and that reform will remedy this, is probably to engage in false advertising that can be counterproductive.

Migration Incentives

The third form of the adverse-incentives argument, which holds that interstate variations in welfare benefits stimulate interstate migration of the poor, also rests on tenuous empirical support. The argument gained currency during the 1960s, as Northern governors attributed rising welfare rolls to the low welfare benefits available in Southern states. As Gilbert Steiner has shown, however, this argument fails on a number of counts. First, if there is any relationship between welfare rates and migration patterns, it holds only for whites. For nonwhites, who were the object of most concern in the 1960s, there was no greater tendency for AFDC recipients to migrate to industrial states than for nonrecipients. Second, in New York, which had no residence requirement, only about 14 percent of AFDC mothers born out of the city obtained assistance within 23 months of moving there. Most came to get jobs, not welfare, and managed without aid for almost two years. Third, most of the increase in poor people in cities through the latter 1960s was not the result of migration, but of the growth of this population within metropolitan areas.

If the migration argument ever had any merit—and this is now in doubt—it did not by the late 1960s.[57] Given what seems to be true about the link of migration to employment, there is little reason to believe that greater equalization of benefits will prompt a remigration to the South. If such migration occurs, it will be the improving employment prospects outside the urban North that will deserve the credit.

Administrative Complexity

While there may be grounds to question whether an indictment of the welfare system based on charges of inadequate benefits, inequity, and disincentive effects is as valid now as it once was, no such grounds exist with regard to the issue of administrative complexity. Welfare is an administrative Alice-in-Wonderland world where life grows "curiouser and curiouser" with each passing regulation. The piles upon piles of training manuals generated not only by state and local administrative offices, but by federal officials and the courts, stand as a physical embodiment of this fact. So do the increasingly shrill complaints of administrative personnel and congressional overseers caught up in the system.

What is the nature of this complexity and why does it exist? Broadly speaking, four sources can be identified. The first, and basic, is the use of both demographic (categorical) and needs-tested criteria for eligibility. Either of these alone would be sufficient to yield a program of great administrative complexity. For, in addition to demonstrating financial need for AFDC, an applicant must establish that she is the mother—or near relative—of a child living with her, whose other parent or guardian is absent from the home. Each of these supplementary conditions, however, involves a series of definitions, forms, and determinations. For example, who is defined as a near relative? An uncle? An aunt? What about a second cousin? Or a godmother? What does "living with" mean? Can the child be away from the home for a period—for example, to stay with a grandparent over the summer? Furthermore, exactly what constitutes absence from the house? Some states define it as 30 days in the case of desertions and three months in the case of imprisonment. Whatever the standard, each point of eligibility must be scrutinized and then checked. Not only does this hold for the intimate details of family circumstances; it also applies to income and assets, the needs-tested half of the eligibility process. Every potential source of income must be explored—earnings, gifts, interest, rent, child support, social security, unemployment insurance, assistance from relatives. Until the mid-1960s, intake workers had to compute the value of birthday gifts and Christmas presents. In addition, asset tests must be applied. This means assessing the value of any property the applicant owns, including a home or an automobile, or a piece of land elsewhere.

Each new wrinkle in the public assistance program adds a new area of administrative procedure. When Congress incorporated a series of earnings exemptions and work requirements into the AFDC statutes in 1967, it added an extra ream of forms to the AFDC eligibility process. AFDC recipients now have to be evaluated for their employability, referred for possible training, screened, processed, monitored in training, provided with child-care aid if necessary. Exemptions for work-related expenses necessitate careful verification of a host of details regarding work activities. For example, California income forms ask applicants how many stops their bus makes on the way to work, how many blocks they have to walk to reach the bus stop, and whether any transfers are needed. Given this level of detail, it is no wonder that the Los Angeles County Social Services Department advises applicants that establishment of eligibility will require "at least three appointments, each one lasting from five to 12 hours." For the staff, however, it will require much more, for each of the major pieces of information must be verified, through checks with other agencies, forms sent to banks, examination of property records, insurance investigation requests, and affidavits from clients and others, such as those required of unrelated adult males living with AFDC applicants. A flow chart showing the intake process in Los Angeles stretches 40 feet long. In response, special units have been developed just to write training materials for intake workers.

The second source of administrative complexity is the additional layer of administrative authority at the federal level. Yet the demarcation between state, local, and federal levels of authority is nowhere clearly articulated. It changes over time, in response to administrative initiative, legislative action, or—increasingly in recent years—federal court action. As a consequence, states are constantly confronted with federal regulatory changes that must be integrated, however imperfectly, into ongoing state administrative practices. When federal rules on the treatment of income of stepfathers in AFDC changed, for example, state social service departments had to revise their data-intake forms accordingly. The number of such changes in the course of a year can be staggering.

The third source of administrative complexity is the newest one, and perhaps the most troubling in terms of long-term prospects. It is the fact that each of the points mentioned above applies not just to one program, but to several, and in a different way for each; there are different procedures, for example, for determining AFDC, food stamp, and Medicaid eligibility. Even the definitions of income differ among these programs, so that determination of the amount of assistance to which a recipient is entitled must be redone for each program. For example, AFDC exempts the income of full-time students and of part-time students who are not full-time employees, and also deducts one-third of all earnings above $30 a month plus work expenses. The food stamp program, however, does not differentiate between full- and part-time students, and provides deductions for, among other things, medical expenses in excess of $10 per month and shelter costs in excess of 30 percent of nonexempt income. Since all AFDC recipients are eligible for food stamps and Medicaid, and extensive overlap and receipt of multiple benefits exist among other programs as well, the result is an elaborate process of churning and rechurning the same numbers. Public assistance is the only place where $400 in monthly earnings equals $233, $141, $330, and $157 in countable income all at the same time.[58]

Not only do separate programs have separate eligibility procedures and definitions; they also frequently have separate administrative structures. Aged food stamp recipients must locate not just the SSI intake office, but the food stamp office as well. What is more, the in-kind programs require additional administrative apparatus to dispense benefits and verify results. Rather than sending a check, the food stamp program requires participants to make monthly or bimonthly visits to stamp-dispensing centers, where they can count on lengthy delays.

The fourth feature of the public assistance system that contributes to the administrative burden is the fact that the welfare population is dynamic, not static. Most recipients are on AFDC for less than two years at a time. Even during this period, situations change. The result is that eligibility must be determined not once, but over and over. Consequently, elaborate recertification procedures are necessary as intake workers repeat, in abridged form, the lengthy eligibility determination process done at the outset, complete with affidavits and verifications.

Whether the public gains very much of value from this administrative complexity is difficult to assess. Perhaps the main beneficiaries are the printers, whose presses are kept humming by the public assistance system's insatiable appetite for forms. What is fairly clear is that the administrative complexity has real costs, three of which deserve mention.

First is the direct cost of administration, which consumes approximately 12 percent of program costs in both AFDC and food stamps. These costs have been increasing rapidly, both absolutely and on per-participant and per-$1,000-in-benefits bases. The overlapping among in-kind programs and cash assistance programs, each of them with their own definitions of need, income, assets, and benefits is, in short, taking its financial toll.

Beyond the direct costs of administration, however, are the indirect costs embodied in error rates. In 1973, HEW conducted a national survey of AFDC cases and discovered that nearly 41 percent were in error either because of overpayment, underpayment, or ineligibility. Although a quality control program was launched in 1974 to correct these errors, 27 percent of the cases were still found to be in error by the end of 1975.[59] And with good reason. As former

HEW Undersecretary John Veneman put it in testimony before the Griffiths Subcommittee in 1972, "it is not welfare recipients cheating the system that constitutes our big problem. It is a chaotic, do-it-yourself system that is cheating the whole nation."[60]

Many doubt whether quality control can eliminate errors without exacting its own inordinate administrative costs. A General Accounting Office report on quality control efforts noted that state officials felt that "many errors disclosed by the quality control system can only be prevented by requiring the eligibility technicians to make as extensive an investigation as the quality control reviewers. However, they doubted whether it was cost effective for them to do so."[61] HEW's assistant secretary for planning and evaluation, William Morrills, put the issue squarely in 1976: "I think we must all recognize that some error results from the current complex of programs we maintain; . . . the system that underlies the program that we are seeking to administer often in and of itself, because of its complexity, invites error."[62]

A third cost of program complexity takes the form of variations in participation rates and participant misperception of program content. Because of the complexity of eligibility formulae and the burdensomeness of the application process, many eligible recipients either remain unaware of their eligibility or consider the benefit not worth the cost. While this may be functional from the perspective of keeping costs down, it seriously challenges the claim that the welfare system has become more equitable in recent years and not a system that impedes participation through complex procedures. Such a system may be no less inequitable than one that impedes it through direct denial of eligibility.

Similarly, to the extent that arguments about the disincentive effects of welfare assume that participants perceive the program accurately, they too may be seriously flawed. That the marginal tax rate on AFDC is now 67 percent, and on food stamps 30 percent, may be immaterial in terms of inducing work effort if the complexity of the programs obscures this point and gives recipients the impression that they are going to end up worse off anyway.

While no one doubts the administrative complexity and resulting costs of the existing system, there is some doubt about the extent to which any alternative program could reduce this complexity and cost, especially if the alternative program maintained some form of means test. Such doubt has been fueled by the experience of the SSI program that was authorized in 1972 and put into operation on January 1, 1974. Although it replaced the cumbersome federal-state program of aid to the aged, blind, and disabled with a uniform, federally administered program utilizing a common eligibility standard and a single benefit scale, SSI has hardly achieved the simplification and savings originally promised.

Despite pressures for simplicity, the SSI law retained a host of special exclusions from income that vary depending on individual circumstances, and that require consideration of over a dozen rules to compute eligibility and benefit levels. Elaborate checks are still required to assess the value of applicants' personal property and resources. State variations that were purged from benefit determination by the adoption of SSI then crept back in via permission— and later requirements—for state supplementation in states where the federal payment is below what recipients were getting under the old categorical programs. Although the federal Social Security Administration typically administers these state supplement programs in addition to basic benefits, it has been obliged to retain the confusing array of state benefit determination criteria for the supplements and to graft these onto the standard criteria used for the SSI benefit. The upshot has been widespread dissatisfaction with the changeover from the categorical programs to SSI,[63] persistent errors, and very limited progress in achieving the reduction in administrative costs anticipated from this switch. The Social Security Administration originally estimated that it would need only half as many employees to administer the simplified, centralized, computerized SSI program as were needed by the states in the old categorical programs. Within a year, however, the agency was back before Congress seeking authority to add 50 percent more permanent employees, as well as more temporary and overtime help, than originally anticipated.[64]

Whether this SSI experience really provides a fair test of the prospects for simplification of public assistance is in hot dispute. For one thing, the Social Security Administration had only 14 months to accomplish the switch from state-operated categorical programs to federally operated SSI. During this period, 2.6 million case files had to be transmitted from some 1,300 state and local government offices to those of the Social Security Administration and then reprocessed using the SSI eligibility determination criteria instead of the 50 separate state criteria previously in force. Under the best of circumstances, this would have been a mammoth undertaking. But the best of circumstances did not prevail for a number of reasons: First, the state files were not uniform or consistent, so that elaborate procedures had to be developed to fill in the gaps; second, Congress changed the law several times between initial enactment and time of implementation, in effect requiring redeterminations of the redeterminations; and, third, the computer system for processing the files proved far more troublesome than anyone expected.

While more time would have solved some of these problems, it seems clear that others are intrinsic to administering a means-tested program. In testimony before the House Ways and Means Committee's Subcommittee on Oversight, Social Security Administration officials conceded that they had "understated" the staffing needs for SSI because of their failure to take sufficient account of the assistance applicants require in filing their claims. They cited the applicants' economic and educational backgrounds and the detailed information required of a means-tested program; the difficulty involved in corroborating claimants' statements regarding income and resources; the court-imposed requirements for due process in adjusting payment levels; the difficulties that arise when death, divorce, or hospitalization occurs, necessitating deviations from provisions in the law establishing payments for couples; and the complex problems of administering state supplementary benefits.[65] Beyond this, there is the problem that

Congresswoman Elizabeth Holtzman had in mind when she complained to the Ways and Means Committee's Subcommittee on Public Assistance in 1975 that "the partial entry of the federal government into the area of direct income maintenance [through SSI] has created confusion about the responsibilities of the three levels of government for the welfare of beneficiaries." According to Congresswoman Holtzman, the pre-SSI system at least fixed responsibility for benefit levels, cost-of-living increases, and emergency and social services for the aged, blind, and disabled poor in one place: state and local welfare offices. SSI, however, splintered these responsibilities:

> The result has been that *no* jurisdiction has primary responsibility for the elderly and disabled poor. This means that while everyone recognizes SSI's failure no one does anything about them. The states say that the federal government has taken over and it is responsible for the program. The federal government says that the states and localities may adapt the program to meet local needs and to provide locally required services. In the meantime, people do not receive an adequate living allowance and some services (such as the provision of emergency living allowance for persons who have not received their monthly benefit checks, or the replacement of furniture and household goods which have been destroyed by fire) have been lost entirely. The net effect is that these already helpless people suffer further deprivation while governments squabble over who should care for them.[66]

All in all, there is a certain irony, in view of the claims made for SSI, in the fact that "the No. 1 problem facing the program," in the eyes of its administrators, is "excessive complexity."[67] Even after making adjustments for the tight deadlines under which the program went into operation and for the legislative changes made just prior to implementation, the experience cannot help leaving us less sanguine about the prospects for reducing administrative costs and complexity elsewhere in the public assistance system. While the existing system leaves room for improvement in this regard, SSI makes it clear that even simplification has its limits as long as public assistance remains means tested.

Welfare and the Individual

The existing system also is criticized for doing damage to self-esteem. Steiner uses the term "crude relief" to depict this problem.[68] Its features are a variety of restrictions on the mobility, conduct, privacy, and personal rights of recipients. Long waits in welfare offices, embarrassing income and asset checks, and the infamous midnight search are just a few of the ways in which welfare comes to pervade a recipient's life. As Steiner has put it: "It is clear that uncomplicated economic need will not bring uncomplicated economic relief. . . . Eligibility in public assistance really turns on how much sacrifice a recipient is prepared to make. . . . In addition to an economic sacrifice, the sacrifice required of a public assistance client may be physical, emotional, moral, or civil libertarian."[69]

In recent years, many of the more punitive and degrading aspects of welfare administration have been eliminated, largely as a result of legal actions brought by welfare recipients; midnight searches and man-in-the-house prohibitions, residency requirements, the so-called suitable-home rule preventing payment to households with illegitimate children are no longer in force. The attitude of many recipients also changed as the 1960s witnessed the first serious organization of welfare mothers and, with it, the burgeoning of the notion of welfare as a right instead of a privilege.

Yet some of the crude relief features are still in evidence in the eligibility process, with its cumbersome verifications of income, assets, work expenses, and family relationships, or in requirements to convery property title to the state as a condition of AFDC eligibility. They are also reflected in provisions such as the Los Angeles County public assistance form 2360 requiring applicants to do the following:

> Assign to the County any support rights you may have. This includes the right to child support and alimony.

> In cases where a parent is absent from the home, cooperate with the County Welfare Department and District Attorney in indentifying, locating, and obtaining financial support and in establishing the paternity of a child born out of wedlock.

The recent shift toward in-kind assistance has exacerbated this paternalistic feature of the relief system, since in-kind benefits are premised on the notion that recipients would misdirect benefits if they were provided in cash. In this area as well, therefore, real progress is more than matched by solid evidence of retrogression, creating the same dilemmas of judgment we have encountered before in assessing whether the cup of public assistance is half empty or half full.

REEXAMINING THE CASE FOR REFORM

Viewed as a whole, it seems clear that the case for welfare reform has changed since the 1960s. The issues of adequacy and equity have been reduced significantly, although the trade-off between the two is now more visible. Mammoth growth rates that prompted concern about a welfare crisis in the 1960s seem to be tapering off and give promise of continuing to do so. Evidence that has been generated on the behavioral consequences of the many disincentives built into the welfare system has tended to discount this line of argument, at least as a major rationale for reform.

While these points are important to insure against any misselling or overselling of reform, however, they hardly add up to a case for no action. To the contrary, disturbing inequities remain in the system. These inequities are aggravated by the administrative complexity that besets public assistance as program has been piled upon program. On administrative grounds alone, a strong case for reform can be made.

What should be clear is that the current system represents one set of decisions about how to resolve a number of conflicting dilemmas among the alternative goals of cost control, adequacy, equity, incentives, and political feasibility. It is not a perfect resolution of these issues, but neither is any other. Every proposed alternative must be judged not on how well it solves one or two of the problems in the current system, but on how its resolution of the full array of trade-offs compares with the resolution achieved by existing programs. Since the existing system will inevitably serve as the standard against which changes will be judged, it is necessary, before turning to a consideration of these alternative changes, to look briefly at how we got where we are. This may help illuminate the road ahead.

NOTES

1. *Social Security Bulletin* 39, no 7 (July 1976):79.

2. *Social Security Bulletin* 41, no. 4 (April 1978):62.

3. Sar Levitan and Robert Taggart, *The Promise of Greatness* (Cambridge: Harvard University Press, 1976), p. 81.

4. U.S. Congress, Joint Economic Committee, Subcommittee on Fiscal Policy, *Income Security for Americans: Recommendations of the Public Welfare Study*, 93d Cong., 2d sess., 1974, p. 1.

5. U.S. Congress, House, Committee on Appropriations, *Hearings on the Departments of Labor and Health, Education, and Welfare Appropriations for 1977*, 94th Cong., 2d sess., 1976.

6. *Social Security Bulletin* 39, no. 1 (January 1976): 58.

7. Daniel Patrick Moynihan, "The Crises in Welfare," *The Public Interest* 10 (Winter 1968): 5.

8. See, for example, Carol Stack, *All Our Kin* (New York: Harper and Row, 1974).

9. Heather Ross and Isabel Sawhill, *Time of Transition: The Growth of Families Headed by Women* (Washington, D.C.: The Urban Institute, 1976), pp. 105–06.

10. The number of AFDC recipients stood at 10.6 million in 1971, and at 11.4 million in 1975. *Social Security Bulletin* 39, no. 7 (July 1976):74.

11. Average benefit level is from *Social Security Bulletin* 39, no. 7 (July 1974): 76; need standard data are from U.S. Department of Health, Education, and Welfare, Social and Rehabilitation Services, *Aid to Families with Dependent Children: Standards for Basic Needs*, DHEW Publication No. (SRS) 76-03200, p. 9. It should be noted, of course, that the food stamp program has diminished these pressures somewhat, since in states where AFDC benefits are low, food stamp benefits are higher.

12. Congressman Wilber Mills, in *Congressional Quarterly*, 90th Cong., 1st sess., August 25, 1967, p. 1641.

13. Senator Russell Long, in U.S. Congress, Senate Committee on Finance, *Social Security Amendments of 1967: Committee Amendments to HR 12080*, 90th Cong., 1st sess. (November 8, 1967), p. 3.

14. Vernon K. Smith, *Welfare Work Incentives*, Studies in Welfare Policy, no. 2 (Lansing: Michigan Department of Social Services, 1974), pp. 25, 30.

15. Based on data from the 1973 HEW AFDC Recipient Survey, summarized in Levitan and Taggart, *The Promise of Greatness*, pp. 53–54.

16. Anne Shkuda, *Former Welfare Families: Independence and Recurring Dependency* (New York: New School for Social Research, Center for New York City Affairs, 1976), pp. 3–4, 65.

17. According to the Michigan estimate, the work incentive exemption increased AFDC payments in Michigan by about $70 million between 1971 and 1974, and increased the average monthly caseload by over 3,400, or 2.7 percent. Smith, *Welfare Work Incentives*, pp. 226–27.

18. John Holahan, *Financing Health Care for the Poor: The Medicaid Experience* (Lexington, Mass.: D.C. Heath and Co., 1975), p. 32.

19. U.S. Department of Housing and Urban Development, *Housing in the Seventies: A Report of the National Housing Policy Review* (Washington, D.C.: Government Printing Office, 1974), pp. 97–98.

20. Program details here are drawn from U.S. Congress, Joint Economic Committee, Subcommittee on Fiscal Policy, *Handbook of Public Income Transfer Programs*, 94th Cong., 1st sess., 1975, pp. 153, 221.

21. Vee Burke, *Federal and State-Local Expenditures for Income Transfers to Persons with Limited Income, Fiscal Years 1975 and 1976*, Congressional Research Service Multilith 76–5ED (Washington, D.C.: Library of Congress, 1976), p. 11.

22. U.S. Bureau of the Census, *County Government Finances in 1974-75*; U.S. Bureau of the Census, *City Government Finances in 1974-75* (Washington, D.C.: U.S. Government Printing Office, 1976).

23. Gilbert Steiner, *The State of Welfare* (Washington, D.C.: The Brookings Institution, 1971), p. 12.

24. According to one study, for example, a 1 percent decrease in average pretransfer income is associated with a .97 percent increase in poverty incidence, and a 10 percent increase in unemployment is associated with a 2.7 percent increase in poverty incidence. Robert D. Plotnick and Felicity Skidmore, *Progress Against Poverty* (Madison: University of Wisconsin, Institute for Research on Poverty, 1975), pp. 117–18.

25. U.S. Bureau of the Census, *Current Population Reports*, Series P-60, no. 103 (Washington, D.C.: Government Printing Office, 1976), pp. 34–35.

26. Edgar K. Browning, *Redistribution and the Welfare System* (Washington, D.C.: American Enterprise Institute, 1975), p. 2. See also Edgar K. Browning, "How Much More Equality Can We Afford?", *The Public Interest*, no. 43 (Spring 1976): 90–111.

27. Congressional Budget Office, "Poverty Status of Families Under Alernative Definitions of Income," Background Paper No. 17 (Revised) (Washington, D.C.: Congressional Budget Office, 1977).

28. On the importance of taking account of life-cycle stages in analyzing income distribution data, see Morton Paglin, "The Measurement and Trend of Inequality: A Basic Revision," *American Economic Review* 65, no. 4 (September 1975): pp. 598–609. Paglin argues that a substantial part of the apparent maldistribution of income merely reflects the fact that people are at different points in their life cycle, and that their income will naturally increase as they grow older. To expect complete income equality is thus not reasonable.

29. Based on data in U.S. Congress, Joint Economic Committee, *Handbook of Public Income Transfer Programs, Studies in Public Welfare, 1975*, 94th Cong., 1st sess., pp. 140–50.

30. Levitan and Taggart, *Promise of Greatness*, p. 74, drawing on data from U.S. Congress, Joint Economic Committee, *Welfare in the 70's*, 93d Cong., 2d sess. (1974), Studies in Public Welfare, no. 15, I have recomputed the figures using San Francisco rather than Contra Costa, California, which is the example Levitan and Taggart use.

31. U.S. Department of Health, Education, and Welfare, Social and Rehabilitation Service, *Public Assistance Statistics*, March 1976, p. 8.

32. Mary Kilkenny, *A Longitudinal Study of Unemployment Insurance Exhaustees* (Princeton, N.J.: Mathematica Policy Research, 1976), pp. 13, 49–50.

33. U.S. Department of Agriculture, Food and Nutrition Survey, National Participation and Cost Impacts of Proposed Changes in Food Stamp Program.

34. Shkuda, *Former Welfare Families: Independence and Recurring Dependency*, pp. 50–51.

35. Subcommitee on Fiscal Policy, *Public Welfare Study*, pp. v–vi.

36. Quoted in Frances Fox Piven and Richard Cloward, *Regulating the Poor: The Functions of Public Welfare* (New York: Vintage Books, 1971), p. 35.

37. Subcommittee on Fiscal Policy, *Public Welfare Study*, p. vi.

38. For further elaboration of this point, see Lester M. Salamon, "Inequality in the Pursuit of Equity: The Dilemmas of Welfare Reform" (Paper read at the 1976 American Political Science Association Convention, Chicago, September 1, 1976).

39. Nathan Glazer, "Reform Work, Not Welfare," *The Public Interest* 40, (Summer 1975): 3.

40. U.S. Department of Labor, Bureau of Labor Statistics, "Marital and Family Characteristics of Workers, March 1970," Special Labor Force Report 130 (Washington, D.C.: Government Printing Office, 1970), p. A-9.

41. Joint Economic Committee, *Welfare in the 70's*, p. 7.

42. Durham *Morning Herald*, November 17, 1976.

43. Henry J. Aaron, *Why Is Welfare So Hard to Reform* (Washington, D.C.: The Brookings Institution, 1973), p. 36.

44. Irwin Garfinkel, "Income Transfer Programs and Work Effort: A Review," in Joint Economic Committee, *Studies in Public Welfare*, Paper no. 13, 93rd Cong., 2d sess., 1974, pp. 1–32; Aaron, *Why Is Welfare So Hard to Reform*, pp. 36–37.

45. For a discussion of these results, see Joseph A. Pechman and P. Michael Timpane, eds., *Work Incentives and Income Guarantees: The New Jersey Negative Income Tax Experiment* (Washington, D.C.: The Brookings Institution, 1975).

46. Irwin Garfinkel and Larry L. Orr, "Welfare Policy and the Employment Rate of AFDC Mothers," *National Tax Journal* XXVII (June 1974): 283.

47. Smith, *Welfare Work Incentives*, pp. iv, 201. This result finds support in the prediction of Garfinkel and Orr that reducing the marginal tax rate on AFDC from 67 percent to 50 percent would be cost effective only if employment increased at least twice as much as their data suggested would happen. Garfinkel and Orr, "Welfare Policy," p. 283.

48. Levitan and Taggart, *Promise of Greatness*, pp. 54–55; Leonard Goodman, *Do the Poor Want to Work: A Social-Psychological Study of Work Orientations* (Washington, D.C.: The Brookings Institution, 1972), pp. 113–14.

49. Data on this point are available in Subcommittee on Fiscal Policy, *Public Welfare Study*, pp. 78–79; Joint Economic Committee, *Welfare in the 70's*, pp. 39–41.

50. Marjorie Honig, "The Impact of Welfare Payment Levels on Family Stability," in Joint Economic Committee, *The Family, Poverty, and Welfare Programs: Factors Influencing Family Instability*, Studies in Public Welfare, Paper no. 12, Part 1, 93rd Cong., 1st sess., 1973, pp. 37–53.

51. Summarized in Ross and Sawhill, *Time of Transition*, p. 10.

52. Robert Lerman attributes 36 percent of the increase in female-headed households between 1950 and 1972 to this factor. Lerman, "The Family, Poverty, and Welfare Programs: An Introductory Essay on Problems of Analysis and Policy," in U.S. Congress, Joint Economic Committee, Studies in Public Welfare, Paper no. 12, 93d Cong., 1st sess., 1974, Part 1, pp. 18–19.

53. Ross and Sawhill, *Time of Transition*, 1975, p. 118.

54. *King v. Smith*, 392 U.S. 309 (1968), and *Lewis v. Martin*, 397 U.S. 552 (1972).

55. Marjorie Honig, "The Impact of Welfare Payment Levels," pp. 49, 53.

56. On the basis of an elaborate computer simulation of a negative income tax

proposal, Ross and Sawhill conclude that "welfare reform probably cannot be viewed as a major policy lever on family organization." Ross and Sawhill, *Time of Transition*, p. 124.

57. Steiner, *The State of Welfare*, p. 88.

58. Figures are based on data provided in *Public Welfare Study*, p. 82; they show how $400 translates into countable income for a family of four under four different programs: food stamps, AFDC, public housing, and SSI, respectively.

59. U.S. Congress, House, Ways and Means Committee, *Hearings Before the Subcommittee on Oversight on HEW Efforts to Reduce Errors in Welfare Programs*, 94th Cong., 2d sess., 1974, p. 76.

60. U.S. Congress, House, Joint Economic Committee, *Problems in the Administration of Public Welfare Programs: Hearings Before the Subcommittee on Fiscal Policy*, 92d Cong., 2d sess., 1972, p. 68.

61. U.S. Congress, House, Ways and Means Committee, *Hearings on AFDC Quality Control Program Before the Subcommittee on Oversight*, 94th Cong., 1st sess., 1975, p. 10.

62. *Ways and Means Committee Hearings on Errors in Welfare Programs*, 1976, pp. 75, 88.

63. See the testimony in U.S. Congress, House, Committee on Ways and Means, *Hearings on the Supplemental Security Income Program Before the Subcommittee on Public Assistance*, 94th Cong., 1st sess., vol. 2, 1975.

64. U.S. Congress, House, Ways and Means Committee, *Hearings on Administration of the Supplemental Security Income Program Before the Subcommittee on Oversight*, 94th Cong., 1st sess., 1975, vol. 2, p. 13.

65. U.S. Congress, House, Ways and Means Subcommittee on Oversight, *Hearings on the Administration of the Supplemental Security Income Program*, vol. 2, 94th Cong., 1st sess., 1975, pp. 13-14.

66. House, Ways and Means Committee, *Hearings on Supplemental Security Income Before Subcommittee on Public Assistance*, vol. 2, 94th Cong., 1st sess., 1975, pp. 153-54.

67. House, Ways and Means Committee, Subcommittee on Oversight, *Hearings on Administration of the Supplemental Security Income Program*, vol. 1, 1975, p. 11.

68. Steiner, *The State of Welfare*, p. 2.

69. Piven and Cloward, *Regulating the Poor*, p. 165.

3

HOW DID WE GET HERE?
THE STRANGE EVOLUTION
OF INCOME ASSISTANCE POLICY

The one almost all-embracing measure of security is an assured income. A program of economic security, as we vision it, must have as its primary aim the assurance of an adequate income to each human being in childhood, youth, middle age, or old age—in sickness or in health. It must provide safeguards against all of the hazards leading to destitution and dependency. . . .

Whatever measures are deemed immediately expedient should be so designed that they can be embodied in the complete program which we must have ere long.

Report of the President's Committee on Economic Security, 1935

It is good . . . to report that public assistance is moving toward greater simplicity, objectivity, and adequacy than in the past. Benefits are no longer paid in kind, such as grocery orders and bushels of coal, but in cash. The recipient therefore has money, as other people do, to spend as he thinks best.

Arthur Altmeyer, 1945

If the previous chapter demonstrated the significant progress public programs have made in relieving poverty over the past decade, it also demonstrated the significant problems that continue to frustrate progress in this field. What is the source of these problems? Why have public assistance programs taken such a peculiar shape in the United States, with severe gaps, wasteful leakage of benefits, numerous overlapping requirements, strange combinations of cash and in-kind assistance, and wide variations in program content from state to state? Why is it that a system endorsed by its designers as the first step toward a single "all-embracing" program of "assured income," and praised by its administrator in the 1940s for eliminating in-kind benefits and for "moving toward simplicity, objectivity, and adequacy," has led instead to today's maze of programs and dramatic expansion of in-kind benefits? Was this pattern of evolution natural and inevitable? Is there a hidden logic in it that will shape subsequent changes as well? Or are we merely the heirs of a set of accidental, ad hoc adjustments with little internal consistency, and therefore little durability?

The answers to these questions have profound implications for the prospects of reform, for they help to define the context within which reform must proceed. To find these answers, it is necessary to look at least briefly at the history of American social welfare policy. This means an examination of the Social Security Act of 1935, the seminal piece of New Deal legislation that spawned virtually the whole array of American income assistance programs, including social security, OASDI, aid to the blind, old age assistance (OAA), unemployment compensation, and Aid to Dependent Children (ADC).* But while the Social Security Act marked, in historian Arthur Schlesinger, Jr.'s words, "a new phase of national history" so far as social policy is concerned,[1] it was not the complete break with tradition that it was popularly assumed to be. To the contrary, the legislation was a compromise, adapted to the political realities of the time and to the prevailing traditions of relief embodied in existing programs. A "piecemeal approach . . . dictated by practical considerations" is how the Committee on Economic Security, which drafted the legislation, described its work in 1935.[2] Similar terms could be used to describe the evolution of this policy since 1935. To understand the peculiar mix of programs that survives today, therefore, it is necessary to look not just at the legislative events of 1935, but also at the developments that preceded and followed them.

The discussion that follows falls into five sections. The first identifies the major elements of the pre-New Deal tradition of public assistance. The second examines how these traditional elements affected the major decisions surrounding the formulation of the social security legislation of 1935. The third explores the strains to which the resulting programs were exposed in the period since 1935. The fourth outlines the changes made in the 1960s in an effort to relieve some of these strains. And the fifth analyzes the abortive attempt at more comprehensive reform represented by the battle over the Family Assistance Plan (FAP) in the early 1970s. On the basis of this glance backward, a concluding section then speculates briefly about the lessons the history of American social welfare policy holds for future reform efforts.

---

*The name of this program was changed to Aid to *Families* with Dependent Children (AFDC) in 1962 as part of an effort to emphasize the provision of services to "stabilize" and aid the families in which dependent children resided. This service strategy is discussed more fully below.

has been near the center of policy debate in America
era. Almost half of the settlers in the New World, after
vants who arrived with no source of support.[3] The uncer-
ntier society plunged thousands more into penury when
uently kept them there. Coping with poverty and want
a central challenge to colonial leadership. By the time of
the Revolution, public assistance was one of the largest items of expenditure in
many of the colonial towns.[4]

While the immediate origins of current American welfare policy go back to
the colonial era, it was the English Poor Laws of the late sixteenth and early
seventeenth centures that colonial leaders drew on in formulating their own approach, establishing thereby a tradition that extends almost unbroken down to
the present. Central to this tradition are three basic elements: first, the concept
of categorization, the notion that some of the poor are not deserving of aid;
second, the related idea that relief must be designed to avoid interference with
the private labor market; and third, the conviction that responsibility for charity
belongs at the local level. Taken together, these three elements have shaped
American relief policy for almost three centuries. They are thus a necessary
starting point for any analysis of the prospects for change.

Categorization: The Deserving and the Nondeserving Poor

The idea of categorizing the poor according to the extent to which they
deserve assistance is a curious byproduct of the stress on individualism that
formed the heart of Enlightenment thought from the fifteenth century onward.
During the Middle Ages, poverty was perceived as a punishment for the sinful-
ness of man in general, and the obligation to care for the needy was placed,
without recrimination, squarely on the shoulders of the feudal lord and the
church. Enlightenment thought, by contrast, stressed the individual's own
responsibility for his circumstances. In the process, it gave rise to the view that
poverty was less a sign of collective human sin than a product of personal failings, for which the poor had only themselves to blame. Faced with the rise in
vagrancy and want that accompanied the collapse of the feudal order, leaders of
opinion in Britain thus jumped easily to the conclusion that the problem lay
with the laziness and viciousness of the poor, who would "rather drink than eat
and rather starve than work."[5] In John Locke's words, it was "the relaxation of
discipline and corruption of manners" that accounted for "the growth of
poverty" in England.[6] Under the circumstances, a certain harshness was appropriate in dealing with the poor. The Protestant religious doctrines that gained
currency during the time gave moral sanction to such an approach. As Reinhold
Niebuhr once put it, "Calvinism has never been able to overcome the temptation

to regard poverty as a consequence of laziness and vice, and therefore to leave the poor and the needy to the punishment which a righteous God has inflicted on them."[7]

As early as the fourteenth century, British authorities made it a crime punishable by imprisonment to give alms to "such, which may labor." Henceforth only those "impotent to serve" were permitted to beg.[8] This distinction between the "impotent" and the able-bodied poor then became the centerpiece of the Poor Laws enacted in the latter sixteenth century. For the first time, these laws made the care of the needy a clear responsibility of public authorities. But they also established the principle that the nature of that care should differ depending on the characteristics of the poor. The "lame, impotent, old, blind and such other being poor and not able to work" were to be provided "the necessary relief" either in their own dwellings or in "abiding places." But the able-bodied poor were to be "set on work," that is, either hired out or placed in workhouses. As a result, a sharp demarcation arose between the deserving poor, who were taken under the public wing, albeit at the price of the near-total surrender of their independence, and the "vicious" or employable poor, to whom aid was extended only under the most restrictive conditions.

This notion of deservingness, and the categorization of the poor to which it gave rise, found ready acceptance and amplification in the American colonies. Lacking a feudal tradition, the colonies also lacked the paternalistic concern for the needy that such a tradition frequently produced. There was little to mitigate the harshness of Enlightenment individualism in the New World, which produced at once a favorable climate for personal liberty and an unfavorable one for protecting the interests of the poor. While the colonists were attentive to their charitable obligations, they found in the Poor Law notion of deservingness a congenial standard for limiting the extent of those obligations. Colonial preachers like Cotton Mather were explicit in sanctioning a policy of "benign neglect" toward the undeserving. "For those who indulge themselves in Idleness," Mather thus declared in one widely circulated sermon, "the Express Command of God unto us is, that we should let them starve."[9] And in the social climate of the day, indulgence in idleness was easily seen as the most common cause of want.

After an early period of benign neighborliness, American relief policy settled into a pattern of relative restrictiveness quite similar to that in Britain. Potential vagrants were barred from cities by residency laws and those already there were confined to workhouses or leased out to local employers. In colonial New York, paupers on outdoor relief were required to wear badges with the letters "N.Y." on their clothes, while the sleeves of recipients in Pennsylvania were appropriately emblazoned with a "P."[10]

As the problem of urban poverty grew more severe in the late eighteenth and early nineteenth centuries, American officials turned increasingly to the almshouse as a solution. One reason for this was the conviction that the deserving poor could be cared for more effectively—and certainly more cheaply—in an institutional setting. Equally important was the view that poverty was a curable disease that could best be treated by separating the poor from the temptations that were assumed to be the cause of their problems and by subjecting them to a vigorous regimen of discipline and hard work. Aside from the curative effects on those actually incarcerated, it was expected that the example of the almshouse would frighten many more of the poor into going to work and thus stem the alarming rise in pauperism that accompanied the rapid urbanization and industrialization of the period. To help guarantee this result, localities cut back severely on outdoor relief, permitting it only during the periodic depressions that punctuated the nineteenth century, and even then only a highly limited basis. The poorhouses themselves were seriously neglected, so that by the latter part of the century they had degenerated into what one observer termed "disgraceful memorials of the public charity."[11]

When Progressive reformers attacked these practices in the late nineteenth and early twentieth centuries, they did little to unseat the basic doctrine of deservingness that underlay the practices. To the contrary, the basic thrust of the reforms achieved during this era built squarely on the longstanding division between the deserving and the undeserving poor by focusing on improvements for the former. The major achievements were the replacement of the all-purpose poorhouse with separate, professionally staffed institutions for the deaf and dumb, the metally ill, the disabled, and the blind; and the reestablishment of home relief for the rest of the impotent poor, especially widows with young children and the aged. Although the state mothers' pension and old age assistance laws enacted in response to these pressures were wholly dependent on local funding and therefore grossly inadequate, they still surpassed what was made available to most of the poor. Categorization, in short, continued to provide the mechanism for dealing with one segment of the poor while neglecting the others.

Welfare and the Labor Market

If the idea of deservingness that forms the core of the Poor Law tradition grew out of the Enlightenment notion of individualism and was reinforced by the harsh morality of Protestant orthodoxy, and later by the doctrines of social Darwinism, it has found ample support in more tangible sources as well. The royal decree that first forbade giving alms to the able-bodied made this point quite explicit, citing the "lack of ploughmen" as the justification for the new policy. "The beggar, in the concern of the Statute of Laborers," historian Karl de Schweinitz notes, "was not a problem in destitution but a seepage from the supply of labor."[12] By denying the benefits of public largesse to able-bodied vagrants, the Poor Laws were to help guarantee a supply of labor.

This economic function of the public assistance system was not restricted to fifteenth and sixteenth century England. It has sustained and buttressed the practice of categorization ever since. As one student of American relief policy has noted: "The goal of forcing the work activity or work seeking of the poor has seldom been forgotten even when welfare aid programs have been expanded somewhat."[13] During the nineteenth century in particular, the need to integrate a mass of new immigrants into the developing industrial labor market argued strongly against liberal public assistance policies. The shift to institutional care of the poor during this period was one reflection of this sentiment. According to one historian of the period:

> Every almshouse became a workhouse, and the work test applied indiscriminately to all paupers—children, aged, blind, and disabled as well as able-bodied. . . . In every city plagued by pauperism in the first half of the nineteenth century, outdoor relief was cut back, and work became the indispensable condition for institutional aid.[14]

What is involved here is not just the conditioning of assistance on work, or the obligation of the poor to support themselves. What is involved is the manipulation of the relief system to affect the terms on which the poor make themselves available for work. What bothered the landlords who pushed for the Statute of Laborers in fourteenth century England was not just that laborers would not work, but that they would "not serve unless they may receive excessive wages"[15] Accordingly, maximum wage rates were specified in the law and laborers obliged to accept them.

This desire to avoid having the public assistance system exert any upward pressure on private wage rates was formally incorporated in the Poor Law system through the principle of less eligibility, which specifies that public assistance payments must be kept below what is paid in the lowest-paying private jobs, whether a work requirement is attached to the assistance or not. To be sure, this principle came to be justified on moral grounds: the poor had to be kept poor lest they have the resources to spend on drink and end up worse off than before.[16] But the real purpose was economic. Along with categorization, it has helped to guarantee not only that the poor would work, but that they would perform the society's worst chores at whatever rates of pay the market would provide. In this way, conditions in the private labor market have been allowed to exert an effective check on the generosity of public assistance, and the assistance system is correspondingly adjusted to avoid any upward impact on the conditions of work.

Localism

The third key element carried over from early British experience to American relief policy was the extensive decentralization of control built into the system. Under the British Poor Law, responsibility for relief was firmly vested in the local, parish authorities. In fact, the Law of Settlement of 1662 gave these authorities the right to deny aid to newcomers, and to pass them on to their place of legal settlement, typically in the custody of a constable.[17]

This practice of local responsibility for public assistance found ready acceptance in the American colonies. In 1641, the colony of Virginia assigned the administration of relief to its parishes. In 1673, Connecticut passed its first general poor law, specifying that "every town shall maintain their own poor." Pennsylvania did likewise in 1705, and the other colonies soon followed suit. This pattern of local control of public assistance changed in only two respects over the subsequent two centuries. One was the shift of responsibility from towns to counties. (By 1934, 24 states had designated the counties as the primary administrative units for relief.[18] The other change, beginning in the nineteenth century, was an expansion in the direct public assistance functions performed by the states. From the earliest times, the states had provided some aid to the so-called unsettled poor, those without a town of settlement. In the nineteenth century, state aid was extended to victims of natural disasters, to military veterans, and to segments of the deserving poor in the form of specialized state institutions. To monitor these specialized institutions, the states created boards of charity or other watchdog agencies and increased their authority to oversee outdoor relief as well.[19] But the primary responsibility for relief remained local, even in the new mothers' pension and old age assistance programs enacted in the early part of the twentieth century.

That local control has remained so important a part of American relief policy is due in part to the traditional distrust of centralized power reflected in the structure of American federalism. When Congress, at the behest of reformer Dorothea Dix, passed a bill in 1854 providing for federal land grants to the states to support facilities for the insane, President Pierce vetoed it with an argument that has echoed through public assistance debates for decades. Noted Pierce:

> Should Congress make provision for such objects, the fountains of charity will be dried up at home, and the several states, instead of bestowing their own means on the social wants of their people, may themselves, through the strong temptation, which appeals to states as to individuals, become humble supplicants for the bounty of the Federal Government, reversing their true relation to this Union.[20]

But the persistence of local control cannot be explained on grounds of tradition alone. Local control also facilitated the linking of the welfare system to the labor market in a nation that has long been characterized by wide regional differences in wage rates and work conditions. Frances Fox Piven and Richard Cloward have argued this point most forcefully. The "old Poor Law principles" of local control embodied in American relief policies are not, they suggest, "merely vestiges of an archaic tradition. They have an important function in our economy, for they make it possible to shape relief practices in accord with widely differing labor practices from region to region, state to state, and locality to locality."[21]

THE NEW DEAL GRAND DESIGN:
A VARIATION ON FAMILIAR THEMES

The Great Depression posed a sharp challenge to th
assistance inherited from the English poor laws.

For one thing, massive unemployment and suffering shook the theory that
poverty was mainly a consequence of individual failings. Suddenly it was clear
that the economy itself was the cause, and that some form of assistance might
therefore be legitimate even for employables. Similarly, the Depression quickly
overwhelmed the resources of state and local relief agencies, demonstrating the
inadequacy of locally determined relief policy in a society increasingly influ-
enced by national economic forces. According to the President's Committee on
Economic Security, the fledgling old-age assistance programs created by the
states in the early 1900s were not only "nonfunctioning" as a consequence of
the economic crisis, but incapable of meeting the need even in the best of
circumstances. The committee concluded that "not more than two or three of
the entire number can be regarded as even reasonably adequate."[22] The need for
a meaningful federal role could no longer be ignored.

Still, the policy innovations flowing out of this emergency situation remained true to the pattern of relief that had evolved over the previous three
centuries. Although the New Deal planners formulated an imaginative grand
design, the ultimate outcome did as much to reinforce as to alter the longstanding categorization of the poor and the central role of state and local discretion. In the process, it left sizable segments of the poor outside the reach of
public assistance, and thus built a variety of inequities and disincentives into the
structure of the relief system.

Since these developments have shaped American social welfare policy ever
since, it is important to understand how and why they occurred. To do so, we
must look first at the early New Deal initiatives in public assistance, which represented a kind of high-water mark of innovation; then examine the grand design
that New Deal planners ultimately formulated to define the long-term role of the
federal government in handling the problems of poverty and dependency; and
finally, explore how this grand design was itself partially unraveled in response
to prevailing political and economic pressures. What emerges most clearly from
such an overview is a sense of the way in which the intellectual, economic, and
political forces traditionally shaping American relief policy ultimately reasserted
their dominance, overwhelming the more innovative emergency provisions
adopted in the heat of the crisis.

Early Initiatives

As we have seen, the Depression of 1929 broke on a country that was still
deeply suspicious of the whole concept of federal involvement in public as-

...ance. As a consequence, despite the intensity of the suffering spawned by the Depression, the federal government avoided serious involvement in relief efforts for three long years. Declaring his opposition to "any direct or indirect government dole,"[23] President Hoover restricted federal involvement to inspirational appeals for the mobilization of local resources through private charities and local governments. When he finally established a President's Organization on Unemployment Relief in 1931, for example, he authorized it only to "gain the benefits of coordination for private philanthropy without accepting Federal responsibility for the unemployment problem."[24] Will Rogers captured the frustration of the situation well in a radio spoof on Walter Gifford, chosen by Hoover to head this new relief organization. "What a job [Gifford] has got," noted Rogers.

> Mr. Hoover just told him, "Gifford, I have a remarkable job for you; you are to feed the several million unemployed."
>
> "With what?" says Gifford.
>
> "That's what makes the job remarkable. If you had something to do it with it wouldn't be remarkable."[25]

While Hoover deferred to private charity and local government, a prolonged debate unfolded in the U.S. Congress over whether the federal government should give Gifford "something to do it with." Not until July 1932, however, did the Congress decide, enacting, with the president's acquiescence, the Emergency Relief and Construction Act, the only federal relief measure of the Hoover administration. Title I of this act authorized a program of loans to the states at 3 percent interest for use in relief activities. But since many of the more hard-hit states were already close to exhausting their constitutional lending authority, the real impact of this act was somewhat limited. Perhaps its main accomplishment was to establish the principle that the constitutional directive to the federal government to protect the general welfare carried with it an obligation to respond to the kind of crisis brought on by the Depression.

Not until May 1933, two months after Roosevelt's inauguration, was this principle translated into programmatic terms. At that time, the Federal Emergency Relief Act was passed and the Federal Emergency Relief Administration (FERA), under Harry Hopkins, created. Because of the severe emergency that confronted it, FERA was permitted to depart extensively from the prevailing practice of American relief. Under the terms of the act, the new agency was authorized to provide $500 million to the states and localities to relieve "the hardship and suffering caused by unemployment." Although the act thus retained a substantial role for states and localities, it established a clearly federal program, with federal funds and federal guidelines. It dropped the categorical distinctions of earlier relief policies, making need, and need alone, the prime determinant of eligibility.[26] As a consequence, local relief agencies were able to respond to the crisis with a broad and flexible program that could accommodate unemployed able-bodied heads of families as well as the traditional recipients of relief. Even some of the working poor, those who were employed full or part time, yet earning hardly enough to survive, received aid under FERA. Thus, FERA changed the whole definition of who deserved public assistance. For the first time, assistance was extended on a broad scale to the able-bodied poor. More than that, the able-bodied were advanced to the head of the class, through instructions to local relief agencies to differentiate between employables and unemployables and then concentrate their resources on the former. "I am not going to hide behind the cloak of the intent of Congress as to what federal funds can be used for," Hopkins told the National Conference of Social Work convention in 1933 in explaining his priorities. "It is my belief that the people who fought for this bill, who tried to get this money, were trying to get it for relief of the unemployed, and not for a number of other perfectly fine and worthy social objectives."[27] In Hopkins's view, the Depression had turned the traditional notions of deservingness on their head. "It is no longer a matter of unemployables and chronic dependents, but of your friends and mine who are involved in this," he pointed out to the social workers. "The whole picture comes closer to home than ever before."[28]

The New Deal's Grand Design

It soon became apparent, however, that FERA's concept of a single, comprehensive assistance program providing benefits solely on the basis of need was an idea whose time had not yet arrived. No one seemed satisfied with this approach as a permanent mechanism for the relief of poverty. The conservatives disliked relief of any sort, let alone relief to the able-bodied, and federal administration. Many social workers feared that inclusion of employables and unemployables in the same program might dilute the quality of individual attention that relief workers could give to the truly dependent. Even Roosevelt and Hopkins had doubts since they remained wedded to the Calvinist notion that relief must be tied to work lest it produce, in Roosevelt's terms, "a spiritual and moral disintegration fundamentally destructive to the national fiber."[29] In fact, Hopkins signaled state relief administrators as early as the spring of 1934 that the FERA was shifting its emphasis from direct relief to "work relief . . . for normally employable people."[30] Justifying the shift some time later, Hopkins put a special twist on the longstanding Poor Law disdain for the undeserving poor, noting that "the family of a man working on a Works Progress Administration [WPA] project looks down its nose at neighbors who take their relief straight."[31] The fact that WPA jobs were available for only a fraction of the unemployed hardly seemed to matter.

While the emergency relief effort went forward, efforts were made to define more clearly—and more narrowly—the appropriate long-term federal role in public assistance. From the outset, two basic principles, both reflecting Roosevelt's own publicly expressed preferences, seem to have guided this search:

...ssistance focus primarily on the long-neglected problems of
...aving to the states, as before, the task of caring for the
...d second, that this federal assistance be work conditioned in
... aim was to extend public protection to those formerly con-
...ng without altering the basic criterion by which deservingness
was judg-

To perform the technical magic needed to translate these seemingly
contradictory principles into a concrete program, Roosevelt appointed the
cabinet-level Committee on Economic Security, headed by Secretary of Labor
Francis Perkins, in June 1934. Working through the summer and fall of 1934,
this committee fashioned an innovative grand design that ultimately became,
with some important modifications, the foundation of the Social Security Act of
1935, and of our social welfare policy thereafter.

In broad outline, this grand design consisted of two sets of programs—one
for employables and one for those not able to work. The program for employables was by far the more complete, containing four major elements: a jobs
program providing for public employment "whenever private employment
slackens";[32] a system of unemployment insurance for industrial workers; old age
insurance; and a temporary program of needs-tested old age assistance.

While these four elements were presented as separate programs, it was clear
that the committee—and the president—perceived them as a single, integrated
package that would work as a unit. Unemployment insurance, for example,
would be the "first line of defense" in times of economic distress, providing cash
assistance to the unemployed workers as a matter of "contractual right," though
only for "a limited period during which there is expectation that he will soon be
reemployed."[33] If the worker remained unemployed at the end of this limited
period through no fault of his own, the prescribed remedy was to be work relief,
not continued cash assistance. The public employment part of the overall program was thus to function not just as a principal line of defense in times of
depression, but as a back-up system at other times as well. Reflecting this, the
Committee on Economic Security argued that public employment should be "a
permanent policy of the Government and not merely . . . an emergency measure."[34] Indeed, it was to play an integral part in a continuing effort to train the
long-term unemployed and thus help relieve the problem of structural
unemployment. Finally, the old age insurance and old age assistance programs
were to operate in similar fashion to relieve the economic insecurity associated
with old age. The former was to be a straight insurance program, funded jointly
by employee and employer contributions. Since this meant in practice that no
payments could be made until a trust fund had accumulated, a noncontributory
cash assistance program was added to fill in until social security payments could
begin, and to aid workers whose jobs were not yet covered by social security or
who were scheduled to reach retirement age prior to building up a sufficient
social security retirement fund.

The benefits for those considered unemployable or hard to employ were less generous and elaborate. In fact, their inclusion in the package was in some sense accidental, the product of special pleadings on behalf of several categories of the state-aided dependent poor by representatives from two or three federal agencies who managed to gain the ear of the president's committee and its staff in the summer of 1934. According to Josephine Brown, a staff member of the FERA who participated in the work of the Committee on Economic Security:

> The major concern of the committee was throughout with insurance against the hazards of unemployment and old age. These measures were designed to provide economic security for that section of the population who are actually employed and able to contribute. . . . Only partial consideration was given, however, to that large section of our population made up of the people who are in greatest need because some disability or other unfortunate circumstance has deprived them of the capacity or ability for work or self support. These "unemployables were never considered as a whole by the committee as presenting a problem of economic security to be dealt with by the Federal Government. Instead certain categories were selected to receive Federal assistance through grants-in-aid to the states.[35]

It was in this way, therefore, that the aid-to-the-blind and ADC programs that have come to dominate our needs-tested public assistance policy came into existence. Although the result was only a partial response to the needs of the unemployables, it represented a major improvement over the benign neglect that had characterized previous federal policy.

The Committee on Economic Security thus produced the blueprint of an economic security program that was far more comprehensive than anything that had existed in this country before. For those previously neglected by social welfare measures in particular, this program offered an ingenious mix of protections, combining cash assistance during short spells of unemployment, long-term protection against the insecurity of old age, and a permanent program of public jobs when private employment lags. In addition, federal aid was provided for the first time to help care for some of the more needy of the unemployable poor, and, in the process, to encourage bolder state action in this sphere.

Still, for all its novelty and breadth, this grand design represented a significant retreat from the more comprehensive assistance program that FERA was then operating. Where FERA conditioned assistance solely on need, for example, the new system would restore the longstanding practice of categorization. Indeed, it would expand on it, segmenting even the unemployable poor into separate program categories, only some of which would be eligible for federal aid (the blind, the aged, the dependent children). In the process, the basic doctrine of deservingness was retained. Now, however, the penalty for failure to become a part of the primary labor force would be all the greater since it would mean no access to the new unemployment insurance or old age protection programs. These new programs, while not means tested, were to be work conditioned: no one could benefit from them unless he had succeeded in getting a private job, and even then, a job in a certain kind of industry, since not all employment was covered. The financing mechanisms built into both social security and unemployment insurance guaranteed this result by making eligibility for assistance in these programs wholly dependent on payroll taxes paid by the worker, or by the employer on his behalf. Thus an employable person would have to be employed in a covered occupation for a specified period of time in order to be eligible for unemployment or retirement benefits. Under the blueprint developed by the Committee on Economic Security, even the proposed public employment program was to be work conditioned. In the committee's view, the admissions process utilized to allocate the necessarily limited jobs created by such a program should be designed to ensure "that only workers who are ordinarily employed are given public employment."[36]

The committee's grand design also upheld the Poor Law tradition by avoiding any interference with prevailing wage rates and working conditions. This was most clearly apparent in the treatment of the working poor, that sizable segment of the able-bodied population that works full time—or tries to—yet earns too little to achieve economic security even in normal times. Under the terms of the needs-tested programs proposed in the grand design, no cash assistance was available to such individuals, unless they were blind, aged, or dependent children. The social insurance programs bypassed them, too, because most of the jobs of the working poor fell in the 45 percent of all employment not covered by these programs. Even as coverage was extended, the payoff to the working poor would be meager. At Roosevelt's insistence, both unemployment insurance and old age insurance were to be self-financing. To achieve this, benefits were related to prior earnings through a system of regressive payroll taxes paid by the employer in the case of unemployment insurance, and jointly by the employer and the employee in the case of social security. As Roosevelt later acknowledged the main motivation for this funding mechanism was political more than economic:

> Those taxes were never a problem in economics. They are politics all the way through. We put those payroll contributions there so as to give the contributors a legal, moral, and political right to collect their pensions and their unemployment benefits. With those taxes in there, no damn politician can every scrap my social security program.[37]

But "with those taxes in there" also, gross regional and industry disparities in wage rates would be translated directly into serious inequities in the unemployment and retirement benefit levels. As a result, those subjected to poverty-level wages while employed would be required by the social insurance funding mechanisms to pay for this failing in their retirement years, or while they were unemployed, as well. Thus, the social welfare package proposed by New Deal planners would not only require the able-bodied to work, but also would require that they accept whatever job was available, at whatever rate of pay, without offering any additional assistance to help with the continued poverty that might—and too often did—result. To be sure, other aspects of the New Deal program—especially minimum wage legislation and the protections afforded unions—offered some potential escape from the dilemmas that resulted, but these were far less certain and, ultimately, themselves incomplete.

In addition to these other manifestations of earlier relief practice, the New Deal grand design also moved closer to the traditional pattern on the question of local control, responding to pressures to decentralize control in order to adjust the assistance system more flexibly to local economic interests. This was apparent to some extent in the limitation of coverage under unemployment compensation to firms employing eight or more persons, and in the exclusion from old age insurance of farm workers and domestics, both prominent in the rural South. It was even more apparent in the decision to place control of the whole unemployment compensation system in the hands of the states, thus avoiding the potential disruption of local labor practices that a national program, with national benefit levels and eligibility provisions, might bring. Similarly, though proposing a significant upgrading and streamlining of the existing state old age, mothers' pension, and aid-to-the-blind programs, the New Deal planners surrendered an important measure of uniformity, equity, and consistency by opting to funnel federal assistance through the existing state-run programs. This problem was aggravated further when Congress went to work on the package and completed the work of returning control over the needs-tested cash assistance programs to the states.

Instead of a single, integrated program of assistance to all in need, what the Committee on Economic Security thus proposed was a far more limited and diverse set of programs that retained the longstanding traditions of categorization, local control, and support for prevailing labor practices and wage rates. The committee justified this approach on the assumptions that general economic recovery would solve whatever problems remained for employables once the federal government made provision for temporary unemployment and retirement; and that the states could handle whatever problems remained for the unemployables, all the more so since the expansion of social security was expected to reduce the pressures on the states for old age assistance payments. As the committee pointed out in its report:

> The measures we suggest all seek to segregate clearly distinguishable large groups among those now on relief or on the verge of relief and to apply such differentiated treatment to each group as will give it the greatest practical degree of economic security. We believe that if these measures are adopted, the residual relief problem will have diminished to a point where it will be possible to return the primary responsibility for the care of people who cannot work to the state and local governments.[38]

But not everyone shared these assumptions. In adopting its approach, the cabinet-level Committee on Economic Security rejected the broader strategy urged on it by its own Advisory Committee on Public Assistance and Relief, which Secretary Perkins had established to aid the cabinet members in their work. According to this advisory committee, "the social hazards to which millions of persons and families are subjected are too varied and too complicated" to justify reliance on work-conditioned assistance alone, or even work-conditioned assistance coupled with federal support for state old age and mothers' pension programs. "If the Federal program should include only old age pensions and mothers' assistance," this expert committee therefore concluded, "the needs of the great bulk of the families would be left to the present local poor relief system, the evils of which are well recognized."[39] As an alternative, the committee vigorously urged a broad program of federal grants to the states for general relief instead of the far narrower program of categorical grants that was ultimately adopted.

Although it is not widely recognized, staffers of the FERA almost managed to incorporate this broader approach into the legislative proposals that President Roosevelt sent to Congress, and that ultimately became the Social Security Act of 1935. In their draft of the ADC title of this bill, FERA professionals intentionally used a definition of dependent children so broad that it could have authorized aid under this title to virtually every family in need in which there was a child under 16. The only restriction placed on the definition was that there be in the child's family "no adult person . . . who is able to work and provide the family with a reasonable subsistence compatible with decency and health." Under this definition, not just the incapacity or absence of a father, but also his inability to find employment or the failure of his job to "provide the family with a reasonable subsistence," could qualify a family for federally supported cash assistance. As Josephine Brown has noted: "'Aid to Dependent Children' as conceived by the FERA meant general relief or assistance on a family basis to all families having children under sixteen" who were in need.[40] This means aid to the working poor and to any of the unemployed who could not find public works jobs. Had this provision been adopted, the whole structure of public assistance might have been different, and much of the criticism of welfare on grounds of inequity and perverse family-splitting incentives avoided. What happened instead was the adoption of a far narrower definition, first in the Committee on Economic Security's report, and ultimately in the legislation.

Unraveling of the Grand Design

If the president's proposals had significant shortcomings compared to FERA practice and the suggestions of some of his advisers, they still were more comprehensive and workable than what ultimately emerged from Congress. The grand design began to unravel almost as soon as it was unveiled.

The first step in this process was paradoxically taken by the administration itself, when it separated the public jobs portion of the program from the rest of the package and introduced two separate bills, one exclusively concerned with public works, and the other containing the rest of the economic security program outlined above. This two-bill approach, which was recommended by budget officials, apparently as a strategy to increase the political prospects of emergency jobs legislation,[41] broke up the integrated approach developed by the president's committee. As we have seen, the logic of this approach rested critically on the availability of public jobs, which were to provide a first line of defense for regularly employed persons in times of depression and a permanent mechanism to help stranded populations and other long-term unemployed persons during other times as well. By separating public jobs from the rest of the program, however, the administration made the jobs component a ready target for Congressional conservatives, who had long opposed a permanent program of public jobs. Even in the halcyon days of the WPA, while Hopkins was encouraging WPA workers to "look down their noses" at recipients of direct relief, federal work assistance was available to less than one person out of five who applied.[42] Thereafter, Congress restricted public works funds even more, despite the fact that recovery continued to lag. The result was widespread suffering, relieved only in part by the residual direct relief program that survived into the latter 1930s. When World War II finally brought a return to full employment, both the direct relief and public works programs of the New Deal years were terminated, deleting permanently, but apparently unconsciously, one of the central elements of the original economic security design, and limiting the government's capacity to cope with the problems that were to face it in the postwar era.

In addition to severly restricting the public jobs component of the administration's package, Congress also imposed a number of other limitations. For example, the coverage of the basic social insurance programs was further restricted, thus delaying the day when such coverage would be universal.[43] In addition, Congress weakened those provisions intended to provide a degree of uniformity in the needs-tested assistance programs for the aged, the blind, and dependent children that the federal government would be funding through grants to the states. In the original version, for example, the FERA would have been given authority to make sure that states would use no criteria other than age and need in determining eligibility for old age assistance, and that benefit levels in all the programs would be sufficient to provide "a reasonable subsistence compatible with decency and health." On both counts, congressional conservatives took serious exception. According to Edwin Witte, who served as executive director of the Committee on Economic Security and chief administration lobbyist on the social security bill, "southern members did not want to give authority to anyone in Washington to deny aid to any state because it discriminated against Negroes in the administration of old age assistance."[44] The southerners wanted no part of a national benefit schedule that might pay the elderly more than could be earned by prime-age field hands for full-time work.

Accordingly, the bill was rewritten to allow states to impose virtually any eligibility criteria they wished beyond the basic federal age and need criteria, and to set benefit levels as low as they wanted without losing federal matching funds.[45] Similar provisions were incorporated in the ADC program, thus fastening onto the welfare system the state-by-state disparities that have been the target of reformers ever since.

Congress also administered the coup de grace to the broad approach to public assistance that had been proposed by the Advisory Committee on Public Assistance and Relief. By adding 18 words to the definition of "dependent children," Congress changed the whole meaning of the aid-to-dependent-children title of the Social Security Act, specifying that only children deprived of parental support "by reason of the death, continued absence from the home, or physical or mental incapacity of a parent" would be eligible for aid.

The programs that ultimately emerged from this critical period of innovation were thus a far cry from a comprehensive, integrated system of income security. What started out in the emergency as a broad program of assistance to anyone in need had become a work-enforcing insurance system providing old age and temporary unemployment protection only to those actively attached to the industrial labor force, and a series of unconnected cash assistance provisions offering limited benefits to selected segments of the dependent poor on terms defined by the states. As the president conceded when signing the law, the Social Security Act, for all its innovations, still constituted just "the cornerstone of a structure which is being built but is by no means complete."

THE MIRACLE ECONOMY AND THE WITHERING-AWAY THESIS

Roosevelt's cautions were soon forgotten, however. In the wake of World War II, with the national confidence restored, it was easy to pretend that the Social Security Act of 1935 had solved the problem of economic insecurity in the United States, at least to the extent that it could be solved. Not until 1962 was this view shaken with the publication of Michael Harrington's powerful portrayal of the persistence of poverty in *The Other America.*[46] Once again the issue of poverty and want attracted national attention, unleashing a new wave of reform activity that rivaled the 1930s in scope and intensity. If we are to understand these reforms of the 1960s, it is necessary to look first at the hopes that gave rise to the optimism of the New Deal planners and at the factors that ultimately frustrated them.

High Expectations

Although the authors of the New Deal's economic security program were well aware that the proposals they were advancing were incomplete in important respects, they took comfort in two assumptions, both of which hardened into dogma in the subsequent 20 years. The first related to the capacity of the American economy to give all those who could work the chance to achieve income sufficiency on their own, once the ravages of the Depression were conquered. To be sure, the President's Committee on Economic Security recognized that widespread unemployment existed even in the prosperous 1920s, and that a residual public works program would therefore be needed even after the Depression.[47] Yet, nowhere was there any recognition of the possibility that a permanent program of income supplementation might be needed for persons who were employed but earning too little to achieve a decent standard of living.

Closely related to this confidence in the economy's ability to supply jobs and income to those able to work was a second set of hopes. This one focused on the capacity of the social insurance programs to displace public assistance expenditures as social insurance coverage expanded. At the outset, these hopes centered on the old age assistance program, which all parties expected to be the only sizable federal public assistance obligation. As we have seen, old age assistance was included in the Social Security Act primarily because old age insurance initially had limited coverage and because its contribution requirements made it largely inapplicable to workers already nearing retirement. With an expansion of insurance coverage expected over time, it was reasonable to expect that an ever larger proportion of the working population would be eligible for the higher social insurance benefits, and that correspondingly fewer persons would thus have to rely on old age assistance. This "withering away" hypothesis, as Steiner termed it,[48] made it easy to rationalize the delegation of old age assistance responsibilities to the states, on the ground that, if old age assistance would ultimately wither away, there was no need to set up a whole new federal apparatus to operate it. With the addition of survivors' insurance to the basic social security insurance package in 1939, this same logic came to apply to the ADC program as well. As we have seen, once the FERA proposals were dropped, ADC was expected to be a small program aimed at providing aid to children whose fathers were deceased. On this assumption, survivors' insurance would be expected to do for potential recipients of ADC what old age insurance was expected to do for potential recipients of OAA: provide a higher level of benefits, and in the more desirable form of an insurance premium available by right instead of a welfare payment available only on demonstration of need.

The assumption that the coverage of the basic social security insurance system would expand continuously until it embraced the entire population, and that this would eliminate the need for public assistance, made policymakers feel confident and complacent about the New Deal's economic security system. President Truman accurately reflected the governing assumptions in 1951, when he confidently observed that "the basic purpose of public assistance . . . is and always has been to supplement our social insurance system. Our aim has been to expand coverage of social insurance and gradually reduce the need for supplementary public assistance programs."[49]

The Reality Beneath the Myth

Why is it, then, that these hopes failed to materialize? What is it that frustrated the expectations of a generation of social welfare policymakers?

The conventional answer points to a variety of social and economic changes that the planners of the New Deal system and their successors "could not have anticipated."[50] A more accurate answer would be that the effect of whatever unforeseeable demographic and economic changes occurred was magnified by a variety of structural defects in the basic assistance machinery, many of which the planners anticipated rather clearly but which they were unable to correct because of entrenched political opposition. Specifically, four basic factors—two foreseeable and two probably not—explain the frustrations that ultimately led to the pressures for reform in the 1960s, and that continue to prompt reform pressures today.

Structural Weaknesses in the Economy. The first of these phenomena are the structural weaknesses in the economy that would have limited the effectiveness of the New Deal's social insurance scheme no matter how complete the coverage. To assume that old age, unemployment, and disability insurance together would eliminate the need for income assistance, it was necessary to overlook the millions of southern blacks trapped in agrarian peonage, the related problems of so-called stranded populations in Appalachia and elsewhere, the dislocations occasioned by large-scale changes in industrial location, and the widespread pattern of discrimination in urban labor markets that consigned blacks and other minorities to permanent low-wage work with little prospect for advancement. To cope effectively with these structurally induced causes of economic insecurity would have required, at a minimum, a system of wage supplementation for those confined to seasonal or low-wage jobs, and, at best, a comprehensive program of public training, public jobs, and equal employment opportunity.

Yet nothing even vaguely approaching this kind of program was forthcoming. To the contrary, by rejecting federally aided general assistance to anyone in need, the New Deal planners foreclosed any chance of aiding the working poor. Similarly, by tying old age benefits to preretirement earnings, the Social Security Act guaranteed that, even with universal coverage, the working poor would remain poor in their retirement years as well. Finally, by scuttling the plan for a residual public works job program, policymakers turned their backs on the stranded populations and other long-term unemployed persons that even the President's Committee on Economic Security had recognized would continue to need help. In none of these cases can the ultimate decision be attributed to lack of foresight on the part of the planners. More plausible as an explanation is the political power of the affected interests.

The Slow March of Coverage Extension. If structural weaknesses in the economy of the sort described above set upper limits on the effectiveness of the New Deal income assistance programs in relieving poverty, the slowness with which the coverage was actually extended explains why even these limits were not met. When the Social Security Act was passed, 45 percent of the paid labor force was excluded from coverage under the act's old age insurance title, and an even larger proportion under unemployment insurance. Although coverage extensions were adopted under old age insurance throughout the postwar period, it was not until 1961 that 90 percent of the potentially eligible population was covered. As a result, instead of declining rapidly, the number of old age assistance recipients climbed steadily throughout the 1940s, and began to decline only in the mid-1950s, and even then fairly slowly.[51]

In the unemployment insurance program, progress was even slower. As of 1950, for example, only 55 percent of the civilian labor force was covered; and as of 1960, 34 percent of the labor force still remained outside the system.[52] What is more, in an effort to make themselves attractive to industry, states competed with each other in reducing the costs of the program to employers by lowering the effective payroll tax. As a consequence, benefits averaged only about one-third of prior earnings instead of the 50 percent figure originally projected. Moreover, the anticipated extension in the maximum benefit period failed to materialize, despite a series of rather deep postwar recessions and mounting evidence of increased structural unemployment resulting from automation and other economic changes. Since there were no back-up programs of public employment or general assistance, considerable insecurity persisted, even for those covered by the system.

The Rise of the AFDC Conundrum. A third factor that frustrated the hopes of New Deal planners is one they could hardly have foreseen, though it might have been less pronounced or less damaging had the system created in the 1930s not been so restrictive. As we have seen, the designs of FERA planners to utilize the ADC program as the entering wedge for a federally subsidized general assistance program were nipped in the bud. ADC was expected to remain a rather small part of the overall public assistance picture, providing aid mainly to the children of widows. In fact, ADC was expected to wither away over time—just like OAA—as survivor's insurance took hold.

While this expectation began to work for OAA by the mid-1950s, however, the opposite happened with ADC. Instead of declining, the number of ADC recipients kept climbing straight through the 1950s and into the 1960s, jumping from 0.9 million children in 1950 to 1.7 million in 1955, and to 2.4 million in 1960.[53] What fueled this growth was a surge in the number of mothers who had to turn to public assistance not because of the death or incapacitation of their husbands, but because they either had no husband or were separated from him. Scholars still dispute whether this occurred because of a basic change in the family patterns of the poor produced by urbanization, or because of the disappearance of low skill jobs for the latest urban immigrants, or because of a rise in illegitmacy, or simply because of an increase in participation rates prompted by better welfare benefits. Whatever the cause, the extent of the change was striking. In 1940, for example, 42 percent of the families on AFDC were there because of the death of the father.[54] As of 1961, death and incapacitation together accounted for only 25 percent of all AFDC fathers. Two-thirds, by contrast, were in the absent-from-the-home category, mostly as a consequence of divorce or separation (22 percent), illegitimacy (21 percent), or desertion (19 percent).[55]

These trends accelerated further in the 1960s. Between 1960 and 1967, AFDC rolls jumped by 2 million, and then doubled again in the next four years.[56] Accompanying this growth in numbers, moreover, was a further decline in the proportion of AFDC cases attributable to the death or incapacitation of the father. This figure declines from 26 percent to 17.5 percent between 1960 and 1967, while the proportion of cases attributable to the father's absence from the home increased from 67 to 74 percent.[57]

Far from decreasing, public assistance expenditures skyrocketed. Worse still, they did so under a program largely ignored in policy debates prior to the mid-1950s and about whose beneficiaries other sectors of society began to raise serious moral questions. The predictable result was a turning of public opinion increasingly against the welfare mother and the assistance programs that helped sustain her and her children. Other factors that might have made for a more thoughtful assessment of the problem got little attention. It did not seem to matter, for example, that divorce and separation were also reaching unusually high levels among middle-class families; that unemployment plagued young, inner-city black males, limiting the financial resources available to sustain durable, two-parent families; or that public policy encouraged the departure of fathers from poor families by making such departure the major requisite for receipt of public assistance. The mothers of dependent children on public assistance still took the blame, altering significantly the traditional concept of who was deserving of public aid.

Contributing importantly to this change was the racial shift that accompanied the growth in AFDC rolls. This racial shift has never been as extreme as in popular perceptions. As of 1961, for example, a clear majority (54 percent) of AFDC recipients were white, and whites still commanded a majority in 1967.[58] However, the black recipients were more highly concentrated in central cities, making them far more visible, and therefore far more vulnerable to adverse stereotyping.[59] As a result, in the AFDC program, the traditional moral outrage over the undeserving poor converged in the 1960s with longstanding attitudes of racial bigotry to produce a highly volatile political brew.

Runaway State Discretion. Because, as a consequence of the factors discussed above, the federally supported categorical assistance programs remained important far longer than anyone would have assumed, a fourth factor soon joined the other three as a cause of the shortcomings of the New Deal relief system: widespread state discretion. In the original design of the public assistance titles, state discretion was to be restrained by federal rules on eligibility standards and minimum benefit levels. But these rules were stricken from the legislation prior to its passage, giving the states considerable freedom. Although federal authorities nevertheless held the states in check during the 1930s, the states seized the initiative soon after, producing the gross disparities in benefit levels, eligibility criteria, and administrative procedures described earlier. The pracical consequence was that recipients in numerous states were left well below adequate levels of income even when they managed to get on the assistance rolls, and the establishment of eligibility was made a complicated, lengthy process.

THE REFORMS OF THE 1960s: A PATCHWORK QUILT?

By the 1960s, the implications of the four factors just discussed could no longer be ignored. The massive migration of southern blacks to northern cities, combined with the outflow of jobs from the central cities to the suburbs, had trapped large segments of the inner-city poor in poverty. Public assistance rolls ballooned, generating anguished reactions from hard-pressed taxpayers. At the same time, a new national leadership took office, committed to a broad array of social welfare changes. Finally, through the civil rights movement and a series of violent urban riots, the masses of the minority poor began to flex their muscles, sending shock waves throughout the nation.

The upshot was a wave of wide-ranging reforms, shaped by two different sentiments: frustration over the inadequacy of New Deal social welfare programs as they had evolved through the early 1960s; and in sharp contrast to this, rising irritation over the seemingly excessive generosity of these same programs. This clash of sentiments focused on the needs-tested public assistance programs. In the social insurance area, the major philosophical issues had already been put to rest by the 1960s, leaving mainly the technical question of how rapidly the coverage and benefits of the program could be expanded, consistent with maintaining the fiscal integrity of the trust funds that provided the financing. Beyond this, the only outstanding social insurance question was whether to expand the system to include medical insurance, a question that was finally resolved in 1965 with the adoption of Medicare.

In the area of public assistance titles, on the other hand, the battle was just warming up. At the very time that pressures to expand aid to the poor were gaining momentum in some quarters, opposition to the existing public assistance programs, particularly the burgeoning AFDC program, was growing in others. The stage was set for an intense political battle. With increasingly hostile opponents of public assistance in command of the legislative power, supporters of more aid found they could make headway only in two basic ways: by characterizing their proposals as devices to reduce AFDC costs; and by designing assistance packages that had particular emotional appeal or that could attract the support of key provider groups through whose hands assistance to the poor could be channelled. The result was a two-pronged strategy that spawned a series of new departures in AFDC and a rich new mix of in-kind benefit programs.

Spending to Save: The Search for Quick Fixes in AFDC

During the 1940s and 1950s, the states had responded to the apparent failure of public assistance to wither away by exercising their discretion to limit benefits and restrict eligibility, and by appealing—successfully, as it turned out—to the federal government to absorb a larger share of program costs.* By the 1960s, however, pressure had mounted for federal officials to take matters into their own hands. The result was three federal initiatives—one adding unemployed fathers to the assistance role; another, substantially increasing federal payments for rehabilitation services; and a third, providing a system of work requirements, work incentives, work training, and day-care services for working mothers, in addition to the basic assistance activities. In each of these cases, the federal initiative proposed to add new costs to the programs. But in each case also, the new costs were justified as necessary to reduce the long-term costs of the system. How was this alchemy to work?

Unemployed-Father Coverage. Under the Social Security Act, as we have seen, able-bodied males of working age were expected to rely completely on the private labor market for their income. While temporary unemployment benefits were provided to some of these individuals to cover short spells of joblessness, no other public assistance was made available to them, no matter what their income or work status. The whole strategy thus hinged critically on the ability of the private labor market to generate sufficient jobs yielding an adequate rate of pay.

The persistence of high unemployment rates among central-city youths, particularly minority youths, in the 1950s and early 1960s, however, threw this strategy into serious question. Was it not possible, after all, that the apparent rise in the number of female-headed households was a consequence of the desperate economic situation confronting ghetto youths? Indeed, was it not possible that AFDC was fueling its own growth by denying aid to a family whose breadwinner—or potential breadwinner in the case of illegitimacy—was unemployed or employed only part time? Did this not give the breadwinner a strong incentive to absent himself from the home in order to make his family eligible for assistance? Under the circumstances, did it not make sense to remove this incentive by extending aid to the family while the father was still present but unemployed, and thus keep the family intact for the day when the father found full-time employment?

It was under the weight of this logic that the Kennedy administration came forward in 1961 with a proposal to extend ADC coverage to families whose children were dependent by virtue of the unemployment—and not just

---

*As of 1945, the federal government was obligated to reimburse states for half the first $40 in monthly state payments to each recipient of OAA and aid to the blind. Thus the maximum federal payment per recipient was $20 per month. From 1946 to 1962, Congress increased the federal contribution in some way in every even-numbered year except 1954, and in 1961 as well. In 1962, the matching formula was changed again, so that the federal government would become liable to pay as much as $51.75 of the first $70 a month in aid-to-the-blind or OAA payments, plus $12 of the next $15 spent for medical care. Corresponding increases also were enacted in the cases of AFDC and aid to the disabled. Almost without exception these changes were initiated by the Congress over the objections of a budget-conscious executive branch.[60]

the absence or incapacitation—of the primary breadwinner. This proposal, which bore obvious resemblance to the plan advanced by FERA staffers during consideration of the Social Security Act of 1935, gained congressional approval on an experimental basis in 1961 and was then extended for five years in 1962. However, the price of passage was the inclusion of a number of qualifying provisions. For example, the new unemployed fathers (AFDC-U) program was made wholly optional: no state would be required to establish one, and no special advantages were gained by those who did. Not surprisingly, only half the states chose to exercise this option. In addition, the definition of unemployment in the program has served to cancel out some of the positive effects that were anticipated. Under this definition, any family whose breadwinner works more than 100 hours per month is abruptly dropped from assistance, thus recreating strong incentives for family splitting, albeit at a different point in the father's employment history. Although the AFDC-U program made cash assistance available to the long-term unemployed for the first time since the Depression, these restrictions have kept the scope of the program rather limited. As of 1977, for example, AFDC-U accounted for less than 4 percent of all AFDC cases.[61]

The Services Strategy. If the unemployed-fathers program was designed to reduce the welfare rolls by eliminating the incentives for family disruption, the second initiative, introduced by the Kennedy administration in its proposed 1962 amendments to the Social Security Act, was aimed at rehabilitating those already on the rolls. Heralded by Kennedy as "the most far-reaching revision of our public welfare program since it was enacted in 1935,"[62] the 1962 amendments greatly expanded federal spending on social services for welfare recipients. Under these amendments, the federal government would henceforth pay 75 percent of the costs of rehabilitative services provided to welfare recipients by the states, a substantial jump from the 50 percent of such funds the federal government provided previously. Armed with these funds, so the argument went, social work professionals in the states could begin the arduous task of rehabilitating relief recipients and ultimately restoring them to productive life free of dependence on AFDC or other forms of assistance. "Professional, skilled services" are "the answer," then HEW Secretary Abraham Ribicoff declared when introducing the new proposal. "We believe," he told the House Ways and Means Committee, "that services represent the key to our efforts to help people become self-sufficient so that they no longer need assistance."[63]

This stress on social services resulted from two important impulses that came to bear on the politics of public assistance in the 1960s. The first was the professionalization of social welfare work and the resulting emergence of an influential community of experts committed to the casework approach to the problems of the poor. This approach originated in the settlement-house movement of the turn of the century and has since come to inform much of professional social work training. It involves the provision of individualized assistance to persons in need by a trained professional equipped with service programs that can be tailored to the individual's situation. Behind this approach is the idea that such difficulties as delinquency, criminality, unemployment, and poverty are in substantial part just the outward manifestation of deep personal maladjustments that must be treated at their source, through careful casework. The public assistance programs authorized by the Social Security Act of 1935, however, made scant provision for such casework or for the services needed to support it. Not until 1956 were state expenditures on casework eligible for federal matching assistance. Even then they were treated merely like administrative costs eligible for 50–50 federal matching, giving the states little incentive to expand them. When the election of a new Democratic administration and the appointment of a sympathetic HEW secretary gave the social welfare community good access to the highest levels of government, they naturally took advantage of the situation to press their case.[64]

This services strategy found additional support in the "culture of poverty" theory that surfaced in scholarly and social services journals at the same time. This theory pointed to the social and intellectual climate of low-income areas as a prime cause of the persistence of poverty. It suggested that the pervasiveness of social problems in low-income areas leads to the development of a vicious cycle in which failure and resulting lowered expectations feed on each other in perverse succession, sapping people of drive and initiative. By providing a variety of social services and a network of caseworkers, the 1962 amendments sought to break this cycle by equipping individuals to escape from the trap and by working with them while they did. This initiative was then supplemented by the Economic Opportunity Act of 1964, which further extended the array of social services made available and the target population eligible to receive them.

Whatever the merits of this approach to the problems of poverty, it did not fulfill the hopes many people had placed in it as a strategy to reduce the welfare rolls. "The great thrust on behalf of prevention and rehabilitation," Steiner wrote after four years of experience with the approach, "seems more gimmicky than substantive." Explained Steiner: "The rehabilitation recommendation . . . was not based on the identification of a new situation in public assistance. If most of the client group did not lend itself to rehabilitation, there would not be much innovation. It didn't; and there hasn't been."[65]

As of 1968, HEW could report the rehabilitation of only 20,000 AFDC recipients out of the 1.5 million families on the rolls.[66] Whether the services strategy had received a fair test or not, it soon became apparent that Congress was ready for yet another new approach.

The Work Approach. This time, following the urban riots, it was congressional conservatives who took the initiative. When Lyndon Johnson proposed a series of major amendments to the Social Security Act on behalf of the elderly in 1967, conservatives in the House took advantage of the occasion to press their case for training and work as a solution to the AFDC "problem." "We want the states to see to it that those who are drawing welfare checks as unemployed fathers or drawing as mothers . . . that they take training and then work," House Ways and Means Committee Chairman Wilbur Mills explained to his House colleagues. "What in the world is wrong with requiring these people to submit themselves, if they are to draw public funds, to a test of their ability to learn a job? Is that not the way we should go?"[67] Four hundred thirteen out of the 419 House members who voted thought it was, and the Senate soon concurred, launching yet another bold assault on the steeply rising AFDC rolls.

The product of this effort was the WIN program. Under it, all AFDC recipients were required to work, or accept training, unless they were incapacitated or needed in the home because of the illness of another family member. Local welfare agencies were instructed to make arrangements with local Labor Department affiliates to set up the necessary training programs, and funds were provided to cover the costs of day-care facilities for the children of AFDC mothers enrolled in training. Finally, as an incentive for welfare recipients to work, $30 a month, plus one-third of all earnings in excess of that amount, was to be excluded from the recipients' incomes when computing the benefit to which they were entitled. This exemption came on top of the deductions for work-related expenses, provided in the 1962 amendments. Clearly, Congress was willing to walk the extra mile to get welfare mothers to work.

At the same time that it strengthened work incentives in the AFDC program, Congress sought to freeze AFDC rolls by denying federal payments to cover any increase in the proportion of children in a state on AFDC. Although this provision was ultimately rescinded in response to the opposition of the social welfare profession and recipient groups, its passage in the first round of voting tells something about the feeling of a substantial segment of Congress toward AFDC.

By allowing welfare mothers to keep a portion of their earnings without a reduction in their benefits, the 1967 amendments built upon a series of earlier provisions allowing recipients under both aid to the blind and old age assistance to do the same. However, by extending this concept to AFDC, and then adding a host of mandatory features that made work a requirement instead of just an opportunity, the 1967 amendments in effect officially reclassified mothers of dependent children from the deserving to the nondeserving category of the poor. The assumption was that sizable numbers of these mothers could be put to work, an assumption that overlooked the fact that many already did work but earned too little to take themselves out of poverty; that many others were physically unable to earn adequate incomes; that child-care responsibilities made it impractical for many others to work without incurring day-care expenses that would cancel out a large part of their earnings; and that many others simply could not find jobs.[68] But these facts could not be overlooked forever.

The In–Kind Approach

In the face of congressional hostility toward further liberalization of AFDC, a hostility that was especially pronounced in the key legislative committees with jurisdiction over the program, a second strategy was pursued to deliver benefits to the poor: in-kind assistance. This approach, too, had its roots in the 1930s, when the federal government inaugurated two major programs of in-kind assistance: commodity distribution and public housing. Under the first, the Department of Agriculture was authorized to distribute to the needy a portion of whatever surplus commodities it purchased in its efforts to stabilize agricultural prices. Under the latter, the federal government made arrangements with local housing authorities to meet the payments on local bonds issued for the construction of housing for the needy. Both programs put the federal government in the position of providing aid to the needy, but in the form of particular commodities instead of cash. Two other in-kind programs were added in the 1950s—one providing limited medical-care benefits for public assistance recipients, and the other providing low-cost loans to college students to finance their education.

In the 1960s, however, in-kind assistance programs mushroomed. In rapid succession, programs were enacted offering food stamps, interest subsidies for the construction of low-income housing, preschool education programs, broad medical-care coverage for the needy, child nutrition programs, as well as the numerous social services mentioned earlier.*

This extraordinary burst of creativity reflected both a strong concern about those trapped in poverty, and some more mundane considerations as well. For one thing, reliance on in-kind assistance appealed to those who believe that the poor are ill-equipped to handle cash. Another factor was that in-kind assistance could generate political support among the relevant provider groups—the home builders, farmers, and others. When assistance is provided in the form of cash, after all, it can be used as the recipient chooses. When it is provided in the form of housing, or food, or medical care, it can be used for that item alone. Given a choice, therefore, provider groups will opt for aiding the poor through in-kind programs rather than through outright grants of cash. The experience of the National Association of Homebuilders (NAHB) is a case in point. Long an opponent of federal social welfare initiatives, the NAHB emerged in the 1960s as a major source of support for an elaborate series of housing subsidy measures enacted during the decade.[69] This pattern was evident in other areas as well.

Although this mode of assistance has naturally led to some leakage of benefits from the poor to the providers, in the end the total volume of resources reaching the poor probably exceeds what would have been made available in cash.

In addition to mobilizing provider groups, in-kind programs also made it easier to generate broad public support by dramatizing the need for assistance. The classic example here is the food stamp program, which had been in existence as a relief measure in the 1930s, and was revived on an experimental basis by

---

*The definition of in-kind assistance varies. Some scholars and administrators include only readily purchasable items, such as food and medical care, and exclude job training, manpower programs, and other less readily available services.

President Kennedy in 1961 as a replacement for the cumbersome commodity distribution program. As concern about poverty in America mounted in the 1960s, the food stamp program became a rallying point for congressional liberals eager to increase federal aid to the poor, for it focused attention squarely on the issue of hungry children. When congressional investigators discovered widespread starvation in the South in 1967, pressures for expansion of the food stamp program became well-nigh irresistible, even though conservatives on the Agriculture Committee tried for a time to resist them. By redefining the issue of aid to the poor as food for hungry children, supporters of food stamps were able to secure votes that may not have been forthcoming for a direct cash relief program. Indeed, as we shall see later, the food stamp program underwent a major expansion in the very year that the Nixon administration's cash assistance reform proposal was headed for defeat.

The in-kind mode of assistance also increased the avenues through which to pursue antipoverty initiatives in Congress. It thus provided a way to pass the generally conservative leadership of the Ways and Means and Finance Committees, which handle cash assistance programs. The committees on Education and Labor, Banking, Commerce, and eventually even Agriculture provided a more hospitable climate for social welfare initiatives than did the tax-writing committees that had jurisdiction over the basic Social Security Act provisions.

Like the payroll taxes that Roosevelt insisted on putting into the social security program, therefore, the numerous in-kind programs adopted in the 1960s, whatever their technical merit, reflected the political circumstances of the time. These circumstances dictated an indirect strategy, in the face of strong hostility toward public assistance in Congress and among the nation. Not surprisingly, the resulting array of programs resembled a patchwork quilt that only partially covered the longstanding shortcomings in the income assistance system inherited from the New Deal.

FAMILY ASSISTANCE PLAN:
THE DIFFICULTIES OF SIMPLIFICATION

Despite a rich harvest of innovative social welfare initiatives, it was apparent by the end of the decade that the programs of the 1960s had only begun to make an impact on the related problems of poverty and welfare dependency. In many cases, new programs were launched and then starved for funds, as budgetary retrenchment and the rising costs of the Vietnam War cut into the promise of the Great Society. In other cases, new departures were ill-conceived in their origins and not suited to the problems they sought to solve. Most disturbing of all, the public assistance rolls continued to rise, at an accelerating rate as the decade wore on. Through it all, the longstanding gaps, inconsistencies, and inequities of prevailing relief practices persisted.

It remained for newly installed President Richard Nixon to offer what to many people was the obvious solution. In a special message to the nation on the

TABLE 3.1

Yearly Benefits and Total Income for a Family of Four under FAP

Family Earnings	Amount of Earnings Disregarded[a]	FAP Payments[b]	Total Family Income[c]
$ 0	$ 0	$1,600	$1,600
500	500	1,600	2,100
1,000	860	1,460	2,460
1,500	1,110	1,210	2,710
2,000	1,360	960	2,960
2,500	1,610	710	3,210
3,000	1,860	460	3,460
3,500	2,110	210	3,710
4,000	2,360	0	4,000

[a]In computing the federal cash payment, a family would be allowed to disregard $60 per month ($720 per year) as work-related expenses, plus one-half of additional earnings up to $3,920.

[b]Federal cash benefits payable to a family would be computed by subtracting the family's earnings, minus the amount disregarded, from the basic FAP benefit of $1,600 for a family of four.

[c]Total family income would be the amount of family earnings plus the federal cash (FAP) payment.

Source: M. Kenneth Bowler, *The Nixon Guaranteed Income Proposal: Substance and Process in Policy Change* (Cambridge, Mass.: Ballinger, 1974), p. 31.

night of August 8, 1969, Nixon proposed to replace the AFDC program with a guaranteed minimum cash income, to be provided to every family with children that needed it. The plan was forged out of a three-way tug-of-war among a few hold-over Democratic economists and social policy advisors in HEW and the White House, a group of liberal Republicans holding key positions in the new administration, and a contingent of conservative economists and administrators operating chiefly out of the offices of the Council of Economic Advisors and the Treasury Department.[70] Called the Family Assistance Plan, it was an unusual mixture of conservative economic reasoning, liberal social planning, pragmatic political strategy, sophisticated technical analysis, and sheer guesswork. Under this proposal, every family with children—whether headed by a female or by an employed male—would be eligible for a family assistance grant of $500 for each of the first two family members, and $300 for each additional family member. Thus a family of four would be entitled to $1,600. These benefits would decline as family earnings increased. But to preserve a work incentive, the benefit reduction would not be dollar for dollar. Rather, the benefit was to decline by 50 cents for each dollar of earnings above $60 a month ($720 a year). Thus, for a family of four making anywhere from nothing to $720 a year, the full $1,600 would be paid. When the same family reached earnings of $3,920, however, the benefit would disappear altogether.* For families with earnings in between, the benefit would be scaled accordingly, as noted in Table 3.1.

Because the level of income provided through FAP would be considerably below that already provided to AFDC recipients in 42 out of the 50 states, the proposal also included a requirement that states supplement the basic benefit so that AFDC recipients would not suffer any decline in income, But as a boon to the states, it included a provision guaranteeing that under the new system no state would have to pay more than 90 percent of what it had spent on public assistance in 1970, thus ensuring a minimum 10 percent cost reduction to every state. In addition, the proposal sought to forestall conservative hostility by including a requirement that recipients register for work or training and accept it when offered, as well as provisions for expanded training and day-care facilities to help make this possible. Although the penalites for violation of this work requirements were to be relatively mild—the primary breadwinner only, and not the entire family, would be required to forfeit his or her benefits—the requirement allowed Nixon to portray the proposal as something other than a guaranteed income, which many conservatives vigorously opposed. Finally, as a complement to the proposed revision of AFDC, the Nixon proposal would have established a basic national minimum standard for state payments under the adult assistance categories (the aged, blind, and disabled), though in this case the payment would continue to be a joint federal-state responsibility.

The proposal that Nixon sent to Congress in October 1969 thus bore a striking resemblance to the "assured income" that Roosevelt's Committee on Economic Security had identified in 1935 as "the one almost all-embracing measure of security" that federal policy was to strive for. What quickly became apparent was that 35 years had not eliminated the opposition to so bold a change. Though the Nixon proposal managed to win the support of leaders on the Ways and Means Committee in the House, who saw it as a possible way out of the seemingly endless AFDC spiral, it ran into solid opposition in the Senate Finance Committee. After clearing the House by a surprisingly comfortable margin of 243 to 155 in April 1970, FAP was sent reeling backward by the conservative bloc on the Senate committee two weeks later. In a dramatic hearing, Senators Williams (R., Del.) and Long (D., La.) strongly attacked the proposal on grounds that, far from encouraging work, it contained severe work disincentives. This was so, they pointed out vividly, because FAP retained the automatic link between participation in the newer in-kind assistance programs, like food stamps and Medicaid, and eligibility for cash assistance, As a consequence, the dollar of earnings that placed one beyond the eligibility cutoff for FAP cost

---

*This is so because at $3,920 in earnings, the benefit is reduced as follows: $3,920 – $720 = $3,200 ÷ 2 = $1,600, which is the total amount of the benefit to begin with.

more than a dollar loss in cash assistance: it means the loss of benefits under these other programs as well. Thus, according to the HEW-prepared charts that Senator Williams unveiled on the second day of Senate Finance hearings on FAP, a welfare mother with three children in Chicago could actually lose $19 in income under FAP by raising her earnings from $720 to $5,560, because in the process she would lose entitlement to food stamps and Medicaid and be liable for income and payroll taxes.[71] The leadership of the Senate Finance Committee could not abide such an arrangement, and FAP was returned to the administration for revision.

One month later, the proposal was back with all these earnings "notches" eliminated. This was done not by altering the FAP proposal itself, but by deleting or reducing benefits under the other programs that would interact with it. The ultimate result, however, was to alienate Senate liberals already skeptical about the low-benefit level offered in the plan without adding measurably to conservative support. In a critical vote in November 1970, the Senate Finance Committee rejected the proposal, and the full Senate confirmed this decision early the next month by a vote of 49 to 21.

Thanks to continued presidential support, FAP resurfaced when the 92d Congress convened in 1971. Once again, Chairman Mills and ranking-minority-member Byrnes of the House Ways and Means Committee gave it their support, but this time not without a painstaking reworking of the measure in an effort to tailor it more sensitively to the tastes of the committee and the House. What emerged after five months of executive sessions was a bill strikingly similar in concept to the original Nixon idea, but with some important changes. Labeled H.R. 1, the Ways and Means Committee bill would have raised the basic benefit level for a family of four with no income from $1,600 to $2,400, but only after eliminating (cashing out) the food stamp program, which was estimated to be worth about $800 in benefits to a family of four. At the same time, H.R. 1 proposed to raise the marginal tax rate (the rate at which a recipient's benefits would decline as his earnings rose) from 50 percent to 67 percent.* At the insistence of Republican Byrnes, H.R. 1 would have eliminated the federal requirement that states supplement the basic FAP benefit if their existing AFDC benefit level exceeded what FAP would have provided, as it would have in most states. H.R. 1 also elaborated on the work requirement features of FAP by providing authorization for public service jobs, rehabilitation and training assistance, and separate payment mechanisms for employables and unemployables. In the process, it dropped a crucial protective feature for recipients by eliminating the

---

*Since the food stamp program had a benefit-reduction rate of about 15 percent, this change did not really constitute a significant alteration for those recipients participating in food stamps. Under the original FAP, they would have found their benefits declining by 65 percent—50 percent from FAP and 15 percent from food stamps—for each dollar earned. However, this point was generally lost in the debate over the measures.

stipulation that they could refuse all but "suitable" employment. Finally, H.R. 1 proposed to extend to the adult assistance categories the same concept of a basic federal payment that it proposed to apply to families with children, and to do so at a more generous level.

All in all, therefore, H.R. 1 was a touch more conservative than the original Nixon proposal, eliminating in particular the statutory protection of existing welfare benefit levels in the high-benefit states and tightening the work features. Yet it was still basically a guaranteed income proposal that would have extended welfare coverage for the first time to millions of the working poor. With Mills, Byrnes, and Nixon behind it, this proposal cleared the House again by a vote of 288 to 132 in late June 1971.

In the Senate, however, the spirit of compromise that Mills and Byrnes were able to generate in the House was missing. Encouraged by outspoken AFDC recipients, liberals criticized the low level of benefits and absence of guaranteed state supplements in H.R. 1, and finally rallied behind Senator Ribicoff to introduce a more generous bill in October 1971. Finance Committee Chairman Long responded with his own plan, the Long "workfare" proposal, which would have replaced AFDC cash benefits with the offer of a job paying welfare mothers $1.20 an hour, and provided limited wage supplements for those in low-wage private jobs as well. When these options came up for a vote in the Senate Finance Committee in late April, the conservative majority on the committee held sway, endorsing Long's workfare plan and rejecting both H.R. 1 and the Ribicoff plan. When the measure finally came before the full Senate in September 1972, in the midst of a presidential campaign in which "guaranteed income" had become a bad term, neither H.R. 1, nor the Ribicoff bill, nor the Long proposal could muster the needed support, and Nixon's initiative was unceremoniously put to rest.

Why is it that so promising an effort should have come to such an end? How could a basically liberal proposal that surprisingly gained the support of a Republican president and a conservative House of Representatives utlimately fail after a bruising and frustrating struggle? Perhaps no question preoccupies social welfare activists more, for the history of FAP teaches much about the value judgments and the political dynamics that bear on welfare reform.

So widespread has been the effort to understand the defeat of FAP, however, that there is a danger of overexplaining it. The FAP episode seems well on its way to becoming the exception that proves John F. Kennedy's rule that "success has many fathers, but failure is an orphan." In the case of FAP, it is defeat for which paternity is hotly contested, and the list of possible reasons is quite long. Under the circumstances, it may be most useful to step back a bit and review what happened, with the benefit of information and perspective yielded by the passage of time. When this is done, three major points emerge.

First, FAP came very close to passing, despite the many explanations of why it failed. The proposal cleared the House on two occasions by substantial margins and might have passed the Senate had eight votes switched in the final tally, 51–35, on October 4, 1972. Although a filibuster might still have killed the plan, there is reason to doubt whether those eight votes were really as immovable as much of the postmortem seems to suggest.

One such reason is evident in the voting patterns on the bill, which constitute the second major point worth making about FAP. Although many analysts attribute the defeat of FAP to liberal defections, an analysis of the votes suggests a different picture. In both the House and Senate, liberal support for the proposal was overwhelming, with over 75 percent of all liberals in both the House and Senate supporting FAP or some version of it, while equal or larger proportions of conservatives opposed it. Paradoxically, the supporters of FAP in both chambers were legislators from the states and localities that would have benefited least from it—the northern and western industrial areas where AFDC benefit levels already exceeded the FAP levels and where private wage rates kept far larger proportions of the labor force out of working-poor status. What spelled the defeat of FAP in the Senate was not the loss of liberal or conservative support, but the loss of the moderates' support that had been present in the House. In the key vote on H.R. 1 in the House, over 70 percent of the moderates gave it their support, providing the critical margin for victory. On the comparable vote in the Senate, less than 40 percent of the moderates ended up on FAP's side.[72]

Why, then, did Senate moderates behave differently on FAP from their House counterparts? And why did legislators from the states with the most to gain from FAP—such as the Southern states— vote most consistently against it? Based on the evidence of House and Senate voting patterns, these two questions hold the key to explaining the defeat of FAP.

As to the first question, the answer probably has to do with so subtle a factor as the absence of leadership to give clear and unmistakable voting cues and to mobilize support. By their very nature, moderates were most likely to take a nonideological approach to FAP, and therefore to be amenable to persuasion, especially—since this was a liberal measure—persuasion from those to the right of them. In the House, such persuasion was provided by Mills, Byrnes, and Nixon. In the Senate, however, Mills's and Byrnes's counterparts—Long and Bennett—were foes of the plan. At the same time, Majority Leader Mansfield, an influential moderate, did not take a stand. Finally, and perhaps most decisively, by the time the measure came up for a vote in the Senate in late 1972, Nixon himself had all but disavowed it, so that there was none of the extra encouragement that was needed to push moderates over the line into support.

So far as the lack of Southern support for FAP is concerned, the issues are more complicated. Once central factor, though, was the limited political potency and lack of leadership on the part of the groups most likely to benefit from FAP—poor southern blacks and whites. The absence of effective southern black support for FAP was both striking and consequential, for it not only left southern legislators much freer to oppose the measure but also weakened the northern liberals in attempts to counter the anti-FAP sentiment mobilized by the northern-based National Welfare Rights Organization.

The third key point about the FAP experience is the way that the public assistance improvements of the 1960s, far from facilitating the adoption of a more comprehensive approach, contributed directly to its defeat. Ironically, had FAP been advanced prior to the expansion of welfare benefits during the 1960s, it might have stood a better chance of passing. But once those benefits were in place, a dilemma arose for policy planners. Because of what we have termed the "work incentive trap," benefits under FAP could not be set as high as those available under existing programs in most states without raising costs well beyond politically tolerable limits, unless the work incentive features were eliminated. But this would have alienated conservatives who insisted that the welfare system did not encourage work. To retain a meaningful financial work incentive, therefore, it was necessary to set the basic benefit level well below what some recipients were already receiving. Under the circumstances, prior benefit levels could be sustained only by requiring the states to supplement the basic federal guarantee. But this threatened another important source of political support, since state government endorsement of welfare reform was heavily conditioned on the capacity of the reform to yield fiscal relief to the states.

This dilemma has, if anything, grown more severe with time. Although numerous states have cut back somewhat on AFDC benefits, the defeat of FAP coincided with a substantial expansion of the food stamp program, thanks to legislation passed in December 1970. As a consequence, fitting a comprehensive income maintenance scheme to the contours of the existing distribution of benefits without leaving anyone worse off has become all the more difficult, yet no less important politically.

Despite its utlimate defeat, the struggle over FAP broke an important mental block in discussions of welfare reform, lifting the concept of a guaranteed income out of the abstract texts of academic economics and making it a subject of practical politics. More than that, the battle did leave behind two living embodiments of the idea. One was the SSI program, the only part of the FAP proposal that passed, establishing a uniform federal income guarantee at least for the needy aged, blind, and disabled. The second was the food stamp program, which after 1970 provided a kind of guaranteed income in the form of food vouchers to anyone in need, complete with a liberal marginal tax rate that reduced benefits by only 30 cents for each dollar increase in earnings. While this is far less than most negative income tax enthusiasts had hoped for, it is probably far more than they originally expected when the election results of November 1968 first became clear.

A FORTY YEAR JOURNEY AROUND A CIRCLE

What emerges most clearly from this discussion of the evolution of American public assistance policy is the durability of the central concepts and concerns that have guided it since its inception, and the lengths to which policymakers have been willing (or forced) to go in order to avoid infringing on these

these concepts and concerns in the process of aiding the needy. To be sure, the principle of localism has fallen victim to the reality of fiscal weakness at the local level. But the twin notions of categorizing the poor according to their employability and then designing relief arrangements that assume the capability of the private labor market to provide a sufficient income to those considered employable remain as potent today as in the early days of the nation.

The problem is that the pursuit of these central principles has left policy-makers with little maneuvering room. The evolution of American relief policy since the Great Depression resembles a journey around a circle, starting in the thirties with a reluctance to acknowledge the limitations of the private labor market—in efforts to relieve the distress of many fully employed persons, let alone that of those trapped in seasonal labor or unemployed—and ending up 40 years later face to face with this same problem. By holding firm to the tradition of denying public assistance on a long-term basis to employables, policymakers in the thirties made it difficult to deal with some of the most severe economic dislocations of the postwar era that contributed to the patterns of dependence that plague the country today. When poverty was rediscovered in the 1960s, a public assistance system whose design left out a sizable segment of the poor was the only channel readily available to deal with the problem. Consequently, the compassionate response of the 1960s intensified the basic inequities of the system, creating a situation in which the benefits available to welfare recipients began to exceed by a substantial margin those avilable to many of the working poor. Then, to complete the circle, it became apparent that the old division be-tween employables and unemployables was breaking down as both the compo-sition of the unemployable group and popular notions about its degree of unemployability began to change. True to tradition, policymakers responded to this situation in the 1960s by grafting a set of financial work incentives onto the public assistance programs, hoping thereby to induce more welfare recipients, particularly AFDC mothers, to work. In the process, the inequities between wel-fare recipients and the working poor were intensified, since the recipients then had available not only the income from work but also a portion of the income from welfare as well, whereas the nonrecipient on the same job had only the in-come from work available. As a result, a measure designed to encourage work was ending up, thanks to the peculiar structure of the relief system as a whole, encouraging greater efforts to get on relief instead. The defeat of FAP, in fact, was a symbol of the resulting trap, for here the beneficiaries of assistance, espe-cially northern AFDC mothers, mobilized successfully to resist the claims advanced on behalf of those long excluded from aid because of their presumed employability.

The central question for the future is whether these dilemmas can be avoided within the constraints of the assumptions guiding relief policy, or whether wholly new assumptions will be needed. In the next chapter we treat this question in detail through an examination of the major reform options now under consideration.

NOTES

1. Arthur Schlesinger, Jr., *The Coming of the New Deal*, Vol. II of *The Age of Roosevelt* (New York: Houghton Mifflin Co., 1958), p. 315.

2. *Report of the Committee on Economic Security* (Washington, D.C.: U.S. Government Printing Office, 1935), p. 3.

3 Raymond A. Mohl, "Three Centuries of American Public Welfare, 1600-1932," *Current History* 65 (July 1976): 6.

4. Josephine Brown, *Public Relief, 1929-1959* (New York: Octagon, 1960), pp. 4-5; Mohl, "Three Centuries," p. 7.

5. Edmund S. Morgan, *American Slavery/American Freedom: The Ordeal of Colonial Virginia* (New York: W. W. Norton and Co., 1975), p. 320.

6. Quoted in Karl de Schweinitz, *England's Road to Social Security* (Philadelphia: University of Pennsylvania Press, 1943), p. 59.

7. Quoted in Joe R. Feagin, *Subordinating the Poor* (Englewood Cliffs, N.J.: Prentice-Hall, 1975), p. 16.

8. de Schweinitz, *England's Road*, pp. 1, 8.

9. Quoted in Neil Betten, "American Attitudes Toward the Poor: A Historical Overview," *Current History* 65, no. 383 (July 1973): 2.

10. Feagin, *Subordinating*, p. 26.

11. Quoted in David Rothman and Sheila M. Rothman, *On Their Own: The Poor in Modern America* (Reading, Mass.: Addison-Wesley Publishing Co., 1972), p. vi.

12. de Schweinitz, *England's Road*, p. 6.

13. Feagin, *Subordinating*, p. 54.

14. Mohl, "Three Centuries," pp. 8-9.

15. Quoted in de Schweinitz, *England's Road*, p. 6.

16. Morgan, *American Slavery/American Freedom*, p. 323.

17. Blanche D. Coll, *Perspectives on Public Welfare: A History* (Washington, D.C.: Government Printing Office, n.d.), pp. 19-20.

18. Brown, *Public Relief*, pp. 5-7.

19. Ibid., pp. 20-23.

20. Quoted in Frances Fox Piven and Richard Cloward, *Regulating the Poor: The Functions of Public Welfare* (New York: Vintage Books, 1971), p. 47.

21. Ibid., p. 47.

22. *Report of the Committee on Economic Security*, 1935, p. 26.

23. Message to Congress, December 1, 1931, quoted in Brown, *Public Relief*, p. 99.

24. Ibid., p. 100.

25. Quoted by Harry Hopkins, *Spending to Save: The Complete Story of Relief* (New York: W. W. Norton and Co., 1936), pp. 62-63.

26. Piven and Cloward, *Regulating the Poor*, p. 74.

27. Quoted in Brown, *Public Relief*, p. 154.

28. Piven and Cloward, *Regulating the Poor*, p. 74.

29. From January 4, 1935 message to Congress, quoted in Piven and Cloward, *Regulating the Poor*, p. 94.

30. Quoted in Brown, *Public Relief*, pp. 161-66.

31. Quoted in Piven and Cloward, *Regulating the Poor*, p. 97.

32. *Report of the Committee on Economic Security*, p. 9.

33. Ibid., p. 14.

34. Ibid., pp. 8-9.

35. Brown, *Public Relief*, p. 164.

36. *Report of the Committee on Economic Security*, p. 10.

37. Quoted in Schlesinger, *Coming of the New Deal*, p. 309.

38. *Report of the Committee on Economic Security*, p. 7.

39. Quoted in Brown, *Public Relief*, pp. 304–05.

40. Ibid., pp. 309–10.

41. Edwin Witte, *Development of the Social Security Act* (Madison: University of Wisconsin Press, 1962), p. 77.

42. Feagin, *Subordinating*, p. 44; Charles H. Trout, "Welfare in the New Deal Era," *Current History* 65 (July 1973): 38–39.

43. Among these changes were an increase in the minimum size of the firm covered by unemployment insurance from four to eight persons, exclusion of state government officials from unemployment insurance, and further intensification of the limitation on coverage of farm workers and domestics on both unemployment insurance and OAA. See Witte, *Development* pp. 111–42, 146–61.

44. Witte, *Development*, p. 144.

45. Witte, *Development*, pp. 144–45; Brown, *Public Relief*, pp. 307–09.

46. Michael Harrington, *The Other America: Poverty in the United States* (New York: Macmillan, 1962).

47. *Report of the Committee on Economic Security*, pp. 1, 8–9.

48. Steiner, *Social Insecurity*, pp. 18–47.

49. *Congressional Record*, July 18, 1951, p. 3847, quoted in Steiner, *Social Insecurity*, p. 22.

50. Steiner, *Social Insecurity*, p. 22.

51. *Social Security Bulletin* 39, no. 7 (July 1976): 74.

52. Labor force statistics are from ibid., p. 82; coverage statistics are from Congressional Quarterly, *Congress and the Nation, 1945–64* (Washington, D.C.: 1965), p. 1290.

53. *Social Security Bulletin* 39, no. 7 (July 1976): 74.

54. Daniel Patrick Moynihan, "The Crises of Welfare," *The Public Interest* 10 (Winter 1968): 13.

55. "Results of the 1961 AFDC Study," cited in Gilbert Steiner, *The State of Welfare* (Washington, D.C.: The Brookings Institution, 1971), p. 42.

56. *Social Security Bulletin* 39, no. 7 (July 1976): 74.

57. 1967 AFDC study, cited in Steiner, *The State of Welfare*, p. 42.

58. Steiner, *State of Welfare*, p. 41.

59. As of 1961, 72 percent of the white children receiving AFDC lived in rural non-farm areas, whereas 75 percent of the Negro children lived in central cities. Moynihan, "The Crises of Welfare," p. 13.

60. Congressional Quarterly, *Congress and the Nation*, p. 1275; Steiner, *Social Insecurity*, pp. 50–59.

61. Steiner, *State of Welfare*, p. 42; U.S. Department of Health, Education, and Welfare, *Findings of the 1973 AFDC Study* (Washington, D.C.: Social and Rehabilitation Services, 1974), Part 1, p. 38; *Social Security Bulletin*, Vol. 41, no. 4 (April 1978), pp. 65–66.

62. Statement of July 26, 1962, *Congressional Quarterly Almanac* 18 (1962): 218.

63. Quoted in Steiner, *Social Insecurity*, p. 146.

64. See, for example, the discussion of the role of the Wickenden report in the formulation of the 1962 amendments in Steiner, *Social Insecurity*, pp. 143–47.

65. Ibid., pp. 47, 173.

66. Piven and Cloward, *Regulating the Poor*, p. 171.

67. Steiner, *State of Welfare*, p. 42.

68. Levitan, *Promise of Greatness*, pp. 53–54.

69. For a more detailed discussion, see Lester M. Salamon, *The Money Committees: A Study of the House Banking and Currency Committee and the Senate Banking, Housing and Urban Affairs Committee* (New York: Grossman Publishers, 1976).

70. For excellent accounts of the dynamics of formulation of the FAP proposal within the administration, see especially M. Kenneth Bowler, "The Nixon Guaranteed Income Proposal: Substance and Process," in *Policy Change* (Cambridge, Mass.: Ballinger Publishing Co., 1974), pp. 36–39; Vincent and Vee Burke, *Nixon's Good Deed: Welfare Reform* (New York: Columbia University Press, 1974), pp. 40–107; and Daniel Patrick Moynihan, *The Politics of a Guaranteed Annual Income: The Nixon Administration and the Family Assistance Plan* (New York: Vintage Books, 1973).

71. Burke and Burke, *Nixon's Good Deed*, pp. 153–55.

72. Bowler, "The Nixon Guaranteed Income Proposal," pp. 144–47, 188.

4

WHERE SHOULD WE GO?
UNRAVELING THE INCOME
ASSISTANCE POLICY PUZZLE

> "There's no use trying," said [Alice]: "One can't believe impossible things."

> "I dare say you haven't had much practice," said the Queen. "When I was your age, I always did it for half an hour a day. Why, sometimes I believed as many as six impossible things before breakfast."
>
> Lewis Carroll, *Through the Looking Glass*

According to medieval philosophy, all human problems would be solved once scientists discovered a special substance known as the "philosopher's stone," which could extend human life indefinitely and transmute base metals into gold. Much of the intellectual energy of the medieval period was consumed in a frantic search for this mysterious substance, a search which, though ultimately futile, nevertheless gave birth to modern science.

Welfare reform is modern America's equivalent of the philosopher's stone. For many, it is the solution that will alleviate at once the suffering of the poor, the fiscal pressures on states and localities, the confusion of the income tax system, the failings of the labor market, and the weakening of basic social institutions like the family—achieving savings for the federal treasury in the process. In search of the right reform plan, therefore, a host of latter-day alchemists have set to work, earnestly pressing reluctant computers to yield the solution that will transmute base welfare programs into golden income assistance proposals, and bring help to the poor and relief to the coffers of state and local governments in the process.

Alas, the search for the perfect welfare reform has so far been no more successful than the search for the philosopher's stone, and for the same reason: there is none. As Henry Aaron of the Brookings Institution put it recently:

> The reason Congress has found it difficult to find a plan that provides universal benefits at a level regarded as reasonable, that preserves work incentives, and that is not vastly more expensive than President Nixon's proposal is that no such plan exists or can be devised: these objectives are mutually exclusive.[1]

Proposals designed to improve benefit adequacy run the risk of undermining work incentives and exhausting available resources. Efforts to preserve work incentives produce inequities between working recipients and working nonrecipients. Restricting aid to narrow categories of people minimizes these inequities, but only at the price of encouraging dysfunctional changes in living arrangements. What becomes apparent is that public assistance policy is really a tangle of trade-offs, a complex puzzle that will yield, if at all, only to careful, systematic thought.

While it has hardly generated the ultimate proposal, however, the search for welfare reform has at least yielded some analytical insights that provide the foundation for decisions. It is the purpose of this chapter to build on this foundation by examining the major welfare reform options available, and the critical choices that underlie them. In the process, this chapter seeks to provide a framework for organizing this complex field, identifying the major issues, and analyzing the trade-offs involved in each.

To do so, the discussion falls into four basic sections. The first explores the nature of the problems that income assistance policy is supposed to address, and the criteria against which this policy should be measured. The second identifies and analyzes the major design choices inevitably involved in the framing of income assistance proposals. The third then examines in some detail three major approaches to reform, each of which has a number of variants, and each of which represents a particular grouping of the design features identified in the second section. The fourth section provides a summary evaluation of these alternative approaches.

IS WELFARE OR POVERTY THE PROBLEM?

At the heart of the current debate over welfare reform is a basic disagreement over what the problem is. For some, the object of the exercise is the reduction of poverty. But for others, it is the reduction of welfare.

This disagreement arises out of the basic tension that exists among the values that undergird the assistance system. As we have seen, welfare is fundamentally an effort to care for the needy, whether out of considerations of charity or prudence. The problem is that care for the needy is constantly in danger of intruding on other cherished social values. Any assistance proposal must therefore be evaluated simultaneously in terms of a number of different criteria, each of which has its own adherents and rationale. For purposes of analysis, these criteria can be grouped conveniently under three basic headings:

1. Adequacy: the extent to which the system provides a level of benefits sufficient to relieve the suffering of those in need, and does so without undue damage to personal pride and self-respect.

2. Equity: the extent to which the assistance system avoids treating some people better than others. Of particular concern here is that those who do not work not be treated better than those who do, which could undermine the incentive to work. We will refer to this criterion as work equity. Other aspects of equity are also important, however, such as equal treatment among those equally in need, so as to avoid creating financial incentives for people to alter their behavior in dysfunctional ways in order to qualify for more aid (for example, by splitting up families or moving). We will refer to this as support equity.

3. Efficiency: the targeting of aid for those most in need (target efficiency), and the use of assistance modes that minimize administrative costs and maximize the chances for careful cost control (administrative efficiency).

As noted in Chapter 3, the existing system has been faulted on each of these criteria. But no system can do equally well on all three. This is so because there are conflicts not only among these goals, but also within them. For example, a system that strives to target benefits efficiently for those in need, and to gear the level and type of benefits to the exact nature of the need, will necessarily be more cumbersome administratively. In other words, greater target efficiency may require sacrificing administrative efficiency. The critical question, therefore, is not whether a new system can give us more of all of these values, but whether the particular mix of adequacy, equity, and efficiency embodied in the existing system can be improved upon. To answer this question, it is necessary to begin by looking at the extent and character of the underlying problem that public assistance is supposed to solve.

The first point to note about the poverty population in the United States is that it is quite large. As of fiscal year 1976, for example, 20.2 million American families, more than one out of every four, had incomes below the official poverty line prior to the receipt of government transfers.[2] Moreover, if a relative, instead of an absolute, definition of poverty were used (for example, earnings of less than 50 percent of the median income), this figure would be even higher.

In addition to its size, the most salient characteristic of the American poverty population is its diversity. Indeed, as one student of the subject has noted, "It is the mixed demographic character of the poorest twenty per cent [of the population] that makes the welfare problem so complex."[3] Segments of the poor differ from each other in terms of age, sex, geographical location, family status, physical condition, race, and a host of other dimensions. Perhaps most important, they differ from each other in terms of their relationship to the world of work, which is the expected route out of poverty for most Americans. In particular, three groups of the poor can be distinguished in these terms—one which is poor because it cannot work; the second, which is poor because it will not work; and the third, which is poor even though it wants to, and frequently does, work. The first group can be divided further into two subgroups, one composed of persons who cannot work because of essentially physical reasons (blindness, disability, old age); and the other composed of persons who cannot work because of essentially social reasons (for example, the need to care for children or other dependents). Four major sources of poverty can thus be identified: first, old age, blindness, or disability; second, the absence of a breadwinner free of home-care responsibilities; third, low wages, unemployment, or seasonal work; and fourth, laziness. How important are each of these sources?

Old Age, Blindness, Disability

The aged, blind and disabled—those prevented from working for essentially physical reasons—are perhaps the biggest category of the poor. Of the 20.2 million American families that had incomes below the poverty line before government transfers in fiscal year 1976, for example, 9.3 million, or 41 percent, were headed by persons aged 65 or over. This figure is likely to grow over time, moreover. According to one recent projection, the number of families headed by persons 65 or over is expected to increase from 16 million in 1976 to almost 21 million in the year 2000.[4] If the same proportion of these are poor as at present, this means approximately 12.2 million poor families. To this must be added some 4.5 million families with disabled heads.[5]

Assuming a continuing growth of social security, most of these pretransfer aged and disabled poor families can be expected to be lifted out of poverty by social insurance payments. However, depending on the rate of social security benefit growth, anywhere from 1.6 to 5.2 million aged and disabled families will need supplementary aid as well.[6]

Single-Parent Families

If the aged and the disabled are the most important segment of the poor in terms of numbers, female-headed households are the most important in terms of public attention and concern. Between 1965 and 1974, female-headed households with children increased ten times as fast as two-parent families in the United States. By 1974, in fact, one out of seven children in the United States lived with a family where the father was absent.[7]

What makes this dramatic social revolution a matter of public concern is that one-half of all female-headed households are poor. Most poor families with children are now headed by women.[8] Despite the existence of a special cash assistance program targeted for this segment of the population (AFDC), some 10 million persons in female-headed families remained poor after cash transfers in 1974, according to Census Bureau figures.[9]

From all indications, there is little reason to anticipate a decline in the rate of female family headship in the foreseeable future. According to one estimate, the population eligible for AFDC is likely to grow from 3.8 million families in 1975 to from 4.1 to 4.9 million families by the year 2000.[10] This does not represent an unchanging pool of individuals, of course. Female-headed families are, as one study puts it, "transitional units," "interim entities of relatively short duration."[11] Public assistance therefore functions typically as a mechanism to keep such units solvent—or at least partially so—during a period of disruption and readjustment. The number of units experiencing such disruption and readjustment has been increasing rapidly, however, and promises not to decline.

The Employed or Employable Poor

The third, and perhaps most troubling, segment of the poor are those in families headed by persons who are in the labor force—or would like to be—but are earning too little to escape poverty. Included here are several different categories of people. First are the unemployed, who, in 1975, numbered 7.8 million people, or 8.5 percent of the labor force.[12] Second are those forced to work only part time because of slack work, job changes, material shortages, and the like. In 1975, close to four million additional workers fell into this category, and many of them doubtless ended up with incomes below the poverty line as a consequence.[13] Beyond these two groups are those who work full time at wages that yield an income below the poverty line. Although data on this group are difficult to get, the Department of Labor estimates that some eight million workers receive the minimum wage or less. Depending on their family size, a sizable proportion of these low-wage workers probably live below the poverty line as well. To this, finally, must be added a portion of the 1.1 million so-called discouraged workers, those who would like a job, but think it is impossible to find one, and have consequently dropped out of the labor force.[14]

Although some aid is available to some segments of these employable persons, it is far from adequate. For younger workers who are new entrants in the labor market, not even unemployment insurance is available. Yet unemployment is especially severe for this group. In mid-1975, nearly half of all unemployed workers were between 16 and 24 years old. This situation is especially severe among black youths. In 1975, almost two out of every five black teenagers in the labor force were unemployed; and slightly more than one out of every five blacks aged 20-24 in the labor force were in the same situation.[15]

Even many of those covered by unemployment insurance have had problems because their benefits have been exhausted by protracted unemployment. And for those in seasonal or low-wage work, assistance has been still more limited. In short, we have a sizable group of poor persons actively involved in the labor market. As of 1975, in fact, half of all the families recorded in poverty were headed by persons in the labor force, and 80 percent of these were employed![16]

Not only does the combination of employment-related factors produce poverty directly; it also does so indirectly, through its impact on family life. According to one recent study, for example, higher unemployment rates and lower wages for black males is "the single most important variable" explaining the higher rate of female family headship among blacks than whites.[17] Indeed, the best predictor of the rate of female family headship in an area, whether for whites or blacks, turns out to be the average wage level for males, not the welfare benefit level as is sometimes assumed.[18]

To be sure, these employment-related sources of poverty reflect the unusually harsh economic circumstances of the past several years. They are, therefore, at least partly cyclical in character and consequently likely to subside as economic recovery proceeds. Yet, there is reason to doubt the speed and extent of the improvement that can be anticipated. For one thing, the number of people seeking jobs has been increasing rapidly due to the dramatic influx of women and youth into the job market. Since many of the new women labor-force entrants have more skills and education than the unemployed or the working poor, they can command better jobs and salaries. In the second place, inflationary pressures continue to inhibit the economic stimulation required to push the unemployment rate down to even 5–6 percent. Finally, many of the employment problems of the poor are structural, not cyclical, in character. In other words, these problems reflect not just the impact of a cyclical downturn in the economy but the longer-term impact of such factors as the reduced demand for low-skilled labor, geographic imbalances in economic growth, and continued race and sex discrimination.[19] Not only are these latter factors likely to persist even in the face of economic recovery, but they promise to grow in importance as a consequence of continued technical change and job dispersal.

Work and Welfare

While old age, disability, ill health, family disruption, unemployment, underemployment, and low wages account for a substantial share of the pre-transfer poor, the expansion of the welfare system over the recent past has given rise to the widespread conviction that laziness, irresponsibility, and promiscuity account for another substantial share. Prior to the 1960s, prevailing concepts of deservingness guaranteed the denial of public assistance to all those who could work, except for the temporarily unemployed and the retired. In the 1950s and 1960s, however, two important sets of changes occurred. For one thing, a dramatic rise in female employment threw into question the notion that female heads of households with children were unemployable and therefore deserving of public assistance. In 1940, for example, only 9 percent of all mothers were in the work force. By 1975, 43 percent were, including 31 percent of those with children under three years old. Under the circumstances, the idea that AFDC mothers need not work was thrown open to challenge, all the more so as the proportion of these mothers who found themselves on AFDC because of illegitimacy or the absence of the father from the home, rather than because of the father's death or incapacitation, began to rise significantly. Similar questions arose as a consequence of the extension of public assistance to male-headed families following the adoption of the AFDC–unemployed parent program in

1962 and the extension of the food stamp program in 1970. Both of these initiatives breached the prohibition of employables on public assistance, built into the structure of previous programs. Coupled with the extension of the unemployment compensation benefit period to 52, and then 65, weeks, these changes made public assistance available to a considerable number of employable people, and thus helped to fuel popular complaints about welfare cheaters who choose to live off public assistance rather than work. According to one estimate, in fact, more than three million employable persons are on public assistance rolls of one sort or another, including close to one million AFDC recipients required to register for training and placement under the WIN program, another million receiving unemployment insurance benefits for more than 39 weeks, and another million on SSI, food stamps, or general assistance.[20]

TABLE 4.1

Employment Status of AFDC Mothers, 1973

Employment Status	Number	Percent
Employed, total	449,051	16
Full time	274,205	10
Part time	174,846	6
Actively seeking work	321,569	12
Needed in home	1,308,993	47
Incapacitated	225,715	8
Not actively seeking work (includes those in a work or training program)	487,316	17
Unknown	903	—
Total	2,793,547	100

Source: U.S. Department of Health, Education, and Welfare, *Findings of the 1973 AFDC Survey* (Washington, D.C.: U.S. Government Printing Office, 1974), p. 58.

While it is undoubtedly true that the improvement in public assistance benefit levels and the extension of coverage to segments of the working poor has brought numerous employable people onto the assistance rolls, it is a sizable leap to consider all of these people work shirkers as a consequence. For one thing, many of them are employed. In the AFDC program, for example, 28 percent of the mothers are either employed (16 percent) or actively seeking work (12 percent), as shown in Table 4.1. Of the remainder, 55 percent are needed in the home to care for young children or are incapacitated, leaving only 17 percent, or 487,000 mothers, not actively seeking work and not otherwise accounted for. At least 100,000 of these are already in work and training programs, and most of the remainder are registered for such programs and awaiting job training or work placement.

TABLE 4.2

Employment Status of AFDC Fathers, 1973

Employment Status	Number	Percent
Employed, total	44,241	11
Full time	20.089	5
Part time	24,152	6
Actively seeking work	104,491	28
Needed in home	5,794	2
Incapacitated	203,800	54
Not actively seeking work (includes those		
in a work or training program)	18,039	5
Unknown	2,683	–
Total	379,048	100

Source: U.S. Department of Health, Education, and Welfare, *Findings of the 1973 AFDC Survey* (Washington, D.C.: U.S. Government Printing Office, 1974), p. 74.

Although some AFDC mothers classified as caring for children could certainly work, this would require some form of day care. Only 14 percent of all AFDC families had no children under age 12 in 1973, and 60 percent of all the families had at least one child under age six. Even with day care, however, few AFDC mothers have the employment experience or educational background to command salaries sufficient to cover day-care expenses and still enable them to escape dependence on welfare. As of 1973, only 25 percent of all AFDC mothers had high school diplomas, and fewer than 5 percent had attended college.

So far as AFDC mothers are concerned, therefore, the search for true shirkers, persons who could work their way off welfare but voluntarily choose not to, is likely to prove disappointing. While many of these recipients are theoretically employable, putting them to work is likely to require expensive training and day care. Even then, the constraints imposed by the supply side of the labor market may still doom the effort, as the recent experience of the WIN program certainly suggests (see Appendix B in this volume).

A similar picture prevails with respect to the males on AFDC. In 1973, close to 400,000 AFDC families, 13 percent of the total, had a natural or adoptive father in the home. As shown in Table 4.2 above, however, 39 percent of these fathers were either employed or actively seeking work, and 54 percent were incapacitated. Of the remainder, only 5 percent—18,000 individuals—were not actively seeking work, and almost all of these were in training or work programs.[21]

Although the data on the other employable adults receiving public assistance are not as complete as those on AFDC recipients, what is available points in the same direction. In the food stamp program, for example, the heads

TABLE 4.3

Distribution of Unemployment Insurance Benefits by Income Class, 1970

Income Class	Percent of Benefits	Percent of all Families
$0–$4,999	17	28
$5,000–$9,999	31	25
$10,000–$14,999	24	18
$15,000–$24,999	20	18
$25,000 and Over	8	11

Source: Martin Feldstein, "Unemployment Compensation, Adverse Incentives and Distributional Anomalies," *National Tax Journal* 27, no. 2 (June 1974): 238.

of over 40 percent of the recipient families in 1975 were either employed or seeking work. Of the remaining 60 percent, a substantial proportion were either female-headed families on AFDC, and hence suffering from the work disabilities already discussed, or aged recipients of social security or SSI payments.[22] In unemployment insurance, the work disincentives that exist operate mainly for the better-off recipients, who alone achieve the employment histories and prior wage levels needed to secure substantial unemployment benefits. As noted in Table 4.3, only 17 percent of all unemployment insurance benefits go to families with incomes below $5,000. If there are work shirkers on unemployment compensation, therefore, they are not stereotyped welfare cheaters, but the stalwart middle class.

Taken together, these data throw serious doubt on the argument that a very significant part of the welfare problem can be attributed to loafers who prefer the dole to work and who have been coddled by an overly indulgent society. To be sure, a substantial share of the current recipients are theoretically employable. But child-care responsibilities, poor training, and inadequate jobs place serious barriers between theoretical employability and actual employment. Overcoming these barriers may turn out to be more costly than paying welfare. While it is always possible to cut welfare, such cuts ought not to be premised on the supposition that only freeloaders are being eliminated. The fact is that most of those on welfare are there because of old age, disability, ill health, family disruption, unemployment, underemployment, low wages, poor training, or some combination of these; and these conditions are likely to persist in the foreseeable future.

If the problem of poverty is likely to persist in its present size and form, and if the system designed to cope with this problem continues to have the shortcomings analyzed in Chapter 2, what can be done to improve things? Is it possible to construct an alternative system that copes with the problem more adequately, equitably, and efficiently than the system now in place, and that does so within the limits of reasonably available resources?

BASIC DESIGN ISSUES: SIX CHARACTERISTICS IN SEARCH OF A PROPOSAL

To answer these questions, it is best to begin with an analysis of the major design choices that lie at the heart of the public assistance policy puzzle. Welfare reform proposals represent different collections of responses to a fairly well-defined set of basic questions. If we can identify these basic questions and explore the possible answers to them, we will have the key to understanding the nature of the current welfare reform debate, and a framework for intelligent policy choice.

Six design issues seem most important in this respect, involving decisions about (1) coverage, (2) how to preserve work incentives, (3) benefit levels, (4) the mode of assistance, (5) administration, and (6) costs. Taken together, these issues define the basic decisions that must go into any welfare reform proposal.

Coverage

The first basic design issue has to do with coverage, the determination of which of the poor are truly deserving of public assistance. This issue involves two different parts: first, the coverage of the income assistance system as a whole, that is, whether some segments of the poor should be dropped from coverage and/or others added; and second, the coverage of particular programs making up that system, that is, whether to have different programs for different categories of the poor.

System Coverage. Historically, public assistance in the United States has not been available to everyone in need. Coverage has been restricted to certain groups of people whose poverty was a consequence of unemployability. What this has meant in practice is that only the first two segments of the poor mentioned previously—the aged, blind, and disabled; and female-headed families with dependent children—have been covered by the income assistance system. By contrast, most of those in the third category—the employed or employable poor— have been excluded from coverage.

This pattern of system coverage is one of the central issues in the current welfare reform debate, posing two questions: whether to cut back on aid to female-headed households; and whether to extend aid to the working poor.

The argument for cutting back on coverage for female-headed households grows out of a concern for the principle of work equity, the notion that those who do not work should not end up better than those who do. As such, it reflects the changing patterns of female labor-force participation cited earlier, and the dramatic rise of divorce, separation, and abandonment—as opposed to widowhood—as causes of female family headship and welfare dependence. The Senate Finance Committee stated this issue clearly in the report that accompanied its version of the FAP in 1972. "Can this nation," asked the committee, "treat mothers of school-age children on welfare as though they were unemployable and pay them to remain at home when more than half of mothers with school age children in the general population are already working?"[23] In the committee's opinion, the answer to this question was a decided no. Accordingly, the committee bill proposed to deny public assistance to all female-headed households except those with children under age six. Altogether, approximately 40 percent of the AFDC families would have been dropped from the program as a consequence. Although this proposal ultimately failed in the full Senate, Congress did strengthen the AFDC work requirements in 1972 under the so-called Talmadge amendment, and at the same time imposed a requirement that fathers who abandon their children be hunted down and forced to pay child support.

While there are thus strong pressures to cut back on aid to AFDC recipients who are now considered employable, it seems doubtful that any net reduction in assistance costs could be achieved in this fashion, given the characteristics of the AFDC mothers and of the job market they face. These women are simply far less employable than they may seem, at least of employability is taken to mean the capacity to earn better than poverty-level wages. To make the cutback in coverage of female-headed families credible, therefore, it is necessary to support some form of training, wage subsidy, and/or public employment program. What this means is that the cutback effort becomes less a coverage issue than a mode-of-assistance issue—it involves a choice between providing aid in the form of cash and providing it in the form of a job. In fact, the Senate Finance Committee's version of H.R. 1 in 1972 would have channeled whatever was saved from the cutback in AFDC into a substantial employment program guaranteeing jobs at three-fourths the minimum wage for all employable AFDC mothers and providing for wage supplements and a work bonus for those who found private employment.

If it thus seems unlikely that coverage of female-headed households will be eliminated or cut back, it seems more likely that coverage will be extended more fully to needy intact families, the so-called working poor. Prior to the food stamp program, as we have seen, the only mechanism available to aid the working poor was the minimum wage, and it provided inadequate protection at best. As a result, the welfare system created perverse incentives and significant inequities.

The Nixon administration proposed its FAP in 1969 largely in response to this situation. The central theoretical innovation of that plan was its proposed extension of coverage to the working poor, an extension that was justified in terms of fairness and as a way to eliminate the perverse incentive to fathers to leave their families in order to qualify them for public assistance.

Yet if this was the central innovation of the FAP, it was also the central point of objection. Given limited resources, the proposed extension of coverage to the working poor meant limiting the benefits made available to those already covered, a prospect that hardly endeared the plan to those representing, or responsive to, existing recipients. In addition, the proposed extension alienated conservative support. The U.S. Chamber of Commerce, one of the most vociferous opponents of FAP, made it clear that "one of our most serious disagreements is bringing in the working poor."[24] Conservatives in Congress echoed this disagreement, arguing that provision of public assistance to those who could work would destroy the work ethic and undermine the moral fiber of the nation.[25] "This is welfare expansion, not welfare reform," trumpeted the Senate Finance Committee in its report on H.R. 1.[26] The AFL-CIO also had reservations on this point. For labor, the extension of aid to the working poor would blunt the push for a higher minimum wage and government job guarantees by placing the government in the position of subsidizing the employers of cheap labor.[27]

Since the defeat of FAP, however, support for the idea of extending income support to the employed or employable poor in two-parent families has grown substantially—for a number of reasons. For one thing, aid was made available to this segment of the poor with the expansion of the food stamp program in the early 1970s, and many people now feel it would be more efficient and effective to provide this aid in the form of cash rather than food vouchers. In the second place, because of the serious employment problems in the economy, increased concern has been voiced about the possible impact of minimum wage legislation on the avilability of semiskilled jobs, prompting greater interest in alternative mechanisms to provide workers the income protection that the minimum wage alone provided in the past.[28] In the third place, in the absence of any support system for the long-term unemployed, the recent economic downturn has put an immense burden on the unemployment insurance system, inducing Congress to extend the benefit period far beyond what the designers of the system ever dreamed of, and consuming most of the trust fund resources in the process. As a result, unemployment insurance has been turned into a public assistance program in everything but name, yet its benefit distribution pattern makes it an immensely inefficient such program. Finally, the results of the New Jersey Income Maintenance Experiment have undercut one of the major arguments against the extension of coverage to the working poor, though not without its problems, this experiment has provided fairly convincing evidence that workers do not significantly reduce their work effort if guaranteed a minimum income, especially if real financial work incentives are included.[29]

The combination of these new arguments and the longstanding equity concerns has generated a broad consensus on the need to extend public assistance in some form to employed or employable persons in need. The National Governors'

Conference, for example, made the extension of income support "to all eligible persons below an established minimum income level" a central plank in its 1976 policy statement on welfare reform. This position has been endorsed as well by a task force of the New Coalition, representing the National Governors' Conference, the National League of Cities, the U.S. Conference of Mayors, and the National Conference of State Legislatures. Perhaps most interestingly, a recent report of the Council on Trends and Perspective of the U.S. Chamber of Commerce reaches much the same conclusion. Calling earlier objections to FAP and other similar schemes "water over the dam today," this council report urges business support for a negative income tax-type proposal that would extend aid to all those in need, regardless of their employment situation or family status. Though not an official statement of Chamber policies, this report certainly signals a new recognition by the business community that the existing system may be more damaging to work incentives than would a comprehensive income assistance system extending benefits in coherent fashion to all those in need.[30]

With the inclusion of this segment of the poor in the coverage of an income assistance program, however, the need to pay close attention to the link between work and welfare becomes all the more urgent. Including the working poor will almost certainly mean a loss in target efficiency since it will necessitate an extension in the benefit structure to guarantee some financial reward for working. As a result, the pursuit of greater equity will likely mean a greater seepage of benefits to persons who are not poor. The Chamber of Commerce's Council on Trends and Perspective stated this point well. "The frequently-heard statement that welfare benefits should be confined to 'the truly needy' may have an appealing sound," notes the council's report,

> but it does not provide an approach to welfare reform. . . . It is a fact of life with respect to welfare that a fairly sizable share of total welfare benefits has to go to 'less needy' people in order to provide adequate rewards for those who work and earn.[31]

Whether this extension of system coverage takes place may very well hinge on how policymakers and the public evaluate this trade-off, between the promotion of equity and the seepage of benefits to the less needy, in order to preserve financial incentives to work.

Program Coverage. As important as the issue of system coverage is the related issue of program coverage, the question of whether to perpetuate the existing practice of handling different segments of the poor in different programs—AFDC, SSI, food stamps—or whether to merge as many programs as possible into one comprehensive program with uniform eligibility criteria and benefit levels. Of all the issues in the current welfare reform debate, this is the one that most clearly distinguishes the major types of approaches, and hence is the basis for the threefold division of reform proposals suggested later in this chapter.

This debate over program consolidation versus categorization essentially involves a trade-off between the efficient targeting of benefits on the one hand

and considerations of equity and administrative efficiency on the other. Advocates of continued categorization typically stress three lines of argument. The first of these flows directly from the diverse demographic character of the poverty population. Since the needs of low-income people are so varied and arise from such different causes, no one sweeping program will be effective in meeting them. In fact, the welfare system may not be the appropriate mechanism to cope with some of these needs, since they really reflect shortcomings in other important systems such as employment, health, education, and social security. To cope with all of these different problems through a single apparatus, therefore, may be wasteful and ineffective.

Closely related to this first line of argument for categorization is the second, which reflects the force of the work incentive trap discussed earlier. As we have seen, any program that includes employable recipients will likely contain a mechanism to allow recipients to keep a portion of their earnings without any loss in benefits, in order to preserve some incentive for them to work. The problem is that to keep such work incentives relatively potent, it is necessary to keep the basic benefit level relatively modest. Otherwise, the coverage and cost of the program quickly escalate. With a 50 percent tax rate on earnings, for example, each dollar increase in the basic benefit level increases the benefit cutoff level by two dollars, and thus takes in a larger share of the population. If unemployables are put in the same program with employables, therefore, they will find themselves subjected to benefit levels designed to accommodate the latter, who are expected to have outside income from work.

The third argument for categorization is what might be called the "multiple track" theory. In this view, numerous categorical programs are preferable to a single program precisely because they afford more numerous tracks through which program expansion can be pursued. Given a generally hostile public climate toward the poor, it is essential to have a variety of arenas in which assistance programs can be advanced. The records of the 1960s gives some credence to this view, for it was only by shifting the arena of conflict that advocates of greater aid to the poor managed to make much headway during this decade. In this view, the loss of control that results from a multitude of categorical programs is something to be applauded, not deplored, for it opens the way for significant improvements in the condition o the poor.

Opponents of categorization are no less vigorous in their attack, citing three main arguments on their side of the issue. The first of these challenges the theoretical validity of the distinction between employables and unemployables, not to mention the additional categories into which the poor are sliced by the categorical assistance programs. In this view, the longstanding distinction between those who are able to work and those who are not has become increasingly arbitrary and artificial. Notes the U.S. Chamber of Commerce in a recent publication:

> Economists have long understood that 'employability' and 'unemployability' have no absolute meaning, that a person is employable or unemployable with reference to a particular job, at a particular wage, or in a particular place, with particular working conditions. A totally disabled person may be perfectly able to work in certain jobs, while an apparently able-bodied, prime-age man may be 'unemployable' if the only jobs available require education, experience, or skills which he does not have.[32]

Under the circumstances, having wholly separate programs for employables and unemployables makes little sense. And this is expecially so in view of the fact that the poor are not a stagnant mass, but a rather dynamic population, with families moving in and out of poverty in response to changes in family situation, health, and employment status. According to a recent study of 5,000 American families, for example, 21 percent of the population fell into poverty at least once during the period 1967–72, but only 2.4 percent found themselves below the poverty line in all six years.[33] To require that needy individuals shift from program to program in response to subtle changes in family and employment situations is thus to guarantee low participation rates, excessive administrative churning, and continual frustration.

A second argument for drastically reducing the number of separate categorical programs stresses the inequities and perverse incentives that the present complicated program structure produces. With each program setting eligibility standards and benefit levels differently, the opportunities are great not only for sizable segments of the population to fail to gain coverage, but also for treatment to vary significantly even among those covered by the system. The piling of separate in-kind assistance programs on top of the basic cash support programs only complicates the problem, creating strange and frequently perverse program interactions that no one seems able to anticipate, let alone control. For some recipients, an extra dollar of earnings can produce a substantial loss in benefits as a consequence, while for numerous others the combination of benefits available from the different programs easily exceed what could be earned from working. Since each part of this complicated system operates autonomously from all the others, the impact of the system as a whole is never taken into account when changes in the component parts are considered. Crackdowns in AFDC can thus be canceled out by liberalizations in food stamp benefits. Improvements in social security benefits can be offset by dollar-for-dollar reductions in SSI. Through it all, the recipient can either be whiplashed by a seemingly arbitrary array of separate program regulations, or placed in the position of playing one program off against the other.

The third argument stressed by critics of the prevailing categorical program structure focuses on the excessive administrative costs that result. Because each of the programs has its own administrative structure, design parameters, and operating procedures, immense duplication of effort occurs. The definition of income for eligibility for food stamps, for example, differs from that for AFDC, necessitating successive recalculations of the same numbers. Beyond this, each of the in-kind programs requires its own local administrative apparatus to dispense the needed vouchers. In the eyes of many, collapsing all the separate programs into one would significantly reduce administrative costs, even if it would make the resulting program somewhat less sensitive to differences in individual need and therefore contribute to a certain loss of target efficiency.

Whatever the merits of the arguments against separate, narrowly defined, categorical programs, it seems clear that there are real limits to how far movement toward a single, all-encompassing program structure can go. Little real consideration is being given, for example, to "cashing out" the Medicaid program and merging it with the other income support programs, even if national health insurance becomes a reality. It seems likely that the basic social service programs will also remain intact, as will mechanisms to deal with emergencies. Similarly, a need will probably remain for many of the employment training programs. To the extent that the elimination of administrative complexities is the major rationale for decategorization, therefore, the case for consolidation is probably being oversold.

How far the extension of coverage and the elimination of separate programs actually proceeds, however, will likely depend on two further factors: on political considerations—how potent the support for the separate categorical programs is; and on how the work incentive problem is handled, since it has been concern about the impact on work effort that has long impeded the extensions of system coverage and program coverage that have been discussed here. Let us look now at the latter of these two factors, the work incentive problem.

Promoting Work Effort

From the very earliest times, the major constraint on the design of public assistance arrangements has been the desire to encourage work effort and self-support among all those able to work. The concept of deservingness, the principle of less eligibility, and the use of narrow, categorical assistance programs can all be traced to this central concern. As the welfare system has grown and changed over the past two decades, however, serious complaints have surfaced about the impact of these changes on work effort. As a consequence, the task of devising a way to protect the work ethic while still providing adequately and equitably for the needy has emerged as the vital missing piece in the welfare policy puzzle.

To fill in this missing piece, three basic devices have so far been proposed: first, some modification of the longstanding practice of categorization; second, legal work requirements for employable recipients; and third, financial work incentives. While each of these devices seeks the same goal, each pursues it in a different way, with different consequences for the mix of adequacy, equity, and efficiency in the system.

Categorization. Historically, American relief policy has sought to insulate the welfare system from the work system through the traditional device of denying aid to those expected to work. But this arrangement has been challenged in recent years by two sets of forces: the changing social values that have undermined the presumption of unemployability with regard to current assistance recipients; and the pressures to extend assistance to other employable persons in need on grounds of equity.

To the extent that categorization means the wholesale denial of aid to employables, therefore, these two forces have made the use of categorization as a way to limit welfare's negative impact on work incentives increasingly untenable. However, a new version of the concept of categorization has emerged in recent years that may offer greater possibilities: the use of categorization as a way to define the kinds of benefits to which different types of recipients are entitled, rather than using it to define who is eligible. This was the basic principle behind the 1972 Senate Finance Committee version of FAP discussed earlier, which would have provided aid in the form of guaranteed jobs to those expected to work. An even more fully developed version of this idea is evident in the recent "triple track" reform proposal, which would establish three distinct bundles of benefits for the three basic groups of the poor: a tax credit for the working poor; job training and placement services plus temporary unemployment assistance for those unemployed persons who are expected to work but cannot find jobs; and traditional public assistance for those not expected to work. The advantage of this approach is that is provides aid where it is needed most, but without destroying work incentives or raising costs exorbitantly. As we will see more fully below, however, it requires some difficult choices about who is employable, and depends critically on the feasibility of making jobs available to those expected to work.

Work Requirements. A second way to provide assistance to all in need without undermining work incentives is to impose legal work requirements on assistance recipients. The 1967 AFDC amendments, for example, made the continued receipt of AFDC benefits contingent on the acceptance of training or work. A similar requirement has long existed in the unemployment insurance system, where benefits are supposed to cease if a recipient refuses a suitable job. Similarly, the Nixon FAP included a provision denying FAP benefits to the head of a household if he (or she) refused to work.

Although the concept of a work requirement sounds simple, it is deceptively so. For one thing, the requirement has little meaning if there are insufficient training slots or jobs that recipients could fill. The frustrating performance of the WIN program speaks volumes to this point. In addition, work requirements necessitate difficult administrative decisions about the suitability of particular jobs. In the unemployment insurance program, this loophole has provided a broad avenue for escape from the impact of the work requirement. Finally, sole reliance on compulsion, instead of financial incentives, is unlikely to elicit the attitude toward work that should be the goal of a free society. As noted in the report of the U.S. Chamber of Commerce's Council on Trends and Perspective: "Substituting coercion for incentives denigrates the value of work. . . . One can speculate that there may be no more effective way to destroy the work ethic than to take away the economic rewards for voluntary work."[34] So long as concern about benefit adequacy leads to assistance levels that create work disincentives, work requirements are unlikely to solve the problem, and may actually prove counterproductive.

Financial Incentives. The third way to promote work effort among assistance recipients is to build financial incentives to work into the benefit structures of assistance programs to make sure recipients end up financially better off from working than from not working. This can be cone through two basic tools: work-expense deductions and fractional benefit-reduction rates.

Work-expense deductions allow welfare officials to deduct the cost of work expenses from the earnings of employed recipients when calculating the welfare benefits to which they are entitled. In this way, recipients are credited with only that portion of their total earnings that really represents the net addition to their purchasing power over what they would have had from welfare alone. This, if an AFDC recipient earns $3,000 from work in a year but incurs $1,000 in work-related expenses (transportation, day care), she would be credited with only $2,000 in income for purposes of benefit computation.

Fractional benefit-reduction rates specify the amount by which public assistance authorities can reduce a recipient's benefits for each dollar he earns. When these rates are at 100 percent, as they are in some programs, each dollar of earnings means a dollar loss in benefits, thus eliminating the incentive to work. With a 50 percent benefit-reduction rate, every dollar of earnings in excess of work expenses causes only a 50 cent decline in each dollar of benefits, so that the recipient gets to keep half of what is earned; the recipient is permitted not to report 50 cents out of each dollar in earnings to the public assistance authorities. Thus, a recipient with $2,000 in benefits who earns an additional $2,000 from work would end up with a total income of $3,000 (the $2,000 from the job plus the $1,000 in benefits left after deducting 50 cents from benefits for each dollar of earnings). If the benefit-reduction rate were 75 percent, this same recipient would end up with total income of only $2,500 ($2,000 + [$2,000 - .75 × $2,000] = $2,000 + $500 = $2,500). Thus, as the benefit-reduction rate rises, the financial incentive to work declines.

Beginning in the 1950s, work expense deductions and fractional benefit-reduction rates were incorporated into the major categorical assistance programs for the blind and aged. In the 1960s, this logic was applied to the AFDC program—first, in 1962, with the inclusion of a deduction from income for work-related expenses; and then, in 1967, with the incorporation of the so-called $30-and-one-third rule, which stipulates that AFDC recipients can keep the first $30 in earnings per month above work-related expenses, plus one-third of the remainder.

Although work incentive features have become quite popular, they have real drawbacks. The basic problem is that the inclusion of a work incentive feature automatically extends the coverage of public assistance. With a benefit-reduction rate of 50 percent and a basic benefit level of $4,000, for example, AFDC recipients could still be receiving public assistance benefits with earnings up to $8,000. In the absence of categorical limits on the AFDC program, anyone else making up to $8,000 would also receive benefits. Without the work incentive feature, benefits would have declined to zero when earnings reached $4,000, instead of $8,000. The addition of a work incentive feature can thus be costly. According to one recent study, in fact, the work incentive feature included in the 1967 AFDC amendments cost one state (Michigan) $70 million in additional benefit payments in its first five years of operation.[35] Since most of the reform proposals now under consideration would likely extend system coverage to take in more employable, or employed, recipients, this problem is likely to be all the more severe.

A close tie thus exists between the way the work problem is handled in any welfare system and the level of benefits provided. If the goal of reform is to improve the financial incentives to work, this can be achieved—assuming overall costs are fixed—only by reducing benefits. If improved benefits are the goal, therefore, some other mechanism, like categorization, may be the more suitable way to stimulate work. The extent of the work incentive that can be afforded thus depends importantly on the level of benefits provided.

Benefit Levels

This link between work incentives and benefit levels is a longstanding one; for public assistance benefit levels have always been constrained not only by aggregate cost considerations but also by the need to avoid interference with the incentive to work. The principle of less eligibility, under which benefits were set at a level below those for the lowest-paying private jobs, was the mechanism by which this adjustment was effected. What the pressures for a more comprehensive assistance system and the use of fractional benefit-reduction rates have done is to complicate the resulting dilemma. With these features in place, benefit improvements not only increase costs directly, by raising the amount each recipient gets; but they also do so indirectly, by increasing the number of recipients who are eligible for aid. FAP, as we have seen, was caught squarely in the vise of this dilemma: to extend coverage and yet retain financial work incentives, it set benefit levels quite low, prompting critics such as Gilbert Steiner (and others) to complain, "Inadequate benefits continue to be inadequate whether they are called family assistance or AFDC."[36]

At what point, however, do benefits become adequate? Historically, of course, this question has been answered differently for different programs. Both social security and unemployment insurance peg benefit levels to prior earnings, though the former has a minimum payment feature that delivers a larger share of preretirement earnings to poor wage earners than to better-off ones. Under the federally aided public assistance programs, the idea of a federally determined minimum benefit requirement proposed by the Roosevelt administration in the original draft of the Social Security Act was rejected by Congress in favor of a system leaving benefit levels wholly to state discretion. Under current practice, therefore, each state establishes a need standard which represents its estimate of what a family needs to live on in that state, and then allocates assistance to families in proportion to the gap between their income and this need standard. Not only do the need standards vary widely among the states, but most states set maximum benefit levels far below their own needs standard, thus formally institutionalizing inadequacy.

TABLE 4.4

Weighted Average Poverty Thresholds in 1976 by Family Size and Sex of Head, by Farm-Nonfarm Residence

	Nonfarm		Farm	
Size of Family	Male Head	Female Head	Male Head	Female Head
1 person, under 65 years	3,030	2,804	2,575	2,383
1 person, 65 years and over	2,723	2,688	2,314	2,284
2 persons, head under 65 years	3,797	3,686	3,222	3,063
2 persons, head 65 years and over	3,404	3,380	2,895	2,893
3 persons	4,508	4,360	3,814	3,634
4 persons	5,745	5,715	4,905	4,820
5 persons	6,792	6,719	5,798	5,842
6 persons	7,646	7,592	6,506	6,375
7 or more persons	9,457	9,208	7,977	7,985

Source: U.S. Bureau of the Census, *Current Population Reports*, Series P-60, "Money Income and Poverty Status of Families and Persons in the United States: 1975 and 1974 Revision," Advance Report, no. 103, (Washington, D.C.: Government Printing Office, 1976), p. 33.

Note: Data are adjusted to fiscal-year 1976 levels.

Only in the past decade has a more or less objective measure of benefit adequacy emerged: the Social Security Administration's poverty threshold. Though far from perfect, this measure has gained widespread support as a reasonable approximation of what minimally adequate benefits should be. As noted in Table 4.4, the poverty threshold varies with family structure and residence. Thus, the poverty threshold of a single, female head of household aged 65 or more and living on a farm is less than one-fourth that of a male-headed, nonfarm family of seven or more.

Utilizing the poverty threshold as the standard for benefit adequacy in a reform proposal is not without its difficulties, however. In particular, four objections can be anticipated. In the first place, this standard would add significantly to costs compared to existing arrangements. Only one program now provides benefits equal to, or above, the poverty threshold: SSI. Bringing the others up to this level would thus require a substantial outlay of new funds. In 1974, for example, the maximum benefit available under AFDC and food stamps together for a four-person family with no income was less than the official poverty threshold in 41 out of the 50 states, accounting for 70 percent of all public assistance recipients. In 25 of the states, representing 40 percent of all AFDC recipients, the maximum assistance level was less than 80 percent of the poverty level. If we were to look only at the federal share of program costs, the disparity would be even sharper. In no state does the combined federal share of AFDC and food stamp costs equal the amount necessary to bring a family of four with no income up to the poverty line. In most states, it is barely half as much.[37] Thus, to bring all current recipients up to the poverty line would require substantial additional expenditures and, very likely, state supplementation.

Even if the resources were available, there would still be opposition to a national minimum benefit floor set at the poverty line because of the impact it might have on work effort and the private labor market in some states. Some evidence that this opposition remains potent came in early 1977, when a task force of the National Governors' Conference sought to translate the welfare reform statement adopted by the governors at their July 1976 convention into programmatic terms. The group encountered substantial opposition to a single national payment standard set at even 75 percent of the poverty level, even if this standard varied with the cost of living. The problem, as the task force report notes, was that "several states indicated upon analysis that in their opinions this benefits package would have an unacceptable detrimental effect on the economies of those states by discouraging work by those with low earnings levels or potential."[38] As an alternative, therefore, the task force recommended a "three tier" payment system under which the federal government would provide a basic annual benefit level of only $2,400 for a family of four (exclusive of food stamps), and states would be given the option to add another $1,200 per year with 90 percent federal financing, plus another $1,200 per year with 50 percent federal financing. In this way, gross disparities in wage rates and employment conditions among the states could continue to be reflected in welfare benefit levels.

While those in the poorer states find the official poverty level too high to serve as the benefit standard in the welfare system, those in the wealthier states find it too low. The official poverty line was developed, as we have seen, by computing the cost of an economy food diet for various family types in 1955, multiplying this figure by three (on the assumption that the poor use one-third of their income for food), and then adjusting the result for price inflation. However, the U.S. Agriculture Department has itself long questioned whether a family could sustain itself for any length of time on the economy food budget without severe nutrient deficiencies. What is more, the idea that a family can live adequately on a budget that necessitates spending one-third of its total income for food is itself open to serious doubt, especially when most families devote only about half as much to this one item. In fact, when the poverty threshold is recalculated using the Department of Agriculture's low-cost food plan instead of the emergency food plan, it turns out that the poverty line in 1974 would have stood at $6,930 for a family of four, rather than at $5,008.[39]

Reflecting these considerations, many states have already boosted welfare benefits above the official poverty line, especially if the value of Medicaid is included. Approximately 14 states, representing about 35 percent of AFDC recipients, fall into this category. Any effort to restrict benefits to the poverty line would thus encounter real opposition from recipients in these states. Yet, maintaining these levels as they are would likely require state supplementation and hence reduce the reform proposal's impact on both state finances and the degree of equity in the system, the latter because it would perpetuate state-by-state variations in benefits.

One final problem with the use of the absolute poverty level as the benefit standard in a reformed welfare system is that this level has not kept pace with the rise in median income. In 1965, the official poverty threshold for a family of four was 46 percent of the median family income in the nation. In 1975, it was down to only 40 percent of the median. By pegging the assistance level at the absolute poverty level, therefore, we would be doing little to change the overall distribution of income in the country. This is reflected in the fact that the decline in the proportion of families in absolute poverty has not been matched by any decline in the proportion in relative poverty, that is, poverty defined as a certain proportion of the median income.[40] A public assistance level built around the absolute poverty line would thus further institutionalize economic inequality, even though providing the poor with a minimally adequate level of income.

Mode of Assistance

As important as the level of assistance is the mode. This involves three different questions: the proper mix of cash and in-kind assistance; the provision of assistance in the form of jobs instead of outright grants; and the degree of reliance to be placed on social insurance programs as opposed to needs-tested assistance.

Cash versus In-Kind Benefits. One of the great ironies of the significant social reforms of the 1960s was the tremendous expansion in the scope of in-kind assistance programs, which had been the bane of nineteenth century reformers. In rapid succession, programs were enacted to supply a wide variety of commodities (food, housing, milk), as well as a long list of services (medical care, family counseling, employment training, preschool education for children.)* As a result, the relative positions of cash and in-kind programs in the total public assistance budget as of 1975 were almost the reverse of what they had been ten years earlier.

This rapid growth of in-kind programs was the product of several factors: concern about treating the causes of poverty rather than the symptoms; a social theory tracing the roots of poverty to the cultural and behavior patterns of the poor; a newfound confidence among social work professionals about their ability to alter these patterns, with the aid of various service programs; a political situation in which support could be gained for in-kind programs that was unavailable for cash grants; and the feeling that the poor are unable or unwilling to make the best use of their resources.

Although many of these arguments still have force today, the trend toward greater reliance on in-kind assistance has recently come under serious attack, for three basic reasons. First, the in-kind commodity programs are criticized for distorting the purchasing patterns of the poor. Under the food stamp program, for example, recipient families must spend at least 30 percent of their income on food, even if they would prefer to divert a portion of this to housing or clothes. As a consequence, food stamps are worth less to recipients than an equivalent amount of cash, giving rise to active black market operations. Although these distorting effects have been justified as a way to keep the poor from squandering their resources on nonessentials, the available evidence does not support this contention. The results of the New Jersey Income Maintenance Experiment, for example, suggest little change in family expenditure patterns following receipt of cash income supplements, and other studies indicate that the poor may actually get more protein and food value per dollar than middle-class families.[41] What the in-kind programs accomplish, therefore, is to provide aid in a way that makes it worth less to the recipient than it costs the public.

A second criticism of the in-kind mode of assistance focuses on the effectiveness of many of the service programs launched by the war on povery and other Great Society initiatives. These programs have been faulted on grounds that, for all their costs, they have little noticeable impact on the lives of the poor. Although this verdict still rests on imperfect data, it has been embraced by many as support for the position Daniel Patrick Moynihan expressed shortly after taking office as head of former President Nixon's Urban Affairs Council: "I would sort of put my faith in any effort that puts more resources into the hands of those that don't now have them . . . cold cash. It's a surprisingly good cure for a lot of social ills.[42]

---

*In traditional usage, the service programs—especially the counseling, training, and general social work programs—are not considered income assistance programs because they cannot readily be replaced by outright cash grants. Nevertheless, these programs are part of what the public has in mind when it thinks about welfare.

The third line of criticism of in-kind programs emphasizes the role that the blossoming of in-kind assistance programs has played in producing many of the baffling notches, overlaps, and high benefit-reduction rates that make public assistance so cumbersome and counterproductive. In this view, a switch from in-kind to cash assistance would help bring this sprawling system under control, forcing into the open the curious arrangements that now give rise to extensive pyramiding of program benefits and strong work disincentives, and reducing the stigmatizing effect of food vouchers and other forms of poor people's money. Notes the American Public Welfare Association in its recent position paper on welfare reform:

> The payment of cash to individuals is not only simpler administratively, but is also beneficial to those who receive assistance. It reduces the stigma which attaches to those who currently purchase necessities with in-kind benefits which clearly identify them as "welfare recipients." Furthermore it allows poor people to spend their money in a manner which is most responsive to their own needs and priorities. In-kind benefits and vendor payments often hinder rather than promote efficient management of resources. For these reasons, the Committee endorses, as a general rule, the conversion of in-kind benefits into cash payments wherever feasible.[43]

But in-kind programs are not without their defenders. In its own influential position paper on welfare reform, for example, the National Association of Counties vigorously defends the advances in social service funding achieved over the past decade on the grounds that such services are a necessary complement to cash assistance because they help to "achieve the full objectives of encouraging self-support, self-reliance, strengthening of family life and the protection of children and adults."[44] Even those who doubt the wisdom of the 1962 AFDC amendments, with their stress on rehabilitation through services, acknowledge the need for some modicum of social services to aid the elderly, the disabled, and the numerous others for whom cash assistance is not enough. What this suggests is a need to distinguish between the numerous in-kind service programs—like counseling, employment, and traditional social work—for which cash cannot readily be substituted, and the commodity-type programs—like food stamps and housing assistance—for which cash can be substituted.

Even with respect to the latter, two lines of argument can be offered in their defense. The first has to do with the failure of the market to provide certain goods needed by the poor, because of artificial rigidities that would inhibit the market from responding to the needs of the poor even if they had additional resources. The housing and health-care markets provide particularly strong cases for this argument, since both have built-in rigidities—the former because of the combination of physical deterioration of central-city housing, the hesitancy of investors to sink funds into low-income neighborhoods, and the pattern of racial exclusion in the suburbs; and the latter because of the reluctance of medical personnel to locate in low-income neighborhoods or rural areas. Whether these rigidities and market imperfections are serious enough to justify the added costs of in-kind forms of assistance, however, is a matter of real debate.

The second argument for continued use of in-kind assistance is far less debatable, however. For whatever reasons, it seems that the public is willing to support greater outlays for in-kind assistance than it is for outright cash grants. The image of providing food or shelter, rather than the cash that will buy food and shelter, reduces the hostility of many people toward welfare. What is more, it generates support among the affected provider groups (for example, home builders). To the extent this continues to be true, therefore, reliance on in-kind modes of assistance may be the price that has to be paid to achieve an adequate level of benefits.

Jobs versus Direct Relief. Closely related to this question of whether public assistance should be given in the form of cash or in-kind benefits is the question of whether it should take the form of benefit payments or jobs. As we have seen, this question surfaced sharply during the New Deal era when a conscious choice was made to cut back on direct relief and substitute work relief instead, essentially leaving the problems of the unemployables to states and localities. In the latter 1930s and early 1940s, however, the federal commitment to work relief itself disappeared, leaving the federal government responsible only for matching payments to state categorical assistance programs for unemployables.

But with the rise in unemployment during the 1970s, the work relief issue is squarely on the political agenda of the nation once again. This is especially true given the number of employable persons now on welfare, the pressures that exist for expanding this number through extensions of coverage to the working poor, and the structural obstacles that impede the employment of the disadvantaged. Under the circumstances, sentiment has shifted strongly in favor of "providing work in lieu of income transfer support for employable persons," as the National Commission for Manpower Policy put it in its 1976 annual report.[45]

The advantages claimed for this approach are numerous. For one thing, it enjoys broad popular support. In 1972, for example, a national opinion poll recorded 72 percent of its respondents in favor of a guaranteed-job plan, compared to only 38 percent favoring a guaranteed-income plan.[46] This support finds ample reflection in Congress. One of the most significant innovations of the "workfare" program that the Senate Finance Committee put forward as an alternative to FAP in 1972 was its proposal for a guaranteed-government-jobs program—albeit with quite low wages—for all employable AFDC recipients. Similarly, the Humphrey-Hawkins bill before Congress at this writing would call on the president to "make recommendations on how income maintenance and employment policies can be integrated to insure that employment is substituted for income maintenance to the maximum extent feasible."

Another argument for such a jobs approach is the promise it offers for overcoming long-term dependence by providing some valuable work experience to those long alienated from the employment system. If this experience is coupled with training, the long-term advantages in terms of promoting economic independence could be substantial. One of the dilemmas of previous job training efforts has been their inability to guarantee employment for most of their graduates.[47] Some form of public employment program, perhaps even a permanent one modeled after what the President's Committee on Economic Security had in mind in 1935, could increase the incentive to take such training programs seriously.

Despite its attractions, the jobs approach has a number of important drawbacks. For one thing, it probably overstates the employability of current welfare recipients.[48] At the very least, many of these recipients will require extensive training, and many more will require child-care assistance. Beyond this, a jobs program is likely to be expensive. Each public service job funded under the Comprehensive Employment and Training Act (CETA) program in 1975, for example, cost approximately $8,300, well above what even a poverty-level cash grant would cost. One reason for this was the inclusion of a "suitable work" requirement in the law authorizing the public service jobs. But it seems doubtful that a public service jobs program offering wages much below the minimum wage will be politically feasible. Administrative expenses aside, this means a cost of about $5,500 per job. Even then, the administrative burdens of such a program would be heavy.[49] There are real questions whether state and local governments could handle even 500,000 new employees, not to mention the three million employables now on welfare. Even a million new employees would represent a 20 percent increase in state and local noneducational employment. Finally, the broader impact of a guaranteed-jobs approach on the operation of the labor market in general must be of great concern. If the guaranteed jobs carry decent wages, they could draw labor away from lower-paying private employers. The real beneficiaries of the effort might then not be the intended beneficiaries. Indeed, if employers react to the loss of their low-wage labor force by investing in labor-saving machinery, the result could be a reduction in the number of low-skill jobs available. Already, there is evidence of "fiscal substitution" in the existing public service employment program. According to one study, as many as 60 percent of the public service jobs provided to state and local governments under CETA Titles II and VI replaced jobs that these governments would have financed out of local revenues instead. Only 40 percent of the public service jobs represented new employment.[50] Although the use of wage subsidies in addition to public service employment might minimize some of these labor market impacts, such subsidies have their own disadvantages because of the incentives they give employers to keep wages low. In short, any shift from direct assistance to a mode of assistance using jobs should probably be undertaken cautiously until the true secondary effects can be determined and the administrative arrangements tested.

Means-Tested Grants versus Social Insurance. One final issue concerning the mode of income assistance has to do with the extent to which the benefits should be means-tested. As we have seen, two-thirds of all income assistance expenditures in the United States take the form of non-means-tested social insurance payments. Under these programs, participants earn a right to their benefits by making contributions during their productive years. The theory is that since these programs are designed to protect against insurable risks—such as disability, temporary unemployment, old age, and early death—beneficiaries are reaping the returns on risks against which they have purchased protection. In the process, they avoid all the cumbersome and stigmatizing administrative procedures and the segregation involved in the means-tested programs.

According to one school of thought, this basic insurance principle could easily be extended to sizable segments of the current welfare population, producing a far more humane and adequate program than the one that now exists. Advocates of this view observe that the sharp division between social insurance and public assistance has always been greater in theory than in fact. The probability of unemployment, for example, cannot really be calculated, making it hardly an insurable risk.[51] Similarly, the basic OASDI operates more like a transfer station with a sizable welfare component than a true insurance policy. This is so not only because low-wage earners get back a higher proportion of their preretirement earnings as benefits than do high-wage earners, but, more important, because both groups get back far more than they pay in. According to one recent estimate, for example, even high-wage earners pay for no more than one-third of the lifetime benefits they receive from social security. The rest comes from the contributions of current workers. The true genius of social security, therefore, is not its insurance properties but its function as a redistributor of income between current workers and their parents' generation. As we have seen, in fact, the use of employee contributions in social security was urged by Roosevelt more on political than economic grounds: it promised to insulate the program from political attack by giving participants at least a symbolic claim on their benefits. In the original design of the system, this basic principle was eventually to have embraced recipients under the needs-tested programs also, as social insurance coverage was extended and the system took hold.

Those who today support further reliance on the social insurance principle argue that much of our current welfare mess can be traced to the failure of policymakers in the intervening years to follow this original design. To help remedy this, social security benefits were substantially increased during the 1960s, reducing the pressures on the needs-tested old age assistance (now SSI) program. In addition, when the economic downturn struck in the 1970s, the unemployment insurance system was expanded by extending the benefit period and reducing the months of covered employment required for eligibility. In the process, the unemployment insurance system was mobilized to help handle a problem that would otherwise have been thrown more completely onto the public assistance system.[52]

But these changes hardly exhaust the agenda of proposals for extending the basic social insurance principle to cope with problems now handled by welfare. One current idea would extend unemployment insurance coverage to new entrants to the labor force (chiefly teenagers and other young workers), as well as to reentrants (for example, women who reenter the labor force after a period away from it during child rearing).[53] Another interesting extension of the social insurance concept to what is now defined as a public assistance problem is Alvin Schorr's proposal to make divorce and long-term separation "insured events."[54] Under this scheme, part of the basic social insurance premium would be considered "divorce insurance," so that dependent children could be cared for out of an insurance trust fund rather than under the maligned AFDC program. One of the advantages of this approach might be that it would minimize the problem of collecting child-support payments from runaway fathers, since such fathers would, in a sense, have made part of these payments in advance in the form of insurance premiums. Also in the same genre of ideas is the long-standing proposal for a children's allowance, a flat grant to each family with children, prorated according to the number of children. Here, again, the goal is to provide aid to the needy in a form that avoids the stigma and separation currently so salient a part of public assistance.

Opponents of the use of the social insurance mechanisms to serve essentially public assistance functions argue that this is an inefficient way to serve these goals, since the social insurance programs cover the nonneedy as well as the needy. Increasing benefits under social security thus inevitably produces widespread leakage of resources to nonneedy participants, who are far more numerous.[55] Similarly, critics point to the danger excessive welfare-type burdens pose for the integrity of the trust funds that finance social security and unemployment insurance. The fear is that general revenue financing will destroy the privileged place that social security now enjoys in American social thought and lead to the introduction into the social security system of the same stigmatizing features that now burden public assistance.[56]

Administration

The fifth basic issue confronting designers of welfare reform proposals concerns the pattern of administration. Under the existing system, administrative responsibilities are scattered among a number of federal administrative units, and between the federal government and the states and localities. One of the primary motivations for reform, in fact, is the desire to streamline this administrative system and thus reduce its costs.

While most of the attention in discussions of welfare administration has focused on the question of the locus of administrative responsibilities, an even more important question concerns the amount of administration to require, that is, the extent to which restrictive provisions requiring administrative scrutiny are built into the program structure. The central point here is that administrative cumbersomeness is the price that must be paid if one wants to be absolutely certain that benefits go to the most needy. The more that controls are added to achieve this target efficiency, the more administratively complex the system becomes. Both the location and the amount of administration must therefore be considered.

The Locus of Administration. Two issues dominate much of the debate over the locus of administrative responsibility in welfare. The first has to do with the appropriate roles to be played by the federal government on the one hand and state and local governments on the other. The second concerns the allocation of administrative responsibilities within the federal government.

So far as the first issue is concerned, it has long been assumed that welfare reform would mean greater federal administrative responsibility. This view grew out of two key considerations. In the first place, the existing pattern of state administration has contributed to the serious inequities that pervade the needs-tested public assistance programs. Under AFDC, for example, needs standards, payment schedules, certification procedures, eligibility criteria, and other program parameters are determined at the state level, so that the nature of the treatment a recipient gets varies dramatically from place to place. Not only does this generate inequities, but also it frustrates effective cost control and fraud detection because of the diversity of state procedures and the inadequacy of some state administrative structures. Since reform is likely to increase the federal share of total welfare expenditures, demands for closer federal control over these matters are therefore likely to increase. Federal administration, it is assumed, would be both more equitable and more efficient, especially if the mode of assistance is shifted more fully to cash, and program coverage is extended.

These easy assumptions about the desirability of federal administration of a reformed public assistance system have recently come under serious challenge, however. The American Public Welfare Association recently endorsed a nationwide minimum public assistance payment financed fully by the federal government, but then proceeded to recommend that administration be lodged with the states.[57] The National Governors' Conference's Welfare Task Force has responded with a formula calling for "federal supervision/state administration."[58] And the National Association of Counties has proposed increasing federal administrative responsibilities for cash assistance payments, while leaving responsibility for social services and for job development and work-related efforts to the localities.[59]

While considerations of organizational self-interest undoubtedly played a role in these recommendations, the case for continued state and local administrative responsibility does not rest on this factor alone. Increasing the equity of the income assistance system clashes with the equally meritorious goal of making the system responsive to individual needs, and hence more target efficient. Although federal administration can advance the goal of equity, state and local administration seems more likely to accommodate the individual adjustments that are necessary to ensure flexibility and responsiveness. This is especially important because of a second factor: the need to integrate the cash assistance programs with social service activities. The argument here is that public assistance recipients are frequently problem families in need of a host of social services. Since state and local officials will most likely continue to operate the social service programs, placing the related cash programs in federal hands would complicate the coordination problems.

A third argument for maintaining a state and local role in public assistance administration results from the fact that some form of state supplementation would be necessary under most welfare reform proposals now under consideration. Since state governments will consequently be devoting considerable amounts of money to public assistance, they can be expected to demand some control over the way these funds are spent.

Finally, supporters of state administration point to the conversion costs in shifting from state-run to federally run programs as a potent argument for keeping administrative arrangements as they are. The conversion to SSI is a telling lesson in this regard, inducing many state officials to resist a total federal takeover of welfare administration. Aside from the horrors of the SSI experience, moreover, state officials might still oppose federal administration because of the pesky personnel issues—like pension coverage, wage scales, and fringe benefits—that would be involved in any conversion. In fact, when FAP was under consideration, public employees' union head Jerry Wurf initially opposed it on just these grounds, in the process accounting for some of the coolness of labor in general toward the proposal.[60]

On the question of the allocation of administrative responsibility at the federal level itself, old assumptions are also in the process of being challenged. For some time, advocates of major welfare restructuring painted a picture of veritable administrative nirvana in selling their proposals. In this newly reformed world, a single federal assistance agency would efficiently dispatch assistance checks to needy recipients without the muss and fuss of the existing creaky system. To be sure, there were disagreements over whether the Internal Revenue Service (IRS) or the Social Security Administration should handle this function, but this was a technical question that hardly affected the basic optimistic conclusion.

Following the SSI debacle, however, a certain modesty has crept into the discussions of the way reform will affect federal administration of welfare. For one thing, critics have pointed to the limits that exist on administrative simplification. For example, it seems likely that many existing in-kind programs, especially the social service and employment training programs, will survive even comprehensive welfare reform. Surviving with them, therefore, will likely be some of the current administrative structures.

In the second place, the frequent assumption that the IRS could easily assume the role of managing a needs-tested public assistance payment system has itself become an open question. The overworked staff of IRS already has its hands full monitoring income tax filings. To handle a monthly check-issuing and verification operation would require, at a minimum, a substantial expansion of staff- and field-office structure and a significant alteration in outlook, orientation, and ethos. Yet bureaucratic agencies frequently find it difficult to make such drastic changes. The experience of the Federal Housing Administration following its assumption of new responsibilities for low-income housing in 1967, for example, hardly makes one sanguine about the capacity of agencies to shift from serving middle-class clients to functioning as administrators of programs for the poor.[61]

Similar problems arise from utilizing the Social Security Administration, which has now been made the centerpiece of a new income assistance division within HEW. Although the Social Security Administration has greater experience than IRS with centralized check-issuing operations, its experience with means-tested programs is limited to the several years of operation of the SSI program. And the administrative success of this operation is in serious question at this writing. At the very least, the SSI experience suggests that the administrative functioning of even a streamlined, noncategorical, means-tested cash assistance program will hardly be automatic. And SSI involved four million persons. By contrast, a unified public assistance system covering the working poor as well as existing recipients would involve 10–12 million filing units and 27–30 million people![62]

The Amount of Administration. Whatever the distribution of administrative responsibility, the real determinant of the extent of administrative streamlining and simplification possible under any reform proposal will be the amount of administration required. Most of the administrative problems with welfare are a direct product of the restrictions intentionally written into the programs. The basic decision to rely on a needs-tested assistance mode, in fact, automatically dictates a certain level of administrative cumbersomeness, since income and assets must constantly be checked and other features of family circumstances and living arrangements verified. Each new restriction designed to target benefits for those truly in need thus brings with it additional administrative impositions.

Even among needs-tested programs, however, administrative requirements can differ widely, depending on a number of technical features. For example, the longer the accounting period—the period of time over which income is evaluated—the less frequently income, assets, earnings, and family circumstances need to be checked. But the longer the accounting period, the less responsive the system will be to short-term family emergencies. Similarly, administrative detail can be eliminated by using standard deductions for living expenses and work expenses rather than making actual cost calculations. Here again, however, administrative simplicity is purchased at the expense of greater program cost, since the actual deductions may frequently be well below the benefit-of-the-doubt standard deductions.

Another key technical decision that creates the same trade-off between costs and administrative simplicity concerns the definition of the filing unit, the group of persons eligible to apply for assistance. Administratively, the simplest procedure would be to treat each individual as a potential filing unit. This would make it unnecessary to take account of any intrahousehold or intrafamily sharing of income, or of the economies of scale that come from living together. Since such sharing and economies of scale exist, however, ignoring them makes the program more expensive. The administratively more complicated alternative, therefore, is to treat the household as the appropriate filing unit and to scrutinize carefully the total amount of income available in the household from all sources, even though some members of the household may not be in need (for example, the case of an AFDC mother living with her parents).

To be sure, these technical details lack the drama of the debates over assistance levels, work requirements, and aggregate costs. Yet they are not less important.

Costs

Ultimately, the major constraint on the design of income assistance proposals is cost. Yet, the cost implications of altering the current welfare system have hardly surfaced seriously in the public debates on welfare reform. Waste, overlap, inefficiency, multiple benefits, fraud and abuse—these are the problems that have dominated the discussion and shaped public perceptions. That welfare reform is likely to mean greater spending for public assistance, rather than less, hardly seems to have attracted serious notice. Yet this is the conclusion that most keen students of the subject have reached. A recent CBO analysis of alternative reform schemes shows, for example, that even the most restrictive reform proposal now under consideration would shave no more than $1.2 billion off the federal government's share of the fiscal-year-1982 cost of welfare, a reduction of less than 3 percent. By contrast, the more comprehensive reform proposals being given serious attention would add anywhere from $13 billion to $16 billion to these projected costs.[63] While these estimates are still preliminary, they clearly suggest that expectations of substantial savings from welfare reform are likely to be frustrated, and that substantially enlarged expenditures can be anticipated instead.

Whether increased welfare expenditures of this magnitude will occur, of course, depends more on overall social priorities and economic circumstances than it does on factors internal to the design of public assistance programs. To discuss what the upper limit on program costs should be, therefore, would take us well beyond the confines of this study. Nevertheless, two cost issues that bear heavily on this question are appropriate for discussion here: the distribution of costs among the levels of government; and the cost of keeping the status quo in welfare policy.

State and Local Costs. The fiscal impact of public assistance on state and local government has become the central source of political pressure for welfare reform. It has mobilized the U.S. Conference of Mayors, the National Governors' Conference, the National League of Cities, the National Urban League, the National Association of Counties, and the American Public Welfare Association, to name just a few organizations, and forged them into a powerful coalition pushing for greater federal assumption of welfare costs.[64] This position has been endorsed by several business groups, including the Committee on Economic Development,[65] and a newly formed Businessmen's Committee for the Federalization of Welfare, concerned that "the burden of poverty is preventing the older urban portions of the country from fulfilling their function in the nation's economy."[66]

As with everything else in the field of welfare policy, however, federalization of welfare costs is not as simple as it seems. For one thing, a total federal assumption of state welfare costs would be quite expensive. According to CBO estimates, the projected fiscal-year-1978 state and local share of all nonadministrative costs in the five major welfare programs (AFDC, SSI, Medicaid, veterans' pensions, and housing assistance) totaled $16 billion, and this is expected to rise to $24 billion by fiscal year 1982.[67] While such an expenditure would ease the fiscal pressures on state and local governments, it would hardly rectify the welfare mess. Rather, it would leave substantial geographic inequities in benefit levels, as well as the other program deficiencies analyzed earlier. Thus, a straight buyout would produce a situation in which the federal government itself paid more to support AFDC recipients in one state than in another, hardly a tenable situation politically. In addition, there is no guarantee that such a buyout approach would solve the fiscal problems of the deficit-ridden city governments of the Northeast since much of the benefit would flow to state coffers.

Some level of fiscal relief can be delivered to the states, while structural reform is pursued, if the federal government establishes a minimum, federally financed benefit level. Given the current pattern of benefits, however, the federal minimum cannot be set at a level that eliminates the need for state supplementation without involving costs well beyond what most observers consider feasible. As of 1974, a program replacing AFDC and food stamps with a $4,200 federal minimum payment would have left 23 states, accounting for 60 percent of the recipient population, still requiring state supplements to maintain prior benefit levels. Since it is unlikely that the basic federal benefit level will go much beyond that level, more than half of all recipients are thus likely to require state supplementation to maintain current benefit levels.

How to structure these state supplements will therefore become a pressing design issue. One question concerns whether they should be optional or required. If they are optional, some recipients may end up worse off after the reforms than before, a prospect that seems quite likely to generate strong pressures to make state supplementation mandatory, at least up to current assistance levels. However, mandatory state supplementation will limit the extent of fiscal relief provided, even if the federal government pays a portion of the supplements. This is especially true to the extent that reform extends coverage to persons not now eligible for assistance—for example, the working poor. In a sense, the working poor and the state treasuries are competitors for whatever additional federal dollars are pumped into public assistance. The more that coverage is extended in any reform proposal, the less fiscal relief the states and localities will reap per dollar increase in federal expenditures. Furthermore, any extension of coverage raises the difficult question of whether state supplements should be provided to the new recipients. Doing so reduces the fiscal relief prospects, but failing to do so retains many of the inequities that the expansion of coverage is designed to eliminate.

This coverage question is especially important in view of increased concern over the regional distribution of federal expenditures in the past several years. Welfare reform has been promoted most vigorously by politicians in the northern industrial states where burdens under the existing programs are most severe. However, to the extent that coverage is extended to the working poor, the major financial benefits of reform may paradoxically accrue to the South instead, where most of the working poor are concentrated. This would certainly have been the outcome in the case of FAP, even though it did not surface as a political issue at the time. The recent revival of regional sensitivity promises to change this the next time around. Reform proposals will consequently be scrutinized not only for the total amount of fiscal relief offered to states in general, but also for the regional distribution of the benefits they produce, introducing a new element into the already complicated calculus of the decision, and raising the price tag on the proposal that will be politically salable.

The Costs of Sitting Tight. As substantial as the costs of reform may be, critics of the existing system point out that there are also substantial costs involved in doing nothing. Even assuming a far more moderate level of program growth over the next five years than occurred over the previous five, federal expenditures under the existing needs-tested programs are expected to grow by $20 billion, from $38 billion in fiscal year 1977 to $58 billion in fiscal year 1981.[68] However, these estimates assume no increase in the participation rates in the in-kind programs, even though eligibility already exceeds participation by more than two to one in many of them. In addition, these estimates necessarily take no account of the pressures that exist to extend the range of in-kind programs even further through the addition of housing allowances and energy vouchers. So long as no overall reform occurs, these pressures will be exceedingly hard to resist, thus raising additional risks of runaway costs, cumulative benefits, notches, and perverse work incentives.

No less important than these direct costs of sitting tight are the indirect ones. These include not only the welfare system's impact on work effort and family stability, but also the consequences that perpetuation of a system that has lost the public's confidence, could have for general public trust in government. Also important is the way current arrangements stigmatize the poor, who come to be blamed for much of the perverseness of the system on which they are forced to rely. Although it is difficult to translate these indirect costs into monetary terms, they ought not to be ignored in calculating the relative costs of reform versus the status quo.

RESOLVING THE DESIGN ISSUES:
THREE ROUTES TO REFORM

Given these six major issues that underlie decisions on welfare policy, it should be clear why designing welfare reform proposals is so difficult a task. Every proposal must pick its way among a mine field of dilemmas, recognizing as it proceeds how choices in one area preclude options in another. How do some of the major proposals now in circulation cope with these difficult policy decisions?

To answer this question systematically, it is useful to divide the multitude of reform proposals into three basic groups, according to the degree to which they preserve the categorical structure of the existing programs. In the first group are those proposals that would eliminate all categorical distinctions among recipients and rely upon a uniform benefit structure providing the same basic assistance to all those in need, regardless of family situation or other demographic characteristics. In the second group are those proposals that would eliminate many of the categorical divisions in the current programs, but still retain a distinction between recipients who are expected to work and those who are not expected to work. Finally, a third set of options includes proposals that would reform the existing system by making modifications in the present categorical program structure, but without overhauling it completely. We will refer to these, respectively, as "consolidated cash assistance" approaches, "multitrack" or "jobs/cash" approaches, and "incremental" approaches. Although each of these approaches contains numerous variants, together they represent the three major routes to welfare reform.

Route One: Consolidated Cash Assistance Proposals

Consolidated cash assistance proposals have as their goal the replacement of the existing categorical programs with a uniform system providing cash assistance to all those in need. This can be done in either of two ways: through demogrants or negative income taxes. The key difference between the two turns on the question of means testing. Under a demogrant plan, a basic, flat payment would be made to every person or family in the nation, regardless of need. This payment would then be treated like any other income, and taxed at whatever rates apply to the taxpayer in question. Thus some of the grant would be returned to the government from taxpayers in the highest tax brackets, whereas most of it would remain in the hands of recipients who are poor. Demogrants would thus avoid the stigmatizing effects of public assistance, but would involve substantial outlays of funds, even if not necessarily substantial net costs to the government (because some of the benefits would return in the form of taxes).

Among numerous versions of the demogrant plan, two are perhaps most well known. The first is the proposal put forward by Senator McGovern in the course of the 1972 presidential election campaign; it would have provided a basic grant of $1,000 to every man, woman, and child in the country as a matter of right. The second is the concept of a children's allowance, which has been in operation in the European countries since the 1930s, and which would provide grants to families with children in amounts proportional to the number of children.[69]

Given the hostility with which such non-means-tested, flat-grant schemes have been greeted in the United States, most attention has focused on the negative income tax variant of the consolidated approach to reform. This approach combines certain features of the demogrant concept with a clearer means test. Three features in particular characterize this negative-income tax approach: first, the guarantee of a minimum, tax-free cash benefit for all those in need, regardless of family composition or other demographic characteristics; second, provision for a benefit reduction as earnings rise, but at something significantly less than dollar for dollar; and third, a resulting break-even point at which benefits reach zero and tax liabilities on further earnings begin.

Although all proposals in this class adhere to these basic principles, they can diverge widely in their application of them. For example, benefit levels, benefit-reduction rates, and break-even points can all vary extensively. Similarly, proposals can differ with regard to the accounting-period and filing-unit definitions they use, their treatment of unearned income (for example, in-kind aid from relatives, child-support payments), handling of work expenses, administrative arrangements, and the extent to which they replace other assistance programs.

Perhaps the most significant difference among negative income tax-type proposals, however, is in the way they relate to the tax system. At one extreme are proposals that deliver all of their benefits through the tax structure (the pure-tax variant). Two recent examples of this approach are the British-inspired tax credit plan recently endorsed by the National Urban League, and the Income Supplement Program (ISP) drafted by HEW officials under the direction of Secretary Caspar Weinberger in 1974. Such proposals have the advantage of great uniformity and simplicity, since all segments of the population are included in a single, integrated tax system with some (the poor) receiving payments from the government and others (the better off) making payments to it. However, such schemes have the obvious drawback of requiring extensive tax reform in order to work smoothly since there are numerous provisions in the present tax code that allow some taxpayers to exempt much of their income from taxation. Unless these provisions are eliminated, many wealthy individuals could end up receiving negative income tax benefits intended for the poor.

To avoid this dilemma, a second type of consolidated cash assistance proposal has been advanced that uses outright grants, instead of tax credits, to deliver its benefits (the pure-grant approach). The FAP of 1969 is perhaps the best-known example of this particular variant, but several other versions are now in circulation. In between these straight-tax and straight-grant negative income

TABLE 4.5

Proposed Benefit Schedule under ISP (1974 dollars)

Family	Benefits at Various Earnings Levels				Total Income at Various Earnings Levels				Break-Even Level of Earnings, Total Income (benefit = 0)	Average Benefit
	$0[a]	$2,000	$4,000	$6,000	$0[a]	$2,000	$4,000	$6,000		
Single individual	1,200	200	b	b	1,200	2,200	b	b	2,400	726
Childless couple	2,400	1,400	400	b	2,400	3,400	4,400	b	4,800	995
Single parent, one child	2,400	1,400	400	b	2,400	3,400	4,400	b	4,800	1,603
Single parent, three children	3,600	2,600	1,600	600	3,600	4,600	5,600	6,600	7,200	2,593
Two parents, two children	3,600	2,600	1,600	600	3,600	4,600	5,600	6,600	7,200	1,269
Aged, blind, or disabled individual	2,300	1,300	300	b	2,300	3,300	4,300	b	4,600	1,281
Aged, blind, or disabled couple	3,150	2,150	1,150	150	3,150	4,150	5,150	6,150	6,300	1,293
Aged, blind, or disabled parent, three children	3,975	2,975	1,975	975	3,975	4,975	5,975	6,975	7,975	3,722

aThe benefit at zero income is the basic benefit. When income is zero the total income of a family will equal the benefit.

bAt this income level the family is above the ISP break-even income and will therefore receive no ISP benefits and might have a positive tax liability.

Source: U. S. Department of Health, Education, and Welfare, *Income Supplement Proposal: 1974 HEW Welfare Replacement Proposal,* Technical Analysis Paper No. 11, Office of Income Security Policy (Washington, D.C.: Department of HEW, 1976), p. E-7.

tax proposals are plans that utilize a combination of tax credits and grants, an approach that is best exemplified by the so-called Griffiths plan formulated by the staff of the Joint Economic Committee's Subcommittee on Fiscal Policy in 1974.

How, then, would these three types of consolidated cash assistance proposals work?

Pure-Tax Variants

Credit Income Tax. The purest form of the negative income tax idea finds reflection in the credit income tax plan that the Conservative government in England proposed in a special Green Paper in 1974, and that the National Urban League endorsed in its 1976 position paper on welfare reform.[70] Under one version of this plan,[71] every household would be entitled to tax credits that vary with age ($1,400 per year per adult, $1,700 per year for aged adults, and $700 per year per child) and against which the family's regular tax liabilities would be charged. To make the system work, however, the tax code would have to be revised so that all deductions and exemptions were eliminated and a straight 33 percent tax levied on all income. For families that ended up owing taxes less than the amount of their tax credits, the government would provide a refund (hence the term "refundable tax credit" to depict this idea). For those families (or filing units) whose tax liabilities exceeded their tax credit, the excess would be paid to the government as taxes.

Income Supplement Program (ISP). Since the credit income tax proposal would require nothing short of a total elimination of all tax deductions, its chances for passage are rather slim. More feasible would be the proposal developed in HEW during 1973 and 1974 under the direction of Secretary Weinberger: the ISP. This proposal would provide a basic benefit of $3,600 to a family of four with no other income, and include a benefit-reduction rate of 50 percent, so that the break-even point (the point at which benefits decline to zero as earnings rise) would be $7,200.* Coverage would embrace all persons and families in need, but different types of families, with different needs, would be entitled to different basic benefits, as noted in Table 4.5.

Although the ISP would build its benefit schedule into the basic income tax apparatus, it would do so far less disruptively (and far less extensively) than the credit income tax plan. To see this, it is necessary to understand something about how the current income tax system operates. Essentially, income tax liabilities are the product of the interaction among three elements: income, deductions from income, and the tax rate. Obviously, the larger the deductions, the smaller the taxable income, and hence the smaller the tax liabilities. But

---

*These figures are based on 1974 dollars. In 1976 dollars, the respective figures were $3,920 and $7,840.

deductions come in four different forms: the personal exemption, which allows every taxpayer to deduct $750 from his income for each dependent; itemized deductions for a host of special expenses (home mortgage payments, interest charges); partial or total exemptions for certain kinds of income (income from municipal bonds or from the sale of property); and standard deductions for those who choose not to take itemized deductions (typically because the standard exceeds what the itemized deductions would be).

The ISP would generate its benefits by changing the last of these types of deductions. In particular, the standard deduction would be raised so that the combination of the standard deduction plus the existing personal exemption would define a break-even point for each family type. (See Table 4.5.) Any family with income below that break-even level would then be entitled to a tax credit (paid out in weekly or monthly installments) that would equal one-half of the difference between the family's earnings and this break-even level. Thus, as shown in Table 4.5, the standard deduction for a family of four would be raised so that the combination of the standard deduction and personal exemptions would equal $7,200. If such a family had no income, it would receive a benefit of $3,600. If it had earnings of $2,000, it would receive a tax refund of $2,600 (½ × [$7,200 - $2,000]), giving it a total income for the year of $4,600 ($2,000 in earnings + $2,600 in tax credits).

By tying income assistance benefits to the size of the standard deduction, ISP would integrate the public assistance and tax systems without necessitating complete tax reform. This would be possible because the standard deduction is used mostly by lower-income taxpayers, whereas middle-income taxpayers typically itemize their deductions. Although a higher standard deduction might allow some nonpoor families to reduce their tax bill by taking advantage of this higher standard deduction, efforts were made to limit the extent to which this would occur by including provisions to scale down the size of the standard deduction as income increased beyond the break-even point. Thus a family with $9,000 in income would have a smaller standard deduction available than one with $4,000 income. In this way, the amount of general tax relief embodied in the proposal would be limited, and the overall net cost of the program reduced. According to the estimates prepared in 1974, ISP would provide $4.1 billion in tax relief in addition to a $3.4 billion increase in the federal cost of the three programs that would be replaced—AFDC, SSI, and food stamps. When account is taken of the 1975 and 1976 tax changes, and the overall benefit level is adjusted for inflation, the estimated overall cost of the program in fiscal year 1978 rises slightly—to $7.8 billion—but the amount of additional tax relief declines to $2.9 billion.[72]

One feature of the ISP proposal promised to undermine its efforts to limit the tax relief delivered to upper-income groups, however: the provision of automatic cost-of-living increases in the benefit schedule. Given the structure of the ISP proposal, such increases could be achieved only by increasing the size of the personal exemption or the standard deduction in the tax code. But such increases mean more to higher-income taxpayers than to lower-income ones, since an additional dollar in personal exemptions is worth 20 cents in tax savings to a family in the 20 percent tax bracket, and 50 cents to someone in the 50 percent bracket. Therefore, although the proposal to link benefit levels to tax exemptions and deductions was justified as a way to control costs,[73] the inclusion of an automatic cost-of-living escalator for benefit levels makes it produce just the opposite result, since ISP would increase standard deductions and personal exemptions for all taxpayers in order to guarantee cost-of-living increases in the benefits available to the poor. The real gainers would consequently be the upper-income groups. According to one estimate, ISP would add $22.6 billion to the cost of current income assistance programs by fiscal year 1982, of which $16 billion, or 71 percent, would take the form of tax relief. Of this $16 billion, $12 billion, or 75 percent, would go to families with income in excess of $20,000, and only $1 billion, or 6 percent, to families with incomes under $10,000.[74]

Thanks to its tight integration with the tax structure and its extension of coverage to the working poor, ISP did promise to streamline the public assistance system significantly and to reduce its longstanding inequities. Given the cost constraints within which this had to be done, however, it was necessary to scrimp a bit on the level of support provided to the poor, and on the extent of state and local fiscal relief. The ISP basic benefit level, for example, though 50 percent higher than the proposed FAP income guarantee, was still 30-35 percent below the poverty level for a family of four with no outside income. In addition, though incorporating a liberal 50 percent benefit-reduction rate, the ISP made no provision for exempting work-related expenses in calculating benefits. Both of these provisions would have meant lower benefits for many current recipients. In fact, 34 states would have had to supplement ISP benefits to bring them up to existing levels. Fiscal relief for the states and localities thus seems to have ranked far behind efficiency and equity as goals for the designers of ISP. And even then, the extensive reliance on state supplements under ISP would have limited the progress made in relieving existing inequities by preserving some of the state-by-state variations in benefit levels.

Although pure-tax proposals of this sort achieve a high degree of uniformity and simplicity by making public assistance part of the regular tax system, they pay for this uniformity and simplicity in terms of somewhat lower benefits and the partial leakage of these benefits to the nonpoor in the form of tax relief. As we have seen, 55-70 percent of the costs associated with ISP represented tax relief of this sort.

Pure-Grant Variants

While some advocates of welfare reform find this linking of welfare reform to tax relief for the middle class politically appealing, another view holds that the resulting leakage of benefits is too costly. To reduce it, a second type of consolidated cash assistance proposal, utilizing outright grants rather than tax credits, has been advanced. Like the pure-tax proposals discussed above, the pure-grant proposals would eliminate the categorical divisions of the existing programs in favor of a unified program extending income assistance to all those in need, with provision for financial work incentives and a resulting break-even point. Unlike the pure-tax proposals, however, no attempt is made under the pure-grant proposals to provide the benefits through the tax system. Rather, a separate payment mechanism is utilized, as in the existing programs, but without the present categorization of recipients.

The most familiar form of this approach was the Nixon administration's proposed FAP, while the proposal published by the National Governors' Conference in February 1977 provides a modified version of the same approach.

Family Assistance Plan. The least costly and least generous of the recent pure-grant consolidated assistance proposals was FAP. As noted in Chapter 3, FAP represented a breakthrough in thinking about income assistance by proposing to extend the benefits of assistance to the working poor for the first time, albeit only to those in families with children. Under the plan, a basic federal minimum payment amounting to $1,600 for a family of four with no other income was to have been made available. This was later enlarged to $2,400 when the food stamp program was folded into the benefit package. As an incentive to work, recipients would have been permitted to keep the first $720 in earnings with no reduction in benefits, and 50 percent of everything earned in excess of that amount, yielding a break-even point of $3,920 for a family of four. The estimated cost of this proposal was $4 billion, almost all of which would have gone to the newly enrolled working poor. Because of its low benefit level, the plan offered far less to state and local governments or to existing recipients. Indeed, had it not been for a special provision promising every state a 10 percent saving on existing welfare costs, the proposal might actually have increased state and local costs since the FAP benefit would have been below what the federal government was paying per recipient in many of the high-benefit states; yet the proposal stipulated that no recipient be left worse off as a consequence of the reform. Only in a handful of states did FAP promise an increase in benefits for those already on AFDC. In short, the major goal of the proposal was what we earlier termed work equity, equal treatment of the employed and the unemployed poor. The proposal was less vigorous in its pursuit of support equity and program efficiency. Even farther down the list of priorities of FAP planners were adequacy and state and local fiscal relief. Therefore, although FAP pointed the way toward easing some of the more egregious problems with the existing system, it was constrained by cost pressures from solving any of them, leaving all sides much to complain about.

National Governors' Conference Plan. In early 1977, a task force of the National Governors' Conference proposed a somewhat more generous version of FAP that would deliver substantially greater savings to state coffers.[75] Under this plan, the federal government would offer $200 per month in benefits, exclusive of food stamps, to all families with children in need, and then make federal aid available, at state option, to finance 90 percent of the costs of an additional $100 per month in benefits, and 50 percent of the costs of yet another $100 per month in benefits. Depending on state reactions, the proposal would thus provide from $2,400 to $4,800 in cash benefits to all needy families. Food stamp benefits under a modified version of the federal food stamp program could then be added to these cash benefits, boosting the minimum benefit level for a family of four to $3,900 (68 percent of the poverty level) and the maximum to $5,600 (just under the 1977 poverty line).

In order to minimize administrative complexity, the Governors' Conference proposal endorsed a flat work-expense deduction of $100 per month, exclusive of child-care costs. To keep costs down, it proposed a benefit-reduction rate of 70 percent, higher than the 50 percent rate proposed in ISP and several other proposals. In addition, the proposal included a work test requiring employable recipients to work or to participate in a work stimulation and training program developed and administered by the states.

Compared with the other consolidated cash proposals, the Governors' Conference task force proposal would be somewhat more cumbersome administratively, since it would retain food stamps and SSI and maintain a sizable state administrative role. By setting the basic federal minimum rather low and providing federal aid to states that choose to increase benefit levels above this minimum, the proposal retains the possibility of considerable benefit variation from place to place. Indeed, the designers of the proposal explicitly rejected the idea of a higher basic benefit that would vary only with regional cost-of-living differences, on grounds that this might be difficult to operate and might interfere with local labor markets. Yet, the Governors' Conference proposal would eliminate many of the coverage inequities of the existing system and achieve a high level of state fiscal relief per dollar of federal expenditure. Altogether, the proposal would add an estimated $10 billion to the federal welfare bill, of which $4 billion to $5 billion would go to states and local governments as fiscal relief.

Combination Tax and Grant Variants

Midway between the pure-tax consolidated cash proposals and the pure-grant consolidated cash proposals are proposals that combine elements of taxes and grants. The most prominent of these variants is the Griffiths plan, named after Congresswoman Griffiths, whose Subcommittee on Fiscal Policy (of the Joint Economic Committee) formulated it following a three-year study of welfare policy in 1972–74. Under this proposal, two interrelated sets of benefit mechanisms would be created, one linked to the tax system and one consisting of outright grants.

The tax-linked portion of the benefit would involve a refundable tax credit of $225 per person that would replace the existing personal exemption of $750 per person now in the tax laws. Where previously a taxpayer would deduct $750 per household member from his income before computing the amount of taxes he owed, each taxpayer under the Griffiths plan would subtract $225 per household member directly from the amount of taxes owed, and would receive a refund if the credit exceeded the tax bill. Thus a family of four with no taxable income would be entitled to $900 in tax credit refunds. A family owing $500 in taxes would receive a refund of $400. Even those owing taxes in excess of $900 would be aided by the shift from personal exemptions to tax credits since a tax credit of $225 is worth more in terms of tax relief than an exemption of $750 for anyone in a tax bracket with less than a 30 percent tax rate (.30 × $750 = $225). This means that anyone with income as high as $25,000 would receive some benefit from the replacement of the exemption with a tax credit. By the same token, however, this proposal would increase tax liabilities for those with higher incomes, since these taxpayers gain more than $225 in tax reductions from the existing $750 personal exemption. Also included in the tax portion of the proposal was the replacement of existing deductions for household and child-care expenses with a standard employment-expense deduction related to family type rather than to actual expenses.

Since $225 per year is hardly enough to live on, the Griffiths proposal would add to this tax credit a second benefit mechanism: a system of grants to all poor persons except the aged, blind, and disabled, who would continue to be served by SSI. The amount of this Allowance for Basic Living Expenses (ABLE) would vary with family characteristics, as noted in Table 4.6. Thus a penniless family of four composed of two parents and two children in 1974 would have had an ABLE grant of $2,700 ($2,050 + $325 + $325) to add to their tax credits of $900, for a total gross income of $3,600. In an updated version of this plan, adjusted to take account of inflation and the new $35 tax credit placed in the tax code in 1975, the same family would have had in 1976 an ABLE grant of

TABLE 4.6

ABLE Grants under Griffiths Plan, 1974
(assumes no outside income)

Member of Filing Unit	Annual Allowances
Married couple filing jointly	$2,050
Head-of-household filer (as defined by IRS)	1,225
Single filer	825
Dependent aged 18 or over	825
First and second child in filing unit (each)	325
Third, fourth, fifth, and sixth dependent child (each)	225
Seventh and successive dependent children	0

Source: U.S. Congress, Joint Economic Committee, Subcommittee on Fiscal Policy, *Income Security for Americans: Recommendations of the Public Welfare Study*, 93d Cong., 2d sess. (Washington, D.C.: Government Printing Office, 1974), p. 156.

TABLE 4.7

Benefit-Reduction Rates in Griffiths Proposal

Benefit-Reduction Rate	Type of Income to Which Rate Applies
50 percent	Earned income (wages, salaries, commissions, tips, net income from self-employment) less social security taxes and special-earnings deductions for single parents and married couples in which both spouses work. These deductions would reduce the ABLE income-offset rate (benefit-loss rate) for most earners to 47 percent or lower.
80 percent	Public housing subsidies.
100 percent	Veterans' pensions, farm subsidy payments, refunds from federal income tax overwithholding.
67 percent	All income not otherwise classified (such as property income, public- or private-employee retirement benefits, child support, alimony, annuities).

Source: U.S. Congress, Joint Economic Committee, Subcommittee on Fiscal Policy, *Income Security for Americans: Recommendations of the Public Welfare Study*, 93d Cong., 2d sess. (Washington, D.C.: Government Printing Office, 1974), p. 158.

$3,400 ($2,650 + $375 + $375) and tax credits of $1,040 (4 × $260), for a total income of $4,440.

As with other negative income tax schemes, the Griffiths plan includes a benefit reduction mechanism to govern the loss of benefits as earnings rise. Unlike some proposals, however, this one would utilize several different benefit-reduction formulas for different types of income, as reflected in Table 4.7. To show how the benefit-reduction mechanism would work in conjunction with the tax credit and ABLE grants of the Griffiths proposal and existing tax provisions, Table 4.8 records the income levels that would result for female-headed families of four with different income levels, using the benefit levels of the original proposal. These figures would have to be adjusted to take account of inflation and tax code changes since 1974.

Unlike FAP, ISP, and H.R. 1, the Griffiths plan would impose no formal work or training requirement on recipients. It would rely wholly on the benefit-reduction rate incentives to encourage work. One reason for this was the desire to avoid the cumbersome administrative apparatus such work requirements always introduce. This same concern for administrative simplicity also finds reflection in the plan's proposal to vest full administrative responsibility for both the tax credit and ABLE grants in the Internal Revenue Service. But the proposal stipulates a monthly accounting period that would complicate IRS's job.

TABLE 4.8

Benefit Schedule under Griffiths Plan for a Mother and Three Children, 1974

Annual Earnings	Federal Income Tax Liability[a]	Tax Credits	Net Federal Income Tax Liability[c]	Social Security Tax	ABLE Grant	Net Cash Income[d]
$0	$ 0	$900	$+900	$ 0	$2,100	$3,000
500	0	900	+900	29	1,914	3,285
1,000	0	900	+900	58	1,729	3,571
1,500	0	900	+900	88	1,644	3,956
2,000	0	900	+900	117	1,358	4,141
2,500	0	900	+900	146	1,173	4,427
3,000	0	900	+900	176	988	4,712
4,000	0	900	+900	234	617	5,283
5,000	0	900	+900	292	246	5,854
6,000	124b	900	+776	351	0	6,425
7,000	495b	900	+405	410	0	6,995
8,000	907	900	7	468	0	7,525
9,000	1,073	900	173	526	0	8,301
10,000	1,260	900	360	585	0	9,055
15,000	2,315	900	1,415	772	0	12,813
20,000	3,695	900	2,795	772	0	16,433
25,000	5,325	900	4,425	772	0	19,803

aBased on the standard deduction but with no low-income allowance. Personal exemptions are replaced by $225 per-person tax credits.

bTax is a reduced amount from regular schedule because of provision for smooth transition from ABLE recipient to nonrecipient status.

cNumbers with plus sign indicate net payments to, rather than from, taxpayers because of tax credits.

dAssuming no state supplementation. Social security taxes, using the current tax rate and taxable wage base, are deductible from earnings in computing ABLE grants.

Source: U.S. Congress, Joint Economic Committee, Subcommittee on Fiscal Policy, *Income Security for Americans: Recommendations of the Public Welfare Study,* 93d Cong., 2d sess. (Washington, D.C.: Government Printing Office, 1974), p. 172.

TABLE 4.9

Distribution of Tax Benefits Under ABLE, Fiscal Year 1978

Pretax, Pretransfer Income	Net Tax Relief (+) or Burden (−)	Percent of Total Tax Relief
Less than $5,000	$5.3 billion	41.4
$5,000–$10,000	3.0	23.4
$10,000–$25,000	4.5	35.2
More than $25,000	−2.9	—
Net	9.9	—

Source: Data compiled by the author, from Congressional Budget Office estimates.

At the time it was formulated, the Subcommittee on Fiscal Policy estimated the net cost of the package, including the cost associated with the tax savings for middle-income taxpayers, to be in the neighborhood of $15.4 billion.[76] A revised estimate completed by the Congressional Budget Office put these net costs at $9.1 billion for fiscal year 1978, when account was taken of the recent changes in the tax laws.[77] This $9.1 billion would be made up of an $0.8 billion reduction in the federal costs associated with the grant programs which ABLE would replace, and a $9.9 billion increase in costs resulting from the tax credit. However, not all of the $9.9 billion in tax relief would flow to the poor. As shown in Table 4.9, the poor would receive only 41 percent of the $12.8 billion in gross tax benefits generated by the proposal. This would make the Griffiths proposal more target efficient than ISP, but it would still mean a significant leakage of benefits.

Compared with ISP, however, more of the tax savings under the Griffiths plan accrues to middle- and lower-middle-income families, precisely the families that shoulder most of the burden of escalating state and local taxes. Therefore, although the Griffiths plan provides less than $1 billion in fiscal relief to state and local governments, it provides in its tax relief features much of what reduction in state and local welfare burdens is supposed to accomplish: reduced financial pressures on middle- and low-middle-income families.

Evaluation

In terms of the criteria identified earlier, consolidated cash assistance proposals generally score high in terms of administrative efficiency, support equity, and work equity; but low in terms of target efficiency and adequacy. On the positive side, by eliminating the categorical distinctions that deny aid to many of the needy, and establishing a single, integrated program structure, such proposals promise to reduce both the administrative costs and the inequitable disparities in the treatment of different types of families under current arrangements. In the case of the tax-linked proposals, moreover, some of the stigma associated with the receipt of welfare is reduced as well, by providing aid directly through the tax system.

On the negative side, however, are some significant drawbacks. In the first place, in order to preserve financial work incentives, such proposals must include marginal tax rates and other devices that raise the break-even level in the benefit structure and thus extend the coverage and increase the costs of the income assistance system. The result is what we earlier termed the work incentive trap. To keep the cost of the program within acceptable limits, basic benefit levels must be kept down if work incentives are to be preserved. But this works a hardship on those not expected to work, since they must subsist on the lower basic benefit even though the work incentive features have little relevance to them. The upshot is to trade off benefit adequacy for the unemployables in order to promote work incentives for the employables. Those who are unable, or not expected, to work are thus penalized by being thrown into the same pot with those able to work.

Even for employables, however, consolidated cash proposals have problems because they tend to assume continuous full employment. They assume, in other words, that everyone has a choice between work and leisure, so that employable recipients can be put to work merely by changing the benefit-reduction rates to make such work financially less costly in terms of benefit losses. Given prevailing unemployment rates and the evidence of structural employment problems, however, this is a dubious assumption.

Finally, in their effort to eliminate the notches and resulting support inequities in the current system, the consolidated cash assistance proposals run a heavy risk of reducing benefits for some current recipients, especially those in the states with the highest benefits. This, in turn, can generate strong political pressures to protect current recipients by stipulating that no one should lose benefits as a result of the reform. Not only can this limit the amount of fiscal relief provided to the states, but also, as the SSI case demonstrates, it can open a pandora's box of administrative problems by requiring program officials to calculate benefits under two separate sets of rules, at least one of which varies from state to state. In the process, many of the projected administrative gains that have been the major rationale for the consolidated proposals in the first place can be lost.

Route Two: Work and Welfare Proposals

A second set of reform proposals avoids some of these problems with the consolidated cash assistance proposals while still retaining the advantages of comprehensiveness. Known variously as the triple-track or cash/jobs approach, this set of proposals would substantially consolidate the existing categorical programs and expand the coverage of the income assistance system. Rather than establish a single, all-embracing program, however, the cash/jobs proposals would group recipients into two basic categories—those expected to work and those not expected to work—and then further subdivide the former group into those with jobs and those without jobs.

Basic to this approach is the conviction that the problems of the poor arise from such different causes that no one sweeping program can be effective in meeting them. Indeed, advocates of this approach argue that most of the difficulties poor people encounter are not caused by the welfare system at all, and therefore cannot be resolved or prevented by it. This means that ultimately there must be substantial changes in a number of other important systems such as employment, health, and education. Grouping recipients is a means to this end, for it permits the tailoring of these other changes to the different needs of different categories of the poor. In particular, most proposals of this type feature three specially targeted sets of benefits: earnings supplements for the working poor, jobs and/or training for those expected to work but unemployed, and cash assistance for those not expected to work (for example, the aged, the disabled, and those families with young children and a single parent).

However, although almost all cash/jobs proposals involve these three basic types of assistance, they differ in the way these types of assistance are provided. Most importantly, these proposals differ in terms of whether they guarantee a job to those expected to work. In these terms, two basic types of jobs/cash assistance proposals can be distinguished: those providing employment assistance but no job guarantees, and those that add a guaranteed job, typically by making the government the employer of the last resort.

Nonguaranteed-Job Variants

The first set of work and welfare proposals focuses on the provision of cash assistance to those not expected to work, and of training, rehabilitation, and caseworkers—but not guaranteed jobs—to aid those expected to work. This approach resembles H.R. 1—the House Ways and Means Committee's substitute for the FAP—which would have channeled payments to families with an employable member through an Opportunities for Families (OFF) program under the Labor Department, rather than through the regular welfare channels. The same idea was embodied in Congressman Al Ullman's REACH proposal and in the recent welfare reform position paper of the National Association of Counties. Two more detailed versions of this approach that deserve attention here are the "mega-proposal" prepared by HEW under Secretary Richardson in the early 1970s; and what has come to be known as the triple-track, or unemployment insurance, approach.

The Mega-Proposal. The mega-proposal, which emerged from planning the reorganization of the Department of Health, Education, and Welfare in 1971–72, exemplifies a number of the early, nonguaranteed-job work and welfare proposals.[78] Central to this plan was a sharp division between families that contain a member available for employment and those that do not. For the latter, the mega-proposal would provide a basic federal grant, modeled after the provisions of FAP and H.R. 1, and set at $2,700 for a family of four, or 65 percent of the poverty level ($900 each for up to two adults, plus $450 for each child).* States would be permitted but not required to supplement this basic benefit. To avoid work disincentives, a 50 percent benefit-reduction rate would be applied against earned income but a 100 percent rate against all other income. Finally, recipients in the not available for work group could take part in employment-related programs if they chose.

For families with a member deemed available for employment, a different apparatus would apply. Such families would be eligible for the basic federal cash assistance grant with one crucial exception: no benefit would be paid for the available member. Thus, in the case of a four-person, two-adult family with one adult available to work, the basic benefit provided would be $1,800 ($900 + $450 + $450) instead of the $2,700 that would be paid were that adult not available for work. To compensate for this and provide an incentive to induce that available adult to work, the first $1,800 of his or her earnings would be disregarded before the 50 percent benefit-reduction rate would apply. This means that the break-even point would be $5,400 [$1,800 + ($1,800/.50)]. Finally, to aid those availables who are unable to find work, a four-pronged approach would be used: a new or upgraded job-search, job-development, and job-training program; a system of tax credits for employers who hire persons enrolled in the assistance program; subsidies for employers who upgrade the skills of eligible workers, so long as the upgrading is really evident in higher earnings and productivity; and, if all else fails, federally subsidized public-sector jobs paying wages set at three-fourths the minimum wage. To avoid undue reliance on public jobs, however, the proposal stipulated that the special disregard of the first $1,800 in earnings would be provided only for those whose earnings come from private jobs.

Assuming that all heads of single-parent families with children requiring day care are classified as unavailable for work, the gross cost of this scheme was estimated to be $12.3 billion in fiscal year 1976, only $0.4 billion more than under existing law and $0.8 billion less than what H.R. 1 would have cost. States would be protected against the cost of increases in the overall caseload under the new program, but no federal financial aid would be provided to states to fund supplementary payments to current recipients who get more under current law than they would under the new program. Hence state and local fiscal relief would be minimal, at least in the short run, until the employment provisions could begin to reduce caseloads. In fact, the low benefit levels in this

---

*In 1976 dollars, this figure would be $3,600.

proposal made it likely that numerous recipients would end up losing benefits that they had under the previous programs unless state supplementation were provided. The proposal even limited the payoffs for recipients in the states with currently low benefits by offering such states the option to specify a minimum federal assistance payment of $2,200 instead of $2,700. The mega-proposal thus represents a kind of mix between the consolidated cash assistance proposals (which tie unemployables to a benefit schedule really designed for employables) and true two-track proposals (which design different benefit packages for these two groups).

Triple-Track Proposal. A far more complete version of the nonguaranteed-job variant of the jobs/cash approach is a proposal developed by a cadre of social welfare activists with support from the labor movement, and known popularly as the triple-track proposal, because it would provide three distinct bundles of benefits for the three identifiable groups of the poor—those who are employed at low-paying jobs, those who are expected to work but are unemployed, and those who are not expected to work.[79]

For the first of these, the working poor, the triple-track plan would provide income supplementation through an improved version of the earned income tax credit (EITC), and, as necessary, through the food stamp program. The EITC, which was added to the tax code in 1975, basically provides families earning less than $8,000 a refundable tax credit computed as 10 percent of gross earnings up to $4,000, declining thereafter at a steady rate until it reaches zero at earnings of $8,000. As presently designed, the EITC thus constitutes a work bonus of as much as $400 per family. Under the triple-track proposal, this earned income tax credit would be enlarged in two ways: by adjusting it for family size, and by extending the phaseout point beyond $8,000. For example, the basic credit of 10 percent of gross income on earnings up to $4,000 could be made available for each family member, so that a family of four with earnings of $4,000 would be entitled to a refundable tax credit of $1,600 (10 percent × $4,000 × 4). This credit could then be designed to decline more slowly than at present, so that it would not disappear until family income exceeded $10,000 or $12,000.

So designed, the expanded EITC, especially when combined with food stamps, would thus provide important income supplementation to the working poor without undermining the financial incentive to work and earn.

For those needy families headed by an employable person who does not have a job, the triple-track proposal would provide two different forms of assistance: improved and restructured employment and training assistance, and a special form of temporary cash payment channeled through the unemployment insurance system and intended to provide transitional aid until the employment assistance can have its effect. This use of the unemployment benefit system is a novel feature of the triple-track plan. It is intended to make clear that the welfare burden represented by this segment of the population is really an employment and labor market problem, not a public assistance problem. In addition, it reduces the stigma attached to the receipt of benefits.

Under this proposal, two changes would be made in the existing unemployment insurance system: coverage would be extended to include new entrants and reentrants to the labor market, who are now barred from receipt of unemployment insurance; and a minimum federal payment standard would be set for the first time. The new entrants and reentrants, plus all those who have exhausted their unemployment insurance benefits, would be eligible for a needs-tested special unemployment assistance benefit (SUAB) financed out of general revenues. Only one SUAB stipend could be paid per household, but the eligibility limit would be set at 125 percent of the poverty line. The SUAB stipend would either be a flat amount equal to what unemployment insurance pays for an unemployed person formerly earning the minimum wage, or a variable amount similar to a pure-grant negative income tax, with a basic benefit level of two-thirds the poverty level, and a benefit-reduction rate of 45 percent. SUAB recipients would also be eligible for food stamps, which would lift their incomes closer to the poverty line.

To complement this cash assistance, those expected to work but who are unemployed would have to enroll in upgraded work-training and job-placement activities operated by the existing CETA and state employment service agencies. These activities would be thoroughly restructured and revitalized, and buttressed by more effective and creative use of public service employment.

With those families with an employable head taken care of in the two employment-related tracks of the triple-track plan, the residual welfare program would then be able to concentrate on its legitimate and appropriate function of providing income support for those not expected to work, including the blind, the disabled, the aged, and single-parent families with preschool children, and others with incapacitating physical or mental disabilities. For this group, the program could provide at least a minimally adequate benefit in an efficient and equitable manner without worrying about the "work incentive trap." The basic benefit would begin at 75 percent of the poverty level with continued eligibility for food stamps, at least until such time as the basic benefit reaches the poverty level. Such relatively generous benefits would be possible under this program because, with employables excluded, there would be no need to include a costly fractional benefit reduction rate. Rather, benefits would be reduced dollar for dollar as earnings rise, although persons in the welfare track can volunteer for the manpower track.

What "triple track" would accomplish would be to avoid the trade-off between adequacy for unemployables and work incentives for employables. It would do so through the simple expedient of putting the two groups in separate program tracks. By providing assistance to employables in a different form from that used for those not expected to work, triple track retains work incentives without sacrificing the principle of work equity, the notion that those who work for a living should end up better off financially than those who do not.

Like other proposals, however, "triple track" is not without its drawbacks. For one thing, it requires a somewhat more complex administrative structure than that envisioned in the consolidated cash assistance approaches. Separate program elements must be created for the three different groups of the poor, creating possibilities for unforeseen notches and program interactions. Especially troublesome is the problem of coping with the changing characteristics of the poor. A household with an employable head who becomes sick might have to shift from track two to track three, necessitating reprocessing. Beyond this, there is a possibility that a share of the SUABs would flow to the nonneedy (for example, second wage earners in families already earning wages above the poverty level), thus increasing cost, even though supporters of the program have added an income limit, which would minimize this problem. Finally, the plan depends importantly on the ability of CETA and the state employment service to develop suitable training and jobs for millions of new assistance recipients participating in the manpower programs, something that past experience suggests will be quite difficult.

Guaranteed-Job Proposals

The second type of work/welfare proposal begins where the first type leaves off—with the failure of the private labor market to generate sufficient jobs. To compensate for this, the second set of jobs/cash proposals would transfer to government a larger share of responsibility for ensuring that at least one member of every family has an opportunity to work and earn a decent living. To the basic premise, of all work and welfare plans, that assistance for the able-bodied must take the form of jobs, this set of proposals adds the corollary that society's expectation that able-bodied assistance recipients should work must be matched by an obligation to make sure that jobs are available to them. Accordingly, this set of proposals would integrate into any expanded public assistance system some form of job guarantee, as well as training and job-placement activities. What form this job guarantee should take and how it should be integrated into the rest of the income assistance system differ among proposals. Three prominent variants of the guaranteed-job approach illustrate the options that are open.

Senate Finance Committee Proposal. The earliest formal acknowledgment of a governmental obligation to guarantee all employable citizens the opportunity to earn an income from working came in the Senate Finance Committee's version of the FAP in 1972.[80] Under this proposal any family headed by an able-bodied father or by a mother with no child under age six would be disqualified from welfare assistance, unless the family is too remote from an employment program or the mother is ill or in school. Such families would not be denied assistance altogether, however. Rather, they would be entitled to one or a combination of three forms of work-linked benefits: the earned income tax credit if the family head is employed and earning less than $8,000; a wage subsidy if the head is employed and earning less than the minimum wage; and a public job if the head is unemployed and unable to find private employment.

TABLE 4.10

Benefits under Senate Finance Committee Bill
(assuming minimum wage of $3 per hour)

Source of Income	Employer		
	Government, at Three-Fourths the Minimum Wage (32 hours)	Private, at Three-Fourths the Minimum Wage (40 hours)	Private, at the Minimum Wage (40 hours)
Wages			
Private employer	–	$ 90.00	$ 120.00
Government	$ 72.00	22.50	–
Special 10 percent work bonus	–	9.00	12.00
Weekly income	72.00	121.50	132.00
Annual income	$3,600.00	$6,075.00	$6,600.00

Source: U. S. Congress, Senate, Finance Committee, *Social Security Amendments of 1972*, Report No. 92-1230, 92d Cong., 2d sess., 1972, p. 415; adjusted to reflect the increase in the minimum wage from the $2 per hour used in the original version to an anticipated level of $3 per hour.

Although the guaranteed public job was perhaps the most innovative feature of this proposal, it was clearly not the preferred type of employment for the poor. To the contrary, the benefit structure was designed to encourage assistance recipients to seek private employment, even at rates below the minimum wage. Thus, the rate of pay on public jobs was set at only three-fourths of the minimum wage, and only 32 hours of work per week were guaranteed. With the minimum hourly wage expected to go to $3 in fiscal year 1978, this would mean a public job worth $72.00 per week, or $3,600 per year—barely 65 percent of the poverty level. In addition, those working on public jobs would not be entitled to the wage subsidy or the earned income tax credit. These benefits were reserved for those in the private labor force. A worker on a job paying at least three-fourths of the minimum wage could thus bring home, in addition to his actual wages, a wage subsidy equal to three-fourths of the difference between his actual wage and the minimum wage; and a tax credit equal to 10 percent of his income up to $4,000, declining to zero at $8,000. Assuming the same $3 per hour minimum wage, such a family would thus have an annual income of $6,075, as shown in Table 4.10. Moving from a public job to a private one at the same, below-the-minimum wage rate would thus have added $2,475, or almost 70 percent, to a poor family's income under the Senate Finance Committee proposal. If the wage earner managed to secure a job at the minimum wage, the combination of wages plus the earned income tax credit would boost his income to $6,600.

To supervise the public jobs program and help the poor train for and find private jobs, the Senate Finance Committee proposed to create a Work Administration that would be separate from the welfare system. This new administration would be responsible for contracting with state and local governments, or with other federal agencies, to employ the participants in the public jobs program. Under the terms of the bill, all families with children were entitled to guaranteed jobs. However, special provisions were included to provide work incentives for those that the bill would disqualify from AFDC. For one thing, the Work Administration was authorized to pay child-care expenses for former AFDC mothers, as well as a portion of transpor.ation expenses in extraordinary cases. More important, states with high AFDC benefits would be required to supplement the incomes of AFDC-eligible participants in the work program by an amount that would bring them up to the benefit level of those who are only on AFDC. For example, if the guaranteed-job program paid a participating family of four, still eligible for AFDC, $300 per month, while AFDC paid a comparable family with a child under six $350 per month, the state would be required to pay $50 per month to the family in the guaranteed-job program. To avoid any adverse state impact on work incentives, the state would be required to disregard any earnings between $300 per month (the amount earned in the guaranteed job) and $550 per month (the amount that could be earned working 40 hours per week at the minimum wage of $3 per hour) in computing the supplement to which a family formerly eligible for AFDC but now enrolled in the work program was entitled. In addition, the committee bill contained a complex series of provisions for cashing out the food stamp program without creating inequities between those on AFDC and those in the new work program. The federal government would pay states the full cost of adjusting AFDC benefit schedules to compensate recipients for the loss of food stamps, and this would extend to the sums going in the form of state supplements to AFDC-eligible participants in the work program. To preserve equity between female-headed (and therefore AFDC-eligible) families in the work program and male-headed families, moreover, the Work Administration would guarantee to the latter a comparable cash replacement for food stamps.

Accompanying its creation of a new series of job guarantees and work-linked benefits, the Senate Finance Committee bill also proposed several changes in the residual AFDC program that would remain available for families without an employable head (for example, female-headed families with a child under six), or families headed by an incpacitated father where the mother either was not in the home or was caring for the father. The federal funding mechanism would be changed so that the federal government would provide the states with a block grant to cover AFDC costs, rather than paying a percentage of state-determined welfare costs. This block grant would equal the lower of two figures—one and one-half times the previous year's AFDC costs or the amount needed to lift benefit levels in a state to $1,600 for a family of two, $2,000 for a family of three, and $2,400 for a family of four or more. Since this formula favored low-benefit states, all states were guaranteed a block grant that would be at least 110 percent of the federal share of AFDC costs in the year before the new program went into effect. The amount of the federal block grant for AFDC was expected to decline as the Work Administration picked up about 40 percent of the former AFDC recipients, as well as millions of newly covered, needy, two-parent families. In this way, a lid would be placed on federal spending for AFDC.

In addition to this funding change, the committee bill also tightened the application requirements for AFDC, required AFDC recipients to sign over child-support payments to state welfare officials, and required state welfare officials to pursue absent fathers more diligently. While guaranteeing low-benefit states enough federal funding to increase benefit levels to $2,400 for a family of four, the committee bill stopped short of requiring the states to draw on this money and provide these benefits. Rather, it strengthened state prerogatives in setting AFDC eligibility criteria.

The Senate Finance Committee bill was thus a mixture of severity and liberality. The bill placed a tight cap on AFDC growth, denying AFDC benefits to numerous current recipients and making benefit increases in high-benefit states improbable. At the same time, the bill protected still-eligible current recipients against any decline in benefits and made federal funds available to raise benefit levels in the low-benefit states. The bill would have instituted an imaginative jobs program that would have made the federal government the employer of last resort for all families with children, including those that would have been excluded from AFDC, though the benefits available from this publicly provided job would have been modest. Formulated prior to the 1970s surge in unemployment, the committee's bill reflected the optimistic assumption that almost all those in need could soon be accommodated in the private labor market. Hence, keeping wage levels in public employment low made sense as part of the impressive incentive mechanism included in the bill to induce those holding public jobs to shift to private employment. Yet, the committee bill did require supplementation of these public employment wages in high-benefit AFDC states, at least for those participants in the work program who would otherwise have been eligible for AFDC. Still, the benefits available to those in the guaranteed-job program would not have been adequate for them to escape poverty, and serious state-by-state inequities would have remained. In addition, the proposed program would have been administratively cumbersome and might have triggered unexpected labor market impacts, if employers used the guaranteed-job program participants to reduce other labor needs.

Whatever its shortcomings, the committee bill established an important principle about the government's obligation to provide every family head the opportunity to earn an income. The question it left hanging was whether the same principle could be combined with a more generous benefit and wage schedule and still be feasible.

Guaranteed Jobs with Cash Assistance. One proposal answering that question has been advanced recently by the policy planners in the Department of Labor and in HEW during the preparation of the Carter Administration welfare reform proposal.[81] A combination of the triple-track plan and a proposal first formulated by Arnold Packer,[82] who became assistant secretary of labor for planning, evaluation, and research in the Carter years, this new proposal espouses much of the basic philosophy of the Senate Finance Committee proposal, but with a more generous guaranteed job, a less generous wage subsidy, and a modified version of a pure-grant consolidated cash assistance program for residual AFDC and food stamp recipients.

The key to this proposal was the marriage of a cash assistance program to a job program guaranteeing a minimum-wage job for the principal adult wage earner in needy families with children, that is, every family in which the total income exclusive of the applicant's earnings, unemployment insurance, and food stamps fell below the poverty line. Eligibility for cash assistance—AFDC—would be ended for any family with at least one parent who was expected to work, that is, who was able-bodied; and with no children under six or other home-care responsibilities. Such families would henceforth have to work for their income, either in private jobs or in the newly created public jobs, where they could earn up to $7,200 per year.

Because the wage scale in the guaranteed-job program would thus exceed what prevails on many private jobs, a combination of food stamps and an expanded version of the earned income tax credit would be included to aid the working poor and thus reduce the impact of the guaranteed-job program on the private labor market. The expanded EITC would basically follow the pattern of the triple-track plan: a refundable credit computed as a percentage of gross earnings per family member up to a certain level, declining gradually to zero. If the credit were 10 percent per person on income up to $4,500, a family of four with earnings of $4,000 would be entitled to credits of $1,600 (4 × 10% × $4,000), bringing its total income to $5,600. The EITC would apply only to income from private employment, not to income from a guaranteed job.

For those families with no parent expected to work, the guaranteed-jobs/cash assistance proposal would replace AFDC and food stamps with a federal cash payment set at 70 percent of the poverty line. The states could then supplement this benefit to the extent they wished, and the federal government would subsidize state supplements, according to a complex formula, up to a certain maximum.

Compared to the Senate Finance Committee proposal, the guaranteed-jobs/cash assistance proposal would achieve a higher degree of adequacy and a greater degree of support equity across the states. By raising the wages on the guaranteed public jobs to the minimum wage level or higher, the proposal would eliminate the need for the elaborate procedures included in the Senate Finance Committee bill for state supplementation of former AFDC eligibles who have guaranteed jobs, and for payment of day-care expenses. These matters would be taken care of simply by offering a more adequate guaranteed-job wage in the first place.

In providing a more adequate wage on the guaranteed jobs, however, the proposal runs a greater risk of putting upward pressures on private wage rates and thus disrupting the low-wage private labor market. Supporters of this approach argue, however, that "disturbing existing labor markets may not be all bad" since it may "force desirable changes throughout the job market for family heads who earn close to $6,000."[83] But such a strategy can backfire if employers respond not by upgrading existing jobs but by eliminating them and shifting to mechanization. Because the proposal includes an expanded EITC program for the working poor, these adverse labor market effects may be reduced somewhat, though it is still anyone's guess how much.

The guaranteed-jobs/cash assistance proposal could also create some troublesome benefit "notches" where additional earnings would be more than matched by loss of benefits. For example, eligibility for a guaranteed job is limited under this proposal to families whose income, exclusive of the guaranteed job and food stamps, falls below the poverty line. Thus, if another family member earns one dollar more than $5,500, the guaranteed-job program participant in the household would lose his job and the family would lose a source of income worth $7,200 a year. This would be a strong disincentive for other family members to increase their earnings. Yet, without some such cutoff, the extent of benefit leakage in the plan would be too great. Already, under the plan, families could retain guaranteed jobs even though they had combined family income in excess of $11,000.

Another problem arises from the restriction of job guarantees to families with children, which creates a kind of baby bonus and effectively delivers a $7,200 reward to needy childless couples or individuals upon the birth of their first child. Yet, without such a limitation, program costs would be much higher. Indeed, even with the limitation, one estimate places the net cost of the guaranteed-job/cash assistance proposal at $30 billion to $40 billion, if the guaranteed jobs pay $3.50 per hour. Of this total, $5 billion to $6 billion would go to the states as fiscal relief.[84]

In the face of these cost estimates, the Carter Administration ultimately backed off from this guaranteed-jobs/cash assistance proposal and introduced instead a modified version that retained the basic features of a two-track, work-and-welfare approach, but eliminated the formal job guarantee, reduced the wages proposed for public service jobs, and included a variety of cost-saving technical changes. In fact, the proposal that ultimately emerged as the Carter Administration's Program for Better Jobs and Income is modelled closely on the "triple-track" proposal outlined above, with the addition of a set of provisions to facilitate cross-overs between the work and welfare "tracks." (For details on the Carter proposal, see the Appendix paper in this volume.)

Evaluation

As a group, the work and welfare proposals have the advantage of being able to provide adequate benefits to unemployables without having to cut back on the financial incentives for work. In the process, they make it possible to reduce the leakage of benefits to the nonpoor. Both the triple-track and the guaranteed-jobs proposals dispense with fractional benefit-reduction rates, at least for families participating in the manpower programs, and rely instead on automatic disqualification mechanisms; the triple-track plan denies aid to anyone who refuses a job offer, and the guaranteed-jobs plan eliminates the job guarantee for families whose other income rises above the povery line. As a result, the benefit cutoff point in these proposals can be lower than in the consolidated cash proposals, targeting benefits more effectively and keeping costs under control. This creates, however, serious benefit "notches." In the case of the triple-track plan, and to a lesser extent guaranteed jobs, moreover, the employment benefits would be extended far enough up the income scale to offset this target efficiency partially.

Work and welfare approaches also make it easier to restrict benefits for employables to jobs and other work-linked assistance, and thus to reinforce the socially valued work ethic and the politically important principle of work equity. In the process, they promise to eliminate some of the stigma attached to the receipt of welfare and reduce the need for checking on the work activity of recipients.

Against these advantages, however, must be set a number of disadvantages. The use of separate program structures for employables and unemployables invariably raises difficult questions about how to divide the needy population between these two categories, and creates disincentives to work among those who are classified in the not-expected-to-work category. In addition, such categorization promises to cause administrative problems because of changes in family circumstances. A female family head who works but who has a child under six would thus have to shift from the employment track to the welfare track if she lost her job or had to quit it because of child-care responsibilities. Since such changes in personal circumstance are quite common, two-track or three-track proposals would require a certain amount of administrative reprocessing. A further problem arises from the mechanisms for implementing the work provisions. If jobs are not guaranteed, it is likely that the same frustrations that have long plagued the existing job-training and placement activities will affect the new system as well, and thus expose it to charges of welfare cheating, and of coddling of people who should be at work. Such charges might be particularly severe in the case of the triple-track proposal, because the coverage of the cash benefits would be so broad. If jobs are guaranteed, however, another set of problems arises because of the potential inflationary impact of decently paid public jobs and the possibility of resulting losses of low-skill private jobs. A guaranteed-jobs program paying decent wages also may attract into the labor force a host of new entrants—for example, women who formerly did not work—and thus end up dissipating its benefits on a recipient population that is far less needy. A guaranteed-jobs program thus requires some difficult decisions about who should be entitled to the jobs that are created, how many jobs there should be, and what they should pay. As we have seen, the Senate Finance Committee proposal and the guaranteed-jobs-with-cash-assistance proposal provide quite different answers to these questions, the former opting for a rather low benefit schedule in public jobs in order to cut costs and encourage private employment, and the latter making provision for more adequate public job benefits in view of existing job shortages in the private labor market and the professed importance of linking assistance benefits to work.

Not only do these proposals raise questions about the link between public jobs and private ones, they also raise equity issues between those on the welfare track and those on the work track. Welfare benefit schedules, for example, adjust benefits for family size. To do the same in the work programs would violate the principle of equal pay for equal work. The Senate Finance Committee proposal would get around this issue by providing for state supplements to former AFDC eligibles now in the work program, but this merely creates a new equity problem between the male-headed and the female-headed families in the guaranteed-job program and adds to the administrative complexity of the system.

None of these issues is insoluble. Yet each involves a number of difficult choices that will leave any proposal subject to criticism by some—which is true, of course, of all proposals in this field.

Route Three: Incremental Reform Approaches

A third set of reform proposals eschews the total revamping of existing programs suggested by the two previously described approaches, in favor of a more fine-tuned set of readjustments. Those who advocate such an incremental or categorical approach differ markedly, however, in the goals they believe such reforms should serve. In particular, three sets of incremental proposals can be distinguished, depending on whether the aim is the expansion of assistance coverage, the reduction of assistance coverage, or basic administrative simplification and modernization.

Categorical Expansion Proposals

The best known of the incremental reform strategies are those aimed at filling in certain critical gaps in the existing programs and thereby expanding coverage and reducing inequities. Advocates of this categorical expansion approach—most notably, Richard Nathan of the Brookings Institution—rest their case on five key arguments.[85] The first is that the growth in welfare programs over the past decade has significantly reduced the poverty problem in the nation, even though the available statistics disguise this fact because of their failure to acknowledge the impact of in-kind benefits. Under the circumstances, major new initiatives are not needed to cope with poverty. In the second place, the existence of multiple programs is perceived not as something to be deplored but as the natural consequence of a pluralistic society with many competing values. It is, moreover, a characteristic feature of the social welfare systems of the Western democracies. Thirdly, the categorical expansion approach is a way to avoid the work incentive trap that causes pressures for downward revisions in benefit levels in negative income tax schemes. This approach is thus justified as a way to preserve the more adequate existing benefit levels in the face of such pressures. A fourth argument advanced for this version of the incremental approach is that the existing system now operates far better than many people—still blinded by earlier images—acknowledge. The expansion of food stamps and the adoption of Medicaid in particular have filled in gaps that justified calls for reforms in the 1950s and 1960s. Finally, growing doubt about the oft-cited claims concerning the administrative efficiency of a consolidated cash approach provides additional support for the categorical expansion approach. The experience of SSI, at any rate, suggests the difficulties involved in administering any need-based program with a mobile and dynamic clientele, no matter how streamlined the assistance system.

Given these arguments and the political opposition to major income redistribution, advocates of the incremental strategy therefore favor the more modest—but possibly more effective—approach of pursuing needed changes through the existing structure. Five such changes are most commonly cited as ways to round out the current system and deal with the remaining inequities without sacrificing benefit adequacy.

AFDC Minimum Benefits. One categorical expansion proposal would establish a federally funded minimum payment for the AFDC program, thus fulfilling a goal that had been included in the original version of the social security legislation. This federal benefit floor would even out some of the variation in AFDC benefits from state to state and, depending on its level, provide a degree of fiscal relief to state and local governments. If this floor were set so that the combination of AFDC benefits and food stamps equaled the poverty level, the added federal cost of this innovation would be an estimated $12.2 billion in fiscal year 1978, of which $6.0 billion would represent savings to the states.[86] Less extreme versions of this proposal could achieve noticeable improvements in benefit levels for many AFDC recipients in low-benefit states at significantly less cost.

Although the establishment of an AFDC benefit floor would contribute significantly to the support equity of the assistance system, it would not alter the existing pattern of inequities between AFDC recipients and the working poor. To the contrary, by raising the benefits of AFDC recipients without extending the coverage of the system, this change might actually aggravate these inequities and intensify the family-splitting incentives of the AFDC program.

Extension of AFDC-Unemployed Parent Coverage. One way to minimize this latter problem would be to mandate the AFDC-unemployed parent program in all states, instead of leaving implementation of this program to state discretion. Under this program, families headed by two parents in which the primary breadwinner is unemployed or employed only part time are made eligible for AFDC benefits. Since the states most likely to be affected by the imposition of a moderate AFDC national benefit standard are precisely the states that now lack AFDC-U programs, making the AFDC-U program mandatory would ensure that employables would reap some benefits as well. The cost of such an AFDC-U extension would depend on the prevailing AFDC benefit levels. This step could be taken whether or not an AFDC minimum benefit level were established.

While the extension of AFDC-U coverage would improve the equity of the public assistance system, it would hardly solve the problem entirely. To the contrary, the provision of aid to additional families headed by unemployed males would only intensify the remaining inequities between these families and the working poor. In the process, it could create incentives for the working poor to cut down on their working hours to qualify for AFDC-U assistance.

Elimination of the Food Stamp Purchase Requirement. A third categorical reform proposal would eliminate the purchase requirement in the food stamp program, as proposed in the McGovern-Dole bill (S. 845), a bill that came close to passage in the Senate Agriculture Committee in 1976. Under current law, all food stamp participants except for the few with no income must purchase the food stamps they receive. The amount they pay is less than the amount of the stamps they receive, and the difference between these two figures represents the real value of the food stamp benefit, or the bonus value of the stamps. Thus, a four-person family with an income of $350 per month is required to pay $95 per month for food stamps worth $182. The bonus value of food stamps for this family is thus $86 per month—$182 minus $95. If the income of this family were smaller, it would have to pay less for its $182 allotment of food stamps, which would mean that the bonus value of the stamps would be larger.

Under the McGovern-Dole bill, this elaborate mechanism of cash payments for stamps would be replaced by a simplified system under which each family would simply receive the bonus value of stamps to which it was entitled by virtue of its income and size. The same family of four with income of $350 would thus simply receive $86 in food stamps, rather than having to pay $95 to receive $182 in food stamps, as under the current law. This would simplify the administrative procedures and give the poor more freedom to allocate their incomes, since less would be tied up in food stamps, and it would eliminate one of the more important impediments to wider participation in the food stamp program. According to one estimate, the elimination of the food stamp purchase requirement, without changing food stamp benefit levels, would add two to three million new participants to the program and increase costs by $1.1 billion, or about 20 percent, by fiscal year 1978. If food stamps were cashed out altogether and replaced by a special food assistance grant of the same amount, the proportion of eligible recipients participating would expand even further, raising costs by another $1 billion by fiscal year 1978. In this way, the food stamp program would reach its full potential as an income guarantee available to all persons in need.

Housing Allowances. A bolder set of categorical reform proposals would add new in-kind assistance packages to those already on the books. Perhaps the most prominent of these is the proposal for a broad-based, needs-tested housing assistance grant modeled closely on the food stamp program. The basic rationale for this approach is that housing cost escalation has placed millions of American families in shelter need even though their gross incomes may not fall below the official poverty line. A program of assistance especially targeted for those suffering from this form of indigence could thus provide what one team of analysts calls "the missing piece" to the welfare policy puzzle.[87] Under a housing assistance program, those in housing need would qualify for a supplement in the form of cash or vouchers based on their housing costs and income, with a maximum rate set on the basis of local housing costs. Under one version of this proposal, such supplements might be as high as $1,600 for a family of four. A housing assistance program of this sort would cost from $4.5 billion to $6.8 billion, depending on whether the recipients took advantage of the assistance to upgrade their shelter. Like the food stamp program, such a housing assistance program would extend income assistance to families now barred from participation in the existing welfare programs because of the categorical eligibility rules. It would eliminate some of the gross inequities and perverse incentives of the existing system, providing aid to intact families in need and not just to those headed by a single parent. As with other in-kind assistance programs, however, this would add further to the complexity of the income assistance system and thus complicate the problems of cost control and overlapping benefits.

Refundable Tax Credit. One final reform proposal that would help fill in the remaining gaps in the existing categorical program structure is the introduction of a small refundable tax credit modeled after the tax feature of the Griffiths plan. Under this proposal, the existing $30 per capita tax credit provided by the Tax Reduction Act of 1975 would be enlarged to $250 and made refundable for those who tax liabilities fell below this amount. This $250 tax credit per person would replace the existing personal exemption of $750. For a family of four with no tax liabilities, this tax credit would provide $1,000 in supplemental income. This income would be available to all families in need, regardless of family composition or geographical location, and would be provided without the hassle normally attached to the receipt of welfare. Since a $225 tax credit is worth more to a middle-income taxpayer than a comparable exemption of $750, middle-income taxpayers would also receive some benefit from this provision. Such taxpayers would benefit indirectly as well, since the $1,000 in tax credits could be treated as ordinary income in calculating AFDC, SSI, and food stamp benefits and thus reduce the costs of these programs. According to one estimate, a refundable tax credit of this sort would generate $5 billion worth of savings in the cost of other welfare programs.[88] The refundable tax credit could be conceived as the first step to a broader consolidated cash assistance system, but a step that, at least for the time being, would leave the existing program structure in place. The real winners in such an innovation would be the lower-income households not covered by the existing system, plus those middle-income households that would benefit from the tax savings generated by the new credit. This proposal would contribute to the equity and administrative efficiency of the welfare system while improving the overall equity of the income tax system as well.

Categorical Reduction Proposals

A far different set of categorical reform proposals seeks to limit public assistance costs by targeting benefits more carefully on those in greatest need and eliminating the leakage of benefits to the nonneedy. The premise behind this approach is that public assistance rolls are bloated as a consequence of excessively liberal eligibility criteria and widespread fraud and deception. Comprehensive reform would only intensify this problem by adding millions of new recipients to the rolls. What is proposed instead is a series of measures to disqualify the less needy for aid under the existing categorical programs, especially AFDC and food stamps.

AFDC Program Tightening. One set of categorical reduction proposals for the AFDC program was embodied in the National Welfare Reform Act (H.R. 5133, S. 1719) introduced in 1975. Under its terms, the open-ended work-expense deductions under current AFDC law would be replaced by a flat deduction of

$60 per month. The extent to which various forms of income could be disregarded would be restricted in computing AFDC eligibility. This bill would also increase the obligations of nonneedy members of an AFDC household to make contributions to support the family, bar strikers from receipt of AFDC benefits, and tighten state reporting requirements and verification procedures to limit the extent of fraud. According to one estimate, this series of measures could yield savings of $1.4 billion in fiscal year 1978, though these savings could be offset by the increases in food stamp and Medicaid costs that would result from lower AFDC benefits.[89]

Food Stamp Program Tightening. Because of the reciprocal link between AFDC benefits and food stamp benefits, efforts to tighten the AFDC program may prove to be ineffective unless accompanied by similar efforts to tighten the food stamp program. Several food stamp reduction proposals have recently been advanced, focusing on one or a combination of three elements in the existing food stamp program: the definition of income that is used to determine eligibility; the amount of money that must be paid to purchase food stamps (the purchase requirement); and the accounting period.

In each of these areas, program critics find fault with existing arrangements. The definition of income is faulted because it exempts a variety of in-kind forms of income, such as school lunches and other child-nutrition benefits, and because it allows exemptions for work expenses, medical costs, and numerous other expenses. Under a proposal introduced by the Ford administration, these exemptions would be replaced by a flat $100 per month deduction to be charged against all income. This proposal would help concentrate food stamp benefits on those in greatest need, who typically have the fewest deductions. Another proposal, the Buckley-Michels bill (S. 1993), would take all in-kind forms of assistance into account in calculating eligibility. This proposal would cut an estimated 4.3 million participants out of the food stamp program by fiscal year 1978, at a savings of $0.8 billion.[90]

Critics of food stamps also complain that the purchase requirement is too liberal, allowing many families to pay little for their stamps and requiring none to pay more than 30 percent of their income. One way to reduce costs, therefore, would be to require all participants to pay 30 percent of their income. Savings could also be achieved by altering the current accounting period in the food stamp program, which bases benefits on projections of the next month's income. Under a proposal introduced by the Ford administration, this procedure would be replaced by one that calculated income and eligibility on the basis of the previous three months' income, thus concentrating benefits on those in longer-term need and limiting benefits for those with immediate, short-term food assistance needs. According to one estimate, this small technical change would exclude three million of the 17 million food stamp recipients and reduce costs in fiscal year 1978 by $0.5 billion.[91]

Program tightening initiatives could be taken in several of the other categorical assistance programs as well. For example, child-nutrition benefits could be restricted to those in greatest need, and efforts could be made to stop price escalation in Medicaid by limiting the extent to which the federal government will cover increases in physician charges.

While these various categorical reduction initiatives would reduce overall program costs, they would pursue greater target efficiency at the price of work equity and of the financial work incentives intentionally built into the existing system; the inclusion of some less needy persons in the assistance system is the other side of the coin of extending financial work incentives to those recipients who could make a more substantial contribution to their own support. Such changes would do nothing to improve the equity of the income assistance system and would leave the system heavily burdened by administrative inefficiencies.

Categorical Modernization Approaches

The third basic type of categorical reform approach focuses less on programmatic changes than on alterations of administrative procedure and casework management. Such changes must be examined with great care, for seemingly technical alterations of administrative practice can significantly alter benefit levels and coverage. For example, the Ford administration's proposal to change the accounting period in the food stamp program from a one-month prospective system to a three-month retrospective one would have eliminated some three million people from the program.

Despite this caveat, the elbow room for significant modernization of public administrative arrangements is ample indeed. Movement toward common definitions of income, work-expense disregards, filing units, and accounting periods among programs just scratch the surface of the simplifications that have been proposed. Similarly, vast administrative improvements could be attained through the use of better data collection and storage facilities to keep track of the voluminous information that must be processed in the operation of public assistance. In the eyes of many, changes of this sort are quite possible within the existing program structure, and, individually and jointly, would greatly improve the efficiency, accuracy, and equity of the system.

Evaluation

The various incremental reform proposals proceed from a far less alarmist view of the existing welfare system than is apparent among supporters of the two previously described reform approaches. In this view, significant improvement has already been made in the income assistance programs, and further progress can best be accommodated within the existing categorical structure. Those who favor this approach are particularly attracted by the opportunity a categorical system provides to target benefits for persons in need, and to finely tune the benefit packages to the extent and character of their needs, thus avoiding the coverage, benefit-level, and work incentive traps of more consolidated approaches. The administrative simplification and the efficiency promised by more comprehensive reforms appear, from this perspective, as unrealistic hopes hardly worth the benefit limitations they frequently bring in their wake.

Yet, it seems clear that any conceivable combination of incremental reforms is likely to leave the public assistance system under a heavy cloud of public suspicion. While many of the categorical reforms cited here would improve benefit adequacy and support equity, they seem unlikely to address the work equity concerns that increasingly lie at the heart of public hostility toward the welfare system. What is more, these proposals do little to address the underlying employment difficulties that help fuel the welfare problem and ultimately impede progress toward its resolution.

BELIEVING IMPOSSIBLE THINGS
IN THE REFORM ARENA

If this chapter has demonstrated the range of options available for improving the American welfare system, it should also have demonstrated why choosing among them is so difficult. In terms of the three criteria of adequacy, equity, and efficiency, there is no clear winner among the three major approaches to reform identified here. Rather, as shown in Table 4.11, each of the proposals has pluses and minuses. For example, the consolidated cash assistance proposals score high in terms of support equity and administrative efficiency, but low in terms of target efficiency and adequacy. The incremental reform approaches tend to score high in terms of adequacy and target efficiency and low in terms of support equity, work equity, and administrative efficiency. The multitrack proposals achieve perhaps the greatest balance, with moderate ratings on several criteria but a high rating on only one.

TABLE 4.11

Evaluating Welfare Reform Proposals
(ratings)

Criterion	Consolidated Cash	Multitrack	Incremental
Adequacy	Low-Moderate	Moderate-High	High
Equity			
Support	High	Low-Moderate	Low
Work	Moderate	High	Low
Efficiency			
Administrative	High	Moderate	Low
Target	Low	Moderate	High

Source: Compiled by the author.

Clearly, the welfare reform arena is no place for Alice's Queen, with her penchant for believing the impossible. Even with practice in this arena, it is difficult to "believe impossible things." Alice's conversation with the March Hare may therefore be more apropos than the one she had with the Queen.

> "Have some wine," the March Hare said in an encouraging tone.
> Alice looked all round the table, but there was nothing on it but tea. "I don't see any wine," she remarked.
> "There isn't any," said the March Hare.

In the public assistance arena, too, there isn't any wine, only tea. What is needed, therefore, is less a capacity to believe impossible things than a willingness to make difficult choices. What this means in practice is that choosing the best welfare reform strategy cannot be done on technical grounds alone. The choice must hinge on the weight to be assigned to the different values served by each competing proposal. And in a democratic society, that weighting must ultimately be the product of a political process. If this study helps to inform and focus that process, it will have amply served its purpose.

NOTES

1. Henry J. Aaron, *Why is Welfare So Hard to Reform?* (Washington, D.C.: The Brookings Institution, 1973).

2. John Korbel, Congressional Budget Office, *Poverty Status of Families Under Alternative Definitions of Income* (Washington, D.C.: Government Printing Office, 1977), p. 10.

3. Arnold Packer, "Employment Guarantees Should Replace the Welfare System," *Challenge*, March-April 1974, p. 3.

4. Mathematica Policy Research Group, *Long-Range Estimates of the Costs and Caseloads of the Major Income Assistance Programs: Technical Description*, prepared for the Congressional Budget Office (October 1975), p. 11 (Princeton, N.J.: Mathematics Inc., 1975).

5. Ibid., p. 28.

6. Ibid., p. 66.

7. Heather Ross and Isabel Sawhill, *Time of Transition: The Growth of Families Headed by Women* (Washington, D.C.: The Urban Institute, 1976), p. 1.

8. Ibid., p. 2.

9. U.S. Bureau of the Census, *Current Population Reports*, Series P-60, No. 103, "Money Income and Poverty Status of Families and Persons in the United States: 1975 and 1974 Revisions" (Washington, D.C.: Government Printing Office, 1976), p. 35.

10. Mathematica Policy Research Group, *Long-Range Estimates*, p. 66.

11. Ross and Sawhill, *Time of Transition*, p. 6.

12. U.S. Department of Labor, *Employment and Training Report of the President, 1976* (Washington, D.C.: Government Printing Office, 1976), p. 25. In 1976, this fell slightly to about 7.3 million.

13. Ibid., p. 256.

14. Ibid., p. 29.

15. Ibid., p. 26.

16. Bureau of the Census, *Current Population Reports*, Series P-60, No. 103, 1976, p. 37.

17. Ross and Sawhill, *Time of Transition*, p. 79.

18. Marjorie Honig, "The Impact of Welfare Payment Levels on Family Stability," in U.S. Congress, Joint Economic Committee, Studies in Public Welfare, 93d Cong., 1st sess., (1973), p. 53.

19. See, for example, National Commission for Manpower Policy, *Second Annual Report: An Employment Strategy for the United States—Next Steps* (Washington, D.C.: National Commission for Manpower Policy, 1976), p. 2; Congressional Budget Office, *Public Employment and Training Assistance: Alternative Federal Approaches* (Washington, D.C.: Government Printing Office, 1977), p. 1.

20. Eli Ginsberg, "The Place of Work in Welfare-Related Reforms" (Unpublished paper, New York, 1976), p. 3.

21. A total of 19,530 AFDC fathers were reported to be in job training or work placement at the time of the 1973 AFDC survey. U.S. Department of Health, Education, and Welfare, *Findings of the 1973 AFDC Study* (1974), Part 1.

22. G. William Hoagland, Congressional Budget Office, *The Food Stamp Program: Income or Food Supplementation* (Washington, D.C.: Government Printing Office, 1977), p. 25.

23. U.S. Senate, Finance Committee, *Report on H.R. 1, Social Security Amendments of 1972*, Senate Report no. 92-1230, 92d Cong., 2d sess., September 26, 1972, p. 411.

24. *Congressional Quarterly*, March 19, 1971.

25. Speaking about the opposition to H.R. 1 in the House, for example, Ken Bowler notes: "It appeared to be the intensity of their concern that poor people would not work if guaranteed an income of $2,400 a year that distinguished the Committee members who opposed H.R. 1 from the other members." Bowler, *The Nixon Guaranteed Income Proposal*, p. 117.

26. Senate Finance Committee, *Report on H.R. 1*, p. 412.

27. Ibid.

28. See, for example, Marvin Kosters and Finis Welch, "The Effects of Minimum Wages on the Distribution of Changes in Aggregate Employment," *The American Economic Review* 62, no. 3 (June 1972).

29. See, for example, the collection of articles in Joseph A. Pechman and P. Michael Timpane, *Work Incentives and Income Guarantees: The New Jersey Income Tax Experiment* (Washington, D.C.: The Brookings Institution, 1975).

30. U.S. Chamber of Commerce, *High Employment and Income Maintenance Policy: A Report of the Council on Trends and Perspective* (Washington, D.C.: U.S. Chamber of Commerce, 1976), pp. 55-56.

31. Ibid., p. 52.

32. Ibid.

33. U.S. Department of Health, Education, and Welfare, *The Changing Economic Status of 5,000 American Families: Highlights from the Panel Study of Income Dynamics* (Washington, D.C.: Government Printing Office, May 1974), pp. 13-14.

34. U.S. Chamber of Commerce, *High Employment and Income Maintenance Policy*, p. 56.

35. Smith, *Welfare Work Incentives*, p. iv.

36. Steiner, *State of Welfare*, p. 315.

37. Data are drawn from U.S. Department of Health, Education, and Welfare, Office of Income Security Policy, *Income Supplement Program*, Technical Analysis Paper no. 11, mimeo. (October 1976), pp. C-7-10.

38. National Governors' Conference, *National Welfare Reform: A Program for Change*, Staff Task Force Report (Washington, D.C.: National Governors' Conference, February 1977).

39. U.S. Department of Health, Education, and Welfare, *The Measure of Poverty: A Report to Congress as Mandated by the Education Amendments of 1974* (Washington: Government Printing Office, 1976), p. 96.

40. In 1965, 15.6 percent of all people in the United States were poor, according to the relative definition of poverty. By 1972, 15.7 percent were still poor, using this definition. During the same period, the proportion in poverty, according to the absolute level, declined from 15.6 percent to 11.9 percent. Robert D. Plotnick and Felicity Skidmore, *Progress Against Poverty* (Madison: University of Wisconsin, Institute for Research on Poverty, 1976), pp. 82–83.

41. Walter Nicholson, "Expenditure Patterns in the Graduated Work Incentive Experiment," in *Final Report of the New Jersey Graduated Work Incentive Experiment*, vol. 3, ed. Harold W. Watts and Albert Rees (Madison: University of Wisconsin, Institute for Research on Poverty, n.d.), pp. DIIIb-1–51. See Also Nick Kotz, *Let Them Eat Promises* (Englewood Cliffs, N.J.: Prentice-Hall, 1969).

42. Congressional Budget Office, *Public Employment and Training Assistance: Alternative Federal Approaches* (Washington, D.C.: Government Printing Office, 1977), pp. 28–29.

43. American Public Welfare Association, "American Public Welfare Association Position on Income Maintenance," Report of the Committee on Income Maintenance Policy (Washington, D.C.: APWA, 1976).

44. National Association of Counties, *Welfare Reform: A Plan for Change* (Washington, D.C.: National Association of Counties, 1976), pp. 3, 5.

45. National Commission on Manpower Policy, *An Employment Strategy for the United States—Next Steps* (Washington, D.C.: National Commission on Manpower Policy, 1976), p. 20. See also Arnold Packer, "Employment Guarantees Should Replace the Welfare System," *Challenge*, March/April 1974.

46. Cited in Robert Lerman, "A Reappraisal of Negative Income Tax and Employment Subsidy Approaches to Reforming Welfare," *Institute for Research on Poverty Discussion Papers* (Madison: University of Wisconsin, 1976), p. 1.

47. For critiques of the WIN program on these grounds, see Sar Levitan and Robert Taggart, *Promise of Greatness* (Cambridge: Harvard University Press, 1976), pp. 53–57; Goodwin, *Do the Poor Want to Work? A Social Psychological Study of Work Orientations* (Washington, D.C.: The Brookings Institution, 1972)

48. Levitan and Taggart, *Promise of Greatness*, pp. 74–77.

49. U.S. Congress, Joint Economic Committee, Subcommittee on Fiscal Policy, *Income Security for Americans: Recommendations of the Public Welfare Study*, 93d Cong., 2d sess., 1974, pp. 150–51.

50. Congressional Budget Office, *Public Employment and Training Assistance*, pp. xiii, 27.

51. Bruno Stein, *On Relief; The Economics of Poverty and Public Welfare* (New York: Basic Books, 1971), p. 68.

52. For a discussion of these changes and the issues they raise, see U.S. Department of Labor, *Employment and Training Report of the President, 1976*, pp. 41–52.

53. Proposal drafted by Tom Joe, mimeo., February–March, 1977.

54. Alvin Schorr, *Explorations in Social Policy* (New York: Basic Books, 1968), pp. 57–69.

55. See Plotnick and Skidmore, *Progress Against Poverty*, p. 56, for data on the leakage of benefits to the nonpoor under social security.

56. For one argument along these lines, see Mark D. Worthington and Laurence E. Lynn, *Incremental Welfare Reform: A Strategy Whose Time Has Passed*, Discussion Paper Number 44D (Cambridge, Mass.: John Fitzgerald Kennedy School of Government, Harvard University, 1976), pp. 22–23.

57. American Public Welfare Association, *APWA Position on Income Maintenance*.

58. National Governors' Conference, *National Welfare Reform: A Program for Change* (February 1977).

59. National Association of Counties, *Welfare Reform: A Plan for Change*.

60. Vincent and Vee Burke, *Nixon's Good Deed: Welfare Reform* (New York: Columbia University Press, 1974), p. 145.

61. For the FHA story, see Lester M. Salamon, *The Money Committees: A Study of the House Banking and Currency Committee and the Senate Banking, Housing and Urban Affairs Committee* (New York: Grossman Publishers, 1976); and Brian Boyer, *Cities Destroyed for Cash: The FHA Scandal at HUD* (Chicago: Follett Publishing Co., 1973).

62. These figures are drawn from estimates under the so-called Griffiths plan formulated by the Subcommittee on Fiscal Policy of the Joint Economic Committee in 1974, and the Income Supplement Program formulated in HEW in 1974. The Griffiths plan estimated 11.2 million families would be involved and the ISP estimated 10.4 million. See *Public Welfare Study*, p. 15; and HEW, *Income Supplement Program*, p. E-9.

63. Congressional Budget Office, *Budget Options for Fiscal Year 1978* (Washington, D.C.: Government Printing Office, 1977), p. 181.

64. Ibid., p. xiv.

65. Committee on Economic Development, *Welfare Reform and Its Financing* (New York: Committee for Economic Development, 1976).

66. Statement of principles of the Businessmen's Committee for the Federalization of Welfare, reprinted in *The Journal of the Institute for Socioeconomic Studies* 1, no. 2 (Autumn 1976): p. 40.

67. Congressional Budget Office, *Budget Options for Fiscal Year 1978*, p. 181.

68. Congressional Budget Office, *Budget Options for Fiscal Year 1977* (Washington, D.C.: Government Printing Office, 1976), p. 138.

69. France adopted a family or children's allowance in 1932, followed by Italy in 1936, the Netherlands in 1939, the United Kingdom in 1945, and Sweden in 1947. Arnold Heidenheimer, Hugh Heclo, and Carolyn Teich Adams, *Comparative Public Policy: The Politics of Social Choice in Europe and America* (New York: St. Martin's Press, 1975), pp. 189, 199.

70. National Urban League, *Income Maintenance: The National Urban League Position* (Washington, D.C.: National Urban League, 1975).

71. Interview with Irwin Garfinkel, Institute for the Study of Poverty, University of Wisconsin, September 3, 1976.

72. Based on Congressional Budget Office estimates.

73. U.S. Department of Health, Education, and Welfare, *Income Supplement Program: 1974 HEW Welfare Replacement Proposal*, Technical Analysis Paper No. 11, Office of Income Security Policy (Washington, D.C.: Department of HEW, 1976), Tab A, p. 2.

74. Based on Congressional Budget Office estimates.

75. National Governors' Conference, *National Welfare Reform: A Program for Change*.

76. Subcommittee on Fiscal Policy, *Public Welfare Study*, p. 162.

77. Congressional Budget Office, *Budget Options for Fiscal Year 1978*, p. 187.

78. "Special Issue on the HEW Mega-Proposal," *Policy Analysis* 1, no. 2 (Spring 1975): 344–67.

79. The discussion of the triple-track plan presented here draws on personal interviews with Tom Joe, Leonard Lesser, and Bert Seidman, as well as on written memoranda on the proposal drafted by Tom Joe, February 14 and March 21, 1977.

80. U.S. Congress, Senate, Finance Committee, *Social Security Amendments of 1972*, Report no. 92-1230, 92d Cong., 2d sess., 1972, pp. 405–32, 499–500.

81. This proposal is outlined in U.S. Department of Health, Education, and Welfare, "Leading Welfare Reform Options: Revised Draft Number Two" (Washington, D.C., April 8, 1977).

82. See Packer, "Employment Guarantees Should Replace the Welfare System."

83. Ibid., p. 6.

84. U.S. Department of Health, Education, and Welfare, "Leading Welfare Reform Options: Revised Draft Number Two," pp. 2-6.

85. See, for example, Richard Nathan, "Food Stamps and Welfare Reform," *Policy Analysis* 2, no. 1 (Winter 1976): 61-70; Richard Nathan, "Alternatives for Federal Income Security Policy," in *Qualities of Life: Critical Choices for Americans* (Lexington, Mass.: D.C. Heath and Co., 1976).

86. Congressional Budget Office, *Budget Options for Fiscal Year 1978*, p. 181.

87. John Heinberg, Joanne D. Culbertson, and James D. Zais, *The Missing Piece to the Puzzle? Housing Allowances and the Welfare System* (Washington, D.C.: The Urban Institute, 1974).

88. John L. Palmer and Joseph Minarik, "Income Security Policy," in *Setting National Priorities: The Next Ten Years*, ed. Henry Owen and Charles L. Schultze (Washington, D. C.: The Brookings Institution, 1976), p. 581.

89. Congressional Budget Office, *Budget Options for Fiscal Year 1978*, p. 182.

90. Ibid., p. 196.

91. Ibid.

APPENDIX A:

WELFARE REFORM REVISITED– PRESIDENT JIMMY CARTER'S PROGRAM FOR BETTER JOBS AND INCOME

Harvey D. Shapiro

INTRODUCTION

On August 6, 1977, at a Saturday morning press conference in Plains, Georgia, President Jimmy Carter released his long-awaited welfare message to Congress, in which he declared: "The welfare system is too hopeless to be cured by minor modifications. We must make a complete and clean break with the past." To replace the existing system, which had developed piece by piece over four decades, President Carter offered a comprehensive reform proposal he called the Program for Better Jobs and Income (PBJI). This program, unveiled just two days short of the eighth anniversary of the Family Assistance Plan, would, President Carter said, "increase job opportunities for the low-income population and consolidate our major income support programs into one simple and efficient system."[1]

The proposal was soon transformed into a 163-page bill and delivered to the House of Representatives on September 12, 1977, where it became H.R. 9030. The Carter administration's proposed new welfare system would accomplish the following:

- Divide the poor into two groups: those expected to work and those not expected to work because of age, disabilities, or responsibilities involving small children.
- Create up to 1.4 million minimum wage jobs for those expected to work and unable to find regular jobs.
- Consolidate AFDC, SSI, and food stamps into a single income maintenance program open to all in need, including for the first time single individuals, childless couples, and low-wage workers.
- Aid the working poor by expanding the earned income tax credit (EITC) as well as by paying them cash benefits.
- Increase the federal share of welfare costs, providing states and localities with $2.1 billion in fiscal relief in the program's first year and the promise of more in subsequent years.
- Potentially decrease the number of people eligible for welfare benefits from 40 million to 36 million while increasing those receiving benefits from 30 to 32 million.

Under this plan, which Carter proposed to put into effect at the beginning of the 1981 fiscal year, the federal government would calculate cash benefits by using a centralized computer system. The program is projected to cost $31.1 billion in fiscal 1981, which, according to administration calculations, represents an outlay of $2.8 billion more than the costs of continuing the existing programs.

Because of the scope of the administration's proposal, it was sent not only to the House Ways and Means Committee, but also to the Education and Labor Committee, which deals with manpower programs, and the House Agriculture Committee, which has jurisdiction over the food stamp program. In the Senate, the proposal was referred jointly to the Finance and Human Resources Committees.

To help expedite the bill through the House of Representatives, a special subcommittee was created, consisting of the entire Ways and Means Subcommittee on Public Assistance and Unemployment Compensation, augmented by selected members of the Agriculture and Education and Labor Committees. This special subcommittee, headed by Representative James C. Corman of California, worked through the winter of 1977–78 in an attempt to report out a bill which would then go before the three full committees in the House and the two in the Senate. But as the Corman subcommittee began its deliberations in the fall of 1977, it was clear that Carter's welfare reform proposal faced an arduous legislative path.

In this study, we will examine the development of the proposal, report on its contents, and then turn to some of the issues raised as the debate began on the Program for Better Jobs and Income.

DEVELOPMENT OF THE PROPOSAL

Jimmy Carter had repeatedly pledged to reform the nation's welfare system during the 1976 presidential campaign. On December 23, 1976, when the president-elect asked Joseph A. Califano, Jr. to serve as secretary of Health, Education, and Welfare, Carter, according to the secretary-designate, "reiterated that campaign pledge and asked that I start work to implement it as soon as possible after assuming office."[2] On January 26, 1977, HEW announced a major study of the existing welfare system, and the White House said it would offer a welfare reform plan on May 1. HEW quickly formed a 32-member consulting group on welfare reform, consisting of representatives of the Congress, the White House, state and local governments, welfare recipients, and public interest organizations. This group conducted weekly public meetings from February 11 through April 15 to consider welfare alternatives. In addition, the ten regional HEW offices solicited views within their areas. A total of 169,000 people were asked for comments, according to HEW figures.

After the May 1 deadline had passed, the president told a news conference the following day that three months of effort had produced the unanimous conclusion that "the present welfare program should be scrapped and a totally new system implemented." but he did not offer a program as projected. Instead, he listed a set of principles. He said those principles would guide the drafting of a legislative proposal which was to be implemented at no increase in federal expenditures. The proposal was to be ready in August. The day after this May 2 press conference, the *Wall Street Journal* reported that "President Carter's statement reflects an inability of the Department of HEW and the Department of Labor to come up with a detailed plan—for that matter any plan at all—that the White House was willing to endorse."[3]

Certainly the broad alternatives open to the president, as discussed earlier in this volume, were clear, and several of these had vigorous advocates in the administration. The office of HEW's assistant secretary for planning and evaluation had strongly supported a negative income tax for years. The Department of Labor emphasized jobs programs and the earned income tax credit. And Tom Joe, a HEW official during the Nixon administration who became a welfare consultant to President Carter, ardently supported the triple-track approach. Others favored incremental change.

The president, however, had made it clear early on that he wanted major changes and that he was "a hawk on job creation," a high HEW official recalled. All plans, therefore, had to have a jobs component. When the president insisted that any plan developed could not cost more than existing programs, "this rapidly moved the alternatives down to three: HEW's, DOL's [Department of Labor's] and the triple track," this HEW official said.[4]

The triple-track plan was soon deemed too costly and elements of it were folded into the Department of Labor plan. Thus two proposals competed for White House approval during much of the spring of 1977: HEW proposed a universal negative income tax with high benefit levels, linked to a relatively small program providing three-quarter-time jobs at the minimum wage. The Department of Labor proposed to create up to two million jobs at relatively high wages and expand the earned income tax credit. This would be linked to a smaller cash assistance program for those clearly unable to work.

As these two separate plans were developed, a HEW official recalled, "the president had linked Califano and Labor Secretary Marshall and said HEW and DOL were coequal. So there was no way to resolve disagreements short of the president, and hard decisions got pushed to the end." Lengthy negotiations between representatives of the two departments and the White House staff, and four briefings with the president were held. "He was more involved in this than any other issue," noted Frank Raines, assistant director of President Carter's domestic policy staff.[5]

Out of these meetings a series of compromises emerged: The president's plan would have a large-scale job-creation component, as the Department of Labor suggested, but with minimum wage jobs, which HEW favored. In line with the Department of Labor's ideas, it would have relatively low benefits, but only initially; people would move up to higher benefits, which HEW favored, if no jobs were available. Compromises were hammered out on benefit-reduction rates, the length of time required for jobhunting, and other questions of incentives. Benefits and wage levels were juggled to bridge differences of opinion and to meet cost constraints. Struggling under the "zero new dollars" constraint imposed by the president, Secretaries Califano and Marshall sent a joint memorandum to the White House in late May, warning:

> The politics of welfare reform are treacherous under any circumstances and they can be impossible at no higher initial cost because it is likely that so many people who are now receiving benefits will be hurt.

The states are our natural allies in welfare reform—most members of Congress would still prefer not to deal with the subjects at all—and there is virtually no relief in this proposal for governors and mayors.[6]

In response to these and other complaints within the administration, the president agreed to some additional expenditures in order to provide fiscal relief. To free even more funds, proposed benefit levels were reduced by leaving the nominal sums the same, but changing them from 1976 dollars to 1978 dollars, which were assumed to be worth significantly less.

By June, the two departments had agreed on the broad outlines of a plan, and over the summer the details were worked out. The result, said Raymond J. Uhaldee, a Department of Labor economist, was that "although Daniel Patrick Moynihan may have been the father of FAP, no one person in the administration is the father of PBJI."[7]

WELFARE REFORM REVISITED

THE CARTER ADMINISTRATION'S PROPOSAL

Rufus Miles, a senior fellow at Princeton University and a former HEW assistant secretary, described the welfare plan unveiled on August 6, 1977 as "the most extensive and complex redesign of a group of governmentally operated social programs ever undertaken in the United States."[8] The Program for Better Jobs and Income, a label that studiously avoided the word welfare, scraps the existing set of categorical aid programs, but creates two new overarching categories: Welfare recipients are divided into those expected to work, and those not expected to work because of age, disability, or child-rearing responsibilities. This division, to be implemented under the direction of the secretary of labor, is essentially a formalization of decisions already being made to meet existing work requirements. But this division of the welfare population becomes significant, on the broad policy level, because the two groups have different benefit levels and because a jobs program for those expected to work is a major element of the Carter program.

THE JOBS PROGRAM

Since President Lyndon Johnson first imposed a work requirement on able-bodied welfare recipients in 1966, succeeding presidents and Congresses have sought, with limited success, to put welfare recipients to work. Like Richard Nixon's Family Assistance Plan, PBJI continued this work requirement, with a Carter pledge to improve the job placement process. However, the president also proposed to create jobs for welfare recipients who couldn't find work in the regular economy.

Carter estimated that 1.4 million jobs would be sufficient to meet the demand. This figure includes 725,000 existing jobs under Title VI of the Comprehensive Employment and Training Act (CETA) program, plus 375,000 newly created full-time positions, and 300,000 new part-time positions. The last category of jobs is reserved for mothers of children aged seven through 13 who have access to day-care facilities. The part-time jobs were added in part to meet the expectations of Senate Finance Committee Chairman Russell Long, among others.

The Carter proposal requires that welfare recipients classified as expected to work engage in an intensive five-week job search, during which they are eligible for limited cash benefits. If, after five weeks, no regular job is found, the family becomes eligible for a subsidized public service job. During the ensuing three weeks an attempt must be made to provide such a job. If a person refuses an offer of a regular or subsidized job, his or her benefits are cut off (though benefits continue to other members of the family). If no job is found or created after eight weeks, that person will begin receiving a higher cash benefit for as long as he/she remains unemployed.

In general, the proposal said, after eight weeks of receiving $44 a week for a family of four, an individual shall be placed in a public service job. That person will then work for 12 months, after which he or she must spend another five weeks looking for a job in the regular job market. If that search is unsuccessful, the person becomes eligible for another subsidized job.

The proposed Job Search Assistance Program is open to all adults in need, but eligibility for the subsidized jobs is limited to single-parent and two-parent families with children. Single individuals and childless couples are excluded, and only one job or training opportunity is available per family. The job goes to either the single parent or, in two-parent families, the principal earner, defined as the parent who had worked the most hours or had the highest earnings in the previous six months.

The basic wage paid on the public service jobs is limited to the higher of the federal or the state minimum wage. However, states may pay a supplement of up to 25 percent of the wage to 15 percent of subsidized workers who are classified as "crew leaders." States which supplement the basic cash payments to those not expected to work also have to supplement the subsidized wages, up to a maximum of 10 percent of the minimum wage. The administration predicted that 39 states would supplement the wage, so that while the minimum wage would be $3.35 per hour in 1981, the average hourly wage paid in the program would be $3.72. Participants in the jobs program are also eligible for cash assistance.

In addition to paying the wages of those in the jobs program, the federal government also provides 30 percent over the basic wages, or double the overhead rate under Title VI of CETA, to cover fringe benefits and administrative costs.

While the jobs program is under the general supervision of the Department of Labor, the jobs search is coordinated by the state employment service offices, and the subsidized jobs themselves are supplied by CETA prime sponsors. Department of Labor officials did not offer specific administrative arrangements, but all used the same formulation in their congressional testimony: "The exact design of the delivery system will probably require a considerable period of interaction with state and local officials."[9]

Because the jobs are to be created by local organizations, the administration said it was impossible to predict what sort of jobs they would be. However, Department of Labor officials said they would be "useful public services which are not normally performed by regular public or private sector workers on the necessary scale."[10] The Labor Department identified 13 major categories of jobs which it said met its requirements and could be filled on a large scale, estimated as follows:

200,000 jobs aiding the elderly and the sick.
200,000 jobs building and repairing recreational facilities.
150,000 jobs improving public safety.
150,000 jobs providing child care.
150,000 jobs as paraprofessionals in the schools.
125,000 jobs running local recreation programs.
100,000 jobs improving school facilities.
100,000 jobs cleaning up neighborhoods and controlling rodents.
 75,000 jobs involving cultural activities.
 50,000 jobs monitoring environmental quality.
 50,000 jobs weatherizing homes to save energy.
 25,000 jobs providing facilities for the handicapped.
 25,000 jobs aiding in waste treatment and recycling.

As is the case in the CETA program, these subsidized jobs can be supplied by state and local governmental agencies, and by many community-based, non-profit organizations.

The PBJI makes several references to training, and Department of Labor Assistant Secretary Arnold Packer noted in Congressional testimony, "We expect that training activities will be a regular component of most subsidized job opportunities."[11] However, no specific training plans or requirements were offered.

The proposal does not specifically guarantee a job to every family unable to find regular employment, but the administration estimates that 1.4 million jobs are sufficient to meet the demand. It assumes these 1.4 million jobs would serve 2.5 million people during the course of a year, as people move in and out of the regular labor force. In making its estimates, the administration assumes that the nation's unemployment rate will be 5.6 percent in October 1980, when the plan would go into effect. This would be a significant reduction from the 7.1 percent unemployment rate in August 1977, when the proposal was released.

THE CASH ASSISTANCE PROGRAM

In addition to the jobs program, the Carter administration proposed that the three existing cash assistance programs—AFDC, SSI, and food stamps—be consolidated into a single, universal program. It provides cash benefits to all in need, including—for the first time—single individuals, childless couples, and low-wage workers. While open to all in need, it is also categorical, in that benefits depend on health, family status, and other factors. The overarching categories of recipients are those expected to work and those not expected to work.

Cash Assistance for Those Not Expected to Work

Those not expected to work include the aged, blind, and disabled (that is, former SSI recipients), plus single parents with children under seven. In addition, single parents with children seven through 13 are not expected to work if no day-care facilities are available. If day care is available, these parents must accept a part-time job if it is available during school hours, or face a reduction in benefits. Those originally categorized as expected to work but without access to a regular or subsidized job also become part of the not-expected-to-work category.

For those not expected to work because of child-care responsibilities the basic benefit for a family of four with no other income is $4,200 in 1978 dollars. The benefit includes $1,900 for the head of the household, $1,100 for the next member of the household, and $600 for each additional child. (Payments increase up to a total of seven persons in a family.) The $4,200 basic annual federal benefit, equal to about two-thirds of the poverty threshold, is higher than the combined total of federal and state benefits in only 12 states under existing programs.

An aged, blind, or disabled person with no other income receives $2,500 a year under PBJI, and a couple gets $3,750. This represents a slight increase over current basic SSI benefits, but would be about the same amount as many currently receive from a combination of SSI and food stamps.

If a person in the not-expected-to-work category does, in fact, work, his or her cash benefits are reduced 50 cents for each dollar of earnings under the basic federal program. This 50 percent benefit-reduction rate, the same rate used in FAP, means that benefits phase out completely when earnings reach $8,400 for a family of four, while benefits to the aged, blind, or disabled cease when earned income hits $5,000 for an individual or $7,500 for a couple. To insure that this federal work incentive is not thwarted by local action, the proposal stipulates that benefits not be reduced by more than 70 percent in states which supplement the federal benefits.

Cash Benefits for Those Expected to Work

The PBJI augments the earnings of those expected to work but whose income is inadequate to support their families: either a direct cash payment called a work benefit, or an expanded earned income tax credit is available to the working poor.

Those expected to work include one of the parents in two-parent families, single parents with no children under 14, childless couples, and single individuals.

Single parents with children seven through 13 are expected to work part time when jobs and day care are available.

For an expected-to-work family of four, the basic benefit is $2,300 per year. This consists of $1,100 for the spouse and $600 for each child. The expected-to-work adult or principal earner receives nothing during the initial eight-week job search and nothing if he or she refuses a proffered regular or subsidized job.

If a member of the family secures a regular or a subsidized job, the family is permitted to keep the first $3,800 of earned income. Beyond that, federal cash benefits are reduced by 50 cents for each dollar of earnings. To maintain this strong work incentive, the benefit-reduction rate is limited to 52 percent in states that supplement the federal payments. Day-care expenses up to a maximum of $150 a month for each of two children are deducted from earnings in computing benefits.

If no job is found and none created, after eight weeks, the family moves up to a higher tier: the head of the household then receives a $1,900 annual cash benefit, in addition to the $2,300 for the spouse and children. This would bring total annual benefits to $4,200, the same amount paid to a family of four with no expected-to-work members.

For single parents with all children over 14, the structure of benefits is the same as for two-parent families. However, for single-parent families in which the youngest child is seven through 13 and the parent was expected to work part time, the adult receives the higher-tier benefits during the initial eight-week job search; he or she loses benefits only after refusing a job.

For childless couples and single individuals, the basic federal benefit is $1,100 per adult, paid during the job search and continued thereafter if no job could be found. This amount is roughly equal to the present food stamp benefit for such recipients. There is no access to subsidized jobs, no higher tier, and the benefit is cut off if the individual refused a job at or above the minimum wage. The benefit-reduction rate is 50 percent, starting with the first dollar of earnings.

Under the existing welfare system, two-parent families in many states are generally ineligible for cash assistance. A working father could increase his family income by leaving, or appearing to leave, home. As President Carter noted, in Michigan a two-parent family with a father working at the minimum wage has a total income, including tax credits and food stamps, of $5,922. But if the father left home, the family would be eligible for benefits totaling $7,076.

The PBJI deals with this problem in two ways: It does not cut off benefits if the father is employed, but rather, permits the family to keep the first $3,800 of earnings and then reduces benefits at a rate which maintains incentives. Moreover, if no job is available, the family receives the same benefits as those not expected to work.

In designing the benefit structures for the expected-to-work and not-expected-to-work groups, the administration sought to ensure that those who work would always end up with more than those who don't, although this may not always be achieved.

The Expanded Earned Income Tax Credit

In addition to creating the work benefit, the president's plan also expands the EITC to provide a second way of supplementing low-income wages while strengthening the incentive to leave public service jobs for the regular economy. Currently the EITC provides a 10 percent tax credit on the first $4,000 of annual earnings, thus saving a maximum of $400. The amount of the EITC is reduced by one dollar for each ten dollars earnings over $4,000, thus disappearing completely when adjusted gross income hits $8,000.

The Carter proposal continues the 10 percent credit on earnings up to $4,000, but adds a 5 percent credit on earnings between $4,000 and $9,100, the point at which a family becomes ineligible for welfare benefits in states with supplementary payments. The credit phases out at the rate of one dollar for each ten dollars of income beyond $9,100. Thus, the credit peaks at $655 for an income of $9,100 and provides some benefits to a family of four with income up to $15,650. The credit is administered by the Internal Revenue Service.

The expansion of the EITC and the structure of the work benefit are designed to aid the working poor while maintaining work incentives. However, the expanded EITC would apply only to workers in regular private- and public-sector jobs and not to earnings from specially created subsidized jobs. Thus, the administration said, there would be a strong incentive to leave public service jobs for the regular economy.

Determination of Program Eligibility and Amount of Benefits

In place of the existing welter of local rules for determining eligibility and calculating benefits, President Carter proposed a new set of rules to provide greater uniformity and tighten eligibility in ways that he said would ensure assistance only for those most in need.

Eligibility for the jobs program has no income or assets tests; to apply, one need only be the unemployed principal earner in a family with children. Willingness to seek a minimum wage job would be considered prima facie evidence of need. The proposed cash assistance program has more elaborate provisions. *Filing Units.* Carter proposed significant changes in the definition of a filing unit, or group of persons who must be considered together when one of the group applies for benefits. The food stamps program has a broad filing unit, including almost everyone living in a household, whether related or not. AFDC and SSI have more narrow filing units, limited generally to a nuclear family living together in the same household.

The administration's proposed definition falls between the narrow and the broad: it stipulates that all related persons who live together are considered as one unit, while all unrelated persons living in the same household are treated as separate units. Aged, blind, or disabled persons without dependents could apply individually for benefits whether living along or not. If such persons have dependents, they are included in the household. Single persons who live in the same household as parents who receive benefits are not eligible to file for separate benefits; but if two related nuclear families live together (such as a couple with their grown children and grandchildren), each family applies separately.

In seeking to establish filing units that conform more closely to actual living arrangements, and which are uniform across the country, the Carter proposals may give some families with members receiving AFDC or SSI benefits less total assistance as a result of combining all members into a single unit.

Retrospective Accounting. The administration also proposes to change the method of counting income for purposes of determining eligibility from prospective to retrospective. While eligibility under existing programs is based on prospective income over the next one to three months, PBJI eligibility is based on income actually received during the previous six-month period. (See Table A.1.) The administration argues that by measuring income received over a lengthy period, welfare will go to those most in need and prevent families with relatively high but irregular incomes from receiving benefits. The administration believes the lengthy retrospective accountability period will help hold down caseloads and costs, while a proposed emergency needs program helps those who require immediate assistance but are not immediately eligible.

TABLE A.1

Waiting Period before Persons Become Eligible for Benefits

Previous Annual Earnings of Persons Applying	Period in Which Persons Become Eligible	
	Under AFDC Current Accountable Period	Under Proposed Six-Month Accountable Period
$5,200 (minimum wage)	1st month	1st month
8,400 (proposed eligibility ceiling)	1st month	1st month
10,600 (average wage in manufacturing)	1st month	2d month
12,000 (city school teacher)	1st month	3d month
15,000 (construction worker)	1st month	4th month

Source: Compiled from Department of Health, Education, and Welfare data.

Retrospective budgeting is also to be used in calculating benefits. Instead of paying benefits on the basis of estimated income—which often leads to overpayments that are difficult to recoup—PBJI bases benefits on actual income received. Thus payments in, say, September will be made minus actual income received in July.

Regular Reporting. The Carter proposal installs a rigorous and uniform system of income reporting to help calculate benefits. Recipients with employment income are required to report monthly while groups with less frequent changes, such as the aged, blind, and disabled, are required to report much less often.

Definition of Income. A nationally uniform definition of income is to determine eligibility and benefits. Countable income is defined as 50 percent of wages; 80 percent of nonemployment income from dividends, property, private pensions, and social insurance programs; and 100 percent of any income from other federal means-tested programs, such as veterans' pensions. Expenses for child care may be deducted from earnings in determining countable income.

Assets Test. In place of current rules stipulating that those whose countable assets exceed certain limits are automatically ineligible for welfare, the Carter plan proposes that 1.25 percent of total assets be added to monthly countable income in determining eligibility. The assets test excludes the first $500 of liquid assets, as well as the value of an owner-occupied house, household and personal belongings, and a car valued up to $3,000. Nonbusiness assets of more than $5,000 or a specified equity value in business assets render an applicant ineligible.

Overall Effect. As a result of the changes in standards of eligibility and the providing of national uniformity, the Carter administration expects changes in both the number of people eligible for benefits and the numbers actually receiving them. It is estimated that some 40 million people are presently eligible for AFDC, SSI, or food stamps, and that three-quarters of those eligible, or 30 million people, actually receive these benefits.

The president's proposal would broaden the categories of eligibility to include single individuals, childless couples, and two-parent families with children. Yet, the president said the total number of people eligible for benefits would decrease from 40 million to 36 million. This reduction results from changes in income ceilings, the longer, retrospective accounting period, and the public jobs program, which would raise the income of many beyond eligibility levels. Of the four million fewer who would be eligible for cash assistance, one million would be AFDC recipients who had high incomes but remained on welfare because of peculiarities in the rules, the president said.

While four million fewer would be eligible, the administration estimates that those who actually receive benefits at some point during the year would increase from 30 million to 32 million. This increased participation is forecast because many of those now eligible for food stamps, particularly the elderly and disabled, have not applied, but are expected to apply, for cash assistance. In addition, participation is expected to increase as a result of simplified application procedures.

THE ROLE OF STATE AND LOCAL GOVERNMENTS

The Carter proposal transforms welfare from hundreds of different state and county programs partially funded by the federal government into a single federal program, supplemented and in part administered by the states. While it does not completely federalize welfare, as many had hoped, the proposal alters the current division of state and federal responsibilities and reallocates financial burdens in ways designed to provide fiscal relief and compensate for local cost-of-living differences.

Administration

The president's plan proposes a major role for the federal government in administering the cash assistance program and a more limited, oversight role in the jobs program. HEW computes benefits and makes payments in the cash assistance program, while the states have the option of retaining the intake and referral portions of cash assistance. The proposal anticipates a total nationwide staff of 100,000 to 120,000 federal and state employees to administer the cash benefit program, compared to the 143,000 currently employed. The total annual cost of administering the new program is estimated by HEW at $2.2 billion in 1978 dollars, compared with current costs of $2.7 billion. Carter said the centralized federal government computer system will not only save administrative expenses, but improve efficiency and reduce fraud and error.

While HEW has the primary role in running the cash assistance program, the states may administer their own supplemental benefit programs, and the Internal Revenue Service will administer the EITC. As noted previously, the U.S. Department of Labor has overall responsibility for overseeing the jobs program, while the state employment services supervise the job search and CETA prime sponsors supply the subsidized jobs. State governments are assigned a vague planning role.

State Supplementation

The Carter proposal permits and helps finance continued state supplementation of basic federal benefits so that, Secretary Califano said, "there will be enough flexibility in the benefit structure to allow for regional variations."[12] The existing range in benefits, which extends from a low of $2,556 for a family of four receiving AFDC and food stamps in Mississippi to a high of $6,132 for such a family in New York, will narrow because the basic federal grant raises the benefit level in states near the low end of the scale.

In addition to paying 90 percent of the basic federal benefit, federal funds pay 75 percent of the state supplements for the first 12.32 percent above the basic grant, and 25 percent of any additional supplement up to the poverty level for those not expected to work. For a family of four, that means the federal government pays 90 percent of the first $4,200 of benefits, 75 percent of the next $500 in annual benefits, and 25 percent of any additional benefits up to the poverty line. For those expected to work, the federal government pays 25 percent of any supplement beyond the basic benefit, up to 75 percent of the poverty level. For the aged, blind, or disabled, the federal government pays 25 percent of any supplement.

In order to be eligible for federal funding for supplementary benefits, state supplements must follow federal eligibility criteria; the benefit reduction-rate is limited to 52 percent for expected-to-work families and 70 percent for not-expected-to-work families.

Beyond these matching supplements, the states may continue offering supplemental assistance using their own rules, eligibility criteria, and money. Indeed, states are encouraged to do so during the transition to the new program in order to protect current AFDC and SSI recipients.

States that supplement the cash assistance payments are required to supplement the work benefits and public service employment wages proportionately, up to a maximum of 10 percent over the minimum wage in the state.

Financial Responsibilities and Fiscal Relief

In addition to paying 90 percent of the basic cash assistance payment and a declining portion of supplemental payments, the federal government reimburses the states for 90 percent of the costs of administering the income maintenance and work benefit programs, and pays up to 110 percent of administrative expenses as a reward for efficiency. Overall, the Carter proposal envisions greater uniformity in the federal-state funding relationship as well as enlarged federal participation and the promise of fiscal relief.

The Carter administration seeks an orderly transition to the new arrangements, including immediate fiscal relief and minimal impact on current recipients. This will be accomplished through the maintenance of current effort requirements coupled with a guarantee of fiscal relief.

To protect current beneficiaries, each state is required to spend at least 90 percent of its current income maintenance expenditures during the new program's first year; in the second year, 75 percent; 65 percent in the third year. Thereafter the states' only obligation would be to pay 10 percent of the basic federal benefits.

While imposing these obligations, the federal government protects the states against increased costs of the new program during a five-year transition period. The federal government reimburses the states for expenditures exceeding 90 percent of current efforts if these additional funds have been spent to maintain current benefit levels or to "grandfather in" current SSI recipients or most AFDC recipients by continuing their supplementary payments.

As a result of this formula, each state is guaranteed a saving of at least 10 percent of its current welfare expenses in the first year of the program, while at the same time minimizing the impact of the transition on current AFDC and SSI recipients. Total first-year fiscal relief for the states is put at $2.1 billion, or 28 percent of the $7.3 billion they would otherwise have spent on welfare. While every state would save at least 10 percent, 34 states would save more, the administration predicts. These projected savings, shown in Table A.2, depend on the states hewing to certain administration assumptions about supplemental payments, benefit-reduction rates, and other factors. The administration figures show the states with the highest benefits and welfare burdens realizing the greatest savings in the first year. In subsequent years, as recipients leave the welfare rolls and the maintenance-of-effort requirements wind down, the administration said, opportunities for fiscal relief will increase.

A pro rata share of fiscal relief to the states must be passed through to localities with welfare expenditures. This means New York City, for example, will receive an estimated $156 million of the $475 saved by New York State in the programs's first year, according to administration figures.

Relation to Medicaid

The Administration said that Medicaid-related issues are best dealt with as part of the national health insurance proposal it expected to present to the Congress in 1978. If the implementation of national health insurance and welfare reform cannot be synchronized, the proposal said, existing Medicaid eligibility criteria should be preserved. Otherwise, new welfare eligibility rules could expand the Medicaid rolls and impose large additional costs.

EMERGENCY ASSISTANCE PROGRAM

To deal with situations that do not fit the proposed eligiblity standards but clearly warrant immediate aid, the Carter proposal establishes a new emergency assistance program under Title XX (Social Services) of the Social Security Act. The federal government will provide $600 million in block grants to the states to handle those whose immediate need is due to events such as natural disasters or to the effects of the retrospective accounting system. A separate allocation of $20 million will be dispensed by the secretary of health, education, and welfare to the states to meet the expenses of special categories of needy families, such as migrant workers, not adequately covered by the basic program.

Federal reimbursement for the administrative expenses involved in operating the emergency needs program is limited to 15 percent of a state's allocation for the program, and participation is contingent upon obtaining federal approval of a state's plans for utilizing the program's funds.

TABLE A.2

Estimated State Fiscal Relief under the Better Jobs and
Income Act ($ millions)

State	Current Effort Plus AFDC Administrative Costs	Fiscal Relief	Fiscal Relief as Percent of Current Effort + Admin.
01 AL	31.1	5.3	17.0
02 AK	11.9	2.4	20.2
03 AZ	21.8	2.7	12.3
04 AR	16.7	1.7	10.0
05 CA	1571.0	433.2	27.6
06 CO	57.0	5.7	10.0
07 CT	96.8	9.7	10.0
08 DE	14.8	4.2	28.2
09 DC	63.3	35.9	56.6
10 FL	44.3	9.9	22.4
11 GA	50.1	7.9	15.8
12 HI	47.5	6.3	13.3
13 ID	10.1	1.2	12.4
14 IL	556.1	222.1	39.9
15 IN	51.7	5.2	10.0
16 IA	49.7	5.0	10.0
17 KS	38.6	3.9	10.0
18 KY	48.3	4.8	10.0
19 LA	44.9	6.9	15.4
20 ME	25.2	4.8	19.2
21 MD	101.1	51.3	50.7
22 MA	419.0	135.5	32.3
23 MI	487.7	123.7	25.4
24 MN	102.6	15.4	15.1
25 MS	9.0	1.8	19.6
26 MO	95.4	20.2	21.2
27 MT	5.9	0.8	14.2
28 NE	16.4	1.6	10.0
29 NV	9.7	1.6	16.3
30 NH	14.7	1.5	10.5
31 NJ	289.5	74.2	25.6
32 NM	12.6	2.2	17.4
33 NY	1415.7	474.9	33.5
34 NC	56.8	5.7	10.0
35 ND	5.4	0.5	10.0
36 OH	260.6	97.4	37.4
37 OK	50.8	6.6	12.9
38 OR	60.4	9.0	14.9
39 PA	533.9	171.8	32.2
40 RI	38.6	10.8	28.0
41 SC	16.6	3.7	22.2
42 SD	8.2	1.5	18.6
43 TN	33.3	5.0	15.0
44 TX	52.3	12.2	23.4
45 UT	14.2	1.4	10.0
46 VT	16.2	1.6	10.0
47 VA	76.7	7.8	10.1
48 WA	116.1	33.3	28.7
49 WV	19.7	2.0	10.0
50 WI	117.3	11.7	10.0
51 WY	3.3	0.9	26.5
TOTAL:	7310.7	2065.0	AVG.: 28.2

Source: U.S. Department of Health, Education, and Welfare.

IMPLEMENTATION OF THE PRESIDENT'S PROGRAM

President Carter proposes that the PBJI be phased in over a three-year period following its enactment in order to minimize errors, confusion, and interruptions of benefit payments. The administration seeks to avoid the administrative chaos that ensued when the SSI program was thrust upon the Social Security Administration after 14 months of planning. The timetable outlined by HEW specifies:

● Within two months after enactment of the program by Congress, each state must declare its choice of state or federal intake.
● The first two years following enactment would be devoted to creating a computer network linking some 4,000 field offices to a centralized computer system. Personnel would also have to be trained.
● Two years after enactment, the first group of recipients would begin to apply for cash benefits.
● Three years after enactment, benefit checks would begin to go out under the new system.

COSTS

Although President Carter originally said his welfare reform proposal would not require any new federal spending, PBJI entails new net federal costs of $2.8 billion in the first year, according to the administration's methods of comparing figures. The gross cost of the program, as shown in Table A.3, is listed as $31.1 billion. Offsetting this is $26.6 billion (see Table A.4) which would otherwise be spent on existing programs and $1.7 billion in savings resulting from the new program. While total offsets come to $28.3 billion, leaving new net costs of $2.8 billion, these calculations ignore the $3 billion in revenue lost

TABLE A.3

Estimated Costs of the Proposed Welfare System
(billions of 1978 dollars)

Program	Cost
Employment	8.8
Cash assistance	20.2
Earned income tax credit*	1.5
Emergency assistance	0.6
Total	31.1

*The EITC above the tax-entry point would cost the federal government an additional $3.0 billion in lost tax revenues.
Source: Department of Health, Education, and Welfare.

TABLE A.4

Current Federal Welfare Expenditures and Projected Savings (billions of 1978 dollars)

Program	Expenditure
AFDC	6.4
SSI	5.7
Food stamps	5.5
Earned income tax credit	1.1
Stimulus portion of CETA public jobs	5.5
WIN	0.4
Extended unemployment insurance benefits (27–39 weeks)	0.7
Rebates of per capita share of wellhead tax revenues to low-income people if passed by Congress	1.3
Subtotal	26.6

	Saving
Decreased unemployment insurance expenditures	0.3
HEW program to reduce fraud and abuse	0.4
Decrease in required housing subsidies due to increased income	0.3
Increases in social security contributions	0.7
Subtotal	1.7
Total	28.3

Source: Department of Health, Education, and Welfare.

to the federal government as a result of expanded EITC benefits to middle-income wage earners. The $1.7 billion in savings is composed of four factors: a reduction in fraud and abuse as a result of the computerized, federally operated cash assistance program, and, as a result of the jobs program and the increased incomes it would provide, reductions in federal spending for unemployment insurance and housing subsidies, and an increase in federal revenues in the form of social security contributions. In the expenditures section, the administration has included $1.3 billion in rebates resulting from the wellhead tax, a provision of the president's energy program which still awaited congressional action when the PBJI proposal was released. The inclusion of this figure, as well as other estimates and methods used in the administration's cost calculations, is controversial, as will be seen below.

ISSUES RAISED BY THE WELFARE REFORM PROPOSAL

The initial reaction and discussion of PBJI was calm in tone, but the range of concerns was as broad as that greeting FAP, stretching from the general to the specific and from the philosophic to the mundane. Some wondered about the impact on the nation's moral fiber and others questioned effects on jobs. Some had abstract hypothetical concerns and others wondered if their own ox would be gored.

The major concerns of the major interested parties sorted themselves out quickly. Since, as was noted by Lester Salamon in Chapter 4, "welfare reform proposals represent different collections of responses to well-defined sets of basic questions," it is not surprising that the basic issues were familiar ones. Salamon identified six design issues that are important in most discussions of welfare reform alternatives: coverage, work incentives, benefit levels, mode of assistance, administration, and costs. It is clear these are the main concerns of those participating in the debate over the president's proposal.

In the next section, we shall first examine the questions raised about the Carter proposal as a whole, and then turn to more specific issues focusing on the jobs program, the cash assistance program, and the proposed relationship between the three tiers of government.

THE OVERALL PROPOSAL

The Pace of Reform: Incremental versus Comprehensive

HEW Assistant Secretary Henry Aaron noted in an Op-Ed page article in the December 12, 1977 edition of the New York *Times*, "the major issue" in the debate over the president's welfare reform proposal is whether it would be "more prudent and efficient to approach welfare reform incrementally, step-by-step, rather than in one major leap forward as President Carter has proposed."[13]

This debate between incrementalists and advocates of comprehensive reform is puzzling in some respects because incrementalists often agree with Aaron that they "seek the same objectives as the president's program for better jobs and income." Yet they differ with aspects of the Carter approach on both substantive and tactical grounds.

A major spokesman for the incrementalists' position is Richard P. Nathan, a senior fellow at the Brookings Institution and HEW deputy undersecretary in the Nixon administration. In congressional testimony, in a number of articles, and in a variety of Capitol Hill meetings, Nathan has challenged the president's approach. In his October 12, 1977 testimony to the House Welfare Reform Subcommittee, which became the basis for an Op-Ed page article in the New York *Times*, Nathan said, "The question to ask today is—Do we still need a *total* reform?" He insisted the answer was clearly no, because "a lot of water has gone over the welfare dam in the past eight years. The amount of program growth and change that has taken place can only be described as tremendous."[14] Federal spending for the poor has roughly doubled during the previous eight years, Nathan argues, filling many gaps in welfare coverage. SSI has established a guaranteed minimum annual income for the aged, blind, and disabled, while the growth of the food stamp program to a $5.4-billion-a-year effort has provided an income floor to the working poor. Congress agreed to eliminate the requirement that recipients put up their own money to buy food stamps in 1977, further broadening the program's coverage, Nathan said. Meanwhile, Congress adopted stringent work requirements, and HEW installed improved controls over fraud and error. The welfare rolls stopped climbing in most areas. In short, Nathan said, it is Medicaid, not welfare, that is now the real "mess," and the chaos that followed the Social Security Administration's attempt to implement the new SSI program should give pause to those who favor rapid changes.

What is needed, Nathan said, is not comprehensive reform, but such incremental steps as an expansion of welfare benefits to intact families, single persons, and childless couples, as well as the establishment of a national floor for benefit payments. Nathan proposed giving states and cities fiscal relief by increasing the level of federal matching funds. All of this would not add up to a dramatic plan, particularly since Nathan would implement his proposals gradually. But precisely because they are undramatic, he said, they could be implemented more readily. In an article in the New School for Social Research publication, *City Almanac*, Nathan noted that national attitudes toward welfare are "decidedly negative." He wrote:

> Under these conditions—when we have a choice of tactics—why should we raise the issue of a new welfare program to a high emotional pitch? The net outcome may involve compromises and concessions to such a degree that little or no improvement of welfare is ultimately achieved.[15]

The advocates of comprehensive reform reply to Nathan by asking: "why not the best?" In his December 12, 1977 Op-Ed page article, Henry Aaron noted:

> It is possible in principle to identify one by one the shortcomings of the present programs—the needs inadequately met, the antiwork and antifamily incentives, and the administrative complexity. Unfortunately, it is not possible to cure them one by one.

Aaron argues, "Some of the goals of welfare reform cannot be achieved by incremental reform at all." Administrative complexity, for example, is a result of incremental development to begin with, and cannot be solved incrementally. In addition, Aaron argues, "Some of the goals of welfare reform *can* be achieved by an incremental strategy, but only at costs far in excess of those entailed by the President's proposal." He noted that extending eligibility to two-parent families would reduce welfare's antifamily bias, but to do so "without adopting the changes recommended by the President in the way income is measured for determining eligibility would result in caseload more than one-third greater and expenditures one-fourth higher than those entailed by the PBJI."

Comprehensive-reform advocates also take issue with the feasibility of the incrementalists' one-step-at-a-time approach. That can only yield confused programs, they insist. "You can't legislate over a ten year period," Michael Barth, HEW deputy assistant secretary argues, because "you need momentum, and committees and people change in the Congress."[16] The rallying cry of the comprehensive-reform group, as stated by Aaron in his Op-Ed page article, was that "the present mess is a product of the incremental strategy." And a favorite analogy of this group was offered by John Palmer, a fellow at the Brookings Institution and former HEW official:

> The dilemma of welfare reformers reminds me of one I recently faced regarding my old, ailing automobile. It was built for conditions which no longer exist. Over the years so many different mechanics had made *ad hoc* repairs and modifications that it resembled a Rube Goldberg creation. Although continued repairs might have kept it running, and perhaps even improved it, it became clear that I could obtain a high level of performance only by trading it in for a new model. We have come to the same point with our welfare system.[17]

Like many a wary owner of an older car, however, Nathan questions whether one could be sure these expensive new models were built to run well. In any case, Nathan says, "This is the wrong approach for social policy. Huge, complex social programs should no longer be thought of in simplistic terms like they were used cars."[18]

The Scope of Reform:
What Goes Into a Welfare Reform Bill

Major concerns about the scope of the president's program focus on the inclusion of the EITC and the jobs program and the exclusion of health care and social services.

Whatever the merits of the EITC as a means of aiding the working poor, many members of the House of Representatives and others are opposed to making tax policy in a welfare bill. The EITC, they argue, should be studied in the context of tax policies, not welfare reform.

Similarly, the administration is accused of establishing employment and training policies in an afterthought to a welfare bill. Ronald Brown, deputy executive director of the National Urban League, argues that "the jobs program should not be a component of welfare reform but rather part of a full employment program."[19] Others argue it should be taken up in the context of a debate on manpower training policies. Still others note that a specific CETA authorization measure was scheduled to come before Congress in the fall of 1978, yet the administration is presupposing a winding down of the CETA Title VI counter-cyclical jobs as part of its welfare reform bill.

In contrast to some critics who fault the proposal for being too broad, other see glaring omissions regarding health care and social services. Though Medicaid eligibility is tied to welfare eligibility, the administration proposes to deal with health care in its upcoming national health insurance proposal. This arouses concern among those who feel that if welfare reform is enacted without a national health insurance proposal, the states will have a Hobson's choice: either expand Medicaid coverage to those newly eligible for welfare, which would run up the already skyrocketing costs; or maintain existing Medicaid eligibility standards, while new and different eligibility standards govern welfare. That would create an administrative morass.

Medicaid expenditures have grown larger than AFDC costs and have involved more people than any other program except social security. Thus, Martin Hochbaum of the American Jewish Congress notes that "failure to deal with the Medicaid program is a serious oversight";[20] and Brown of the National Urban League said it is "critical that the health insurance package be developed as a companion piece to this proposal."[21] The Carter administration felt, however, that Medicaid reform would create even more problems within the scope of the welfare proposal.

Much the same dilemma affects social services. The welfare reform bill says little about social services that states and localities provide in conjunction with welfare payments. But as Robert Fersh of the American Public Welfare Association (APWA) notes:

> As in the case of Medicaid, it is thought that demand for social services will go up due to the expanded number of people eligible for cash assistance. Increased participation should alone result in more referrals and increased familiarity with services provided by states. In addition, the jobs component should create greater demands for child care and other services.[22]

The Carter proposal offers no indication of what it might do about this increased demand for social services, Fersh notes; and it also fails to come to grips with the prospect of greater administrative problems in coordinating the cash assistance and social service programs.

Both the perceived infringement on tax and manpower policymakers and the failure to deal with Medicaid and social services are seen by the incrementalists as support for their position. By breaking up the proposal, they argue, each element could be handled in the proper time and place. The comprehensive-reform advocates differ. They argue that the Carter administration's proposal has to be broad since welfare affects nearly 20 percent of the nation's population in myriad ways and, inevitably, abuts and overlaps a variety of policy areas.

The Complexity of Reform: Will It Work?

Interwoven with concerns about the scope of the proposal are questions about its complexity. Many wonder if the plan contained in H.R. 9030's 163 pages is too complex to legislate, to complex to implement, and too intricate to operate successfully. Barth of NEW insisted, "The issue is inherently complex." But Leslie Lenkowsky, a consultant to Senator Moynihan, spoke for many when he noted, "The plan is overly complex—they tried to get too much into it." Although many regard simplification as a goal of welfare reform, John J. Korbel of the Congressional Budget Office (CBO) mused, "It's not a simplification, and it could be a complication."[23]

The cash assistance program, for example, consolidates the existing array of programs, but the result is not a simple, universal program; benefits, work requirements, benefit-reduction levels, and work opportunities vary widely. Moreover, the links between the jobs program and the cash assistance program require constant monitoring as households move between the upper and lower tiers. Some administrative features may be cost effective and simplify certain actions, but retrospective accounting, monthly income reporting, and the imputation of income from assets all add complex administrative responsibilities.

The increased complexity of the procedures is accompanied by a division of responsibility among several tiers of government and a variety of agencies. If it takes 163 pages to turn the proposal into legislation, it will take much more to turn it into an operational program. Fersh of the APWA argues:

> While the sophisticated computer apparatus that is anticipated should accommodate some of these complexities more efficiently than current technology, the computer cannot solve all. [Social] workers will still have to deal with a great many factors which will vary from case to case. And it is unlikely recipients will comprehend the program's many complexities.[24]

This last problem was considered particularly troublesome by the Center for Social Welfare Policy and Law, which notes in its analysis of the Carter proposal:

> Even leaving aside the basic question of the merits of the substance of the proposal, this incredible complexity is a defect serious enough by itself to call the entire program into question. Those who have created this proposal seem to have lost sight of the fundamental fact that the program is intended to serve real living human beings, not computers. There is simply no sense in establishing a program which cannot be understood and in which only a few will be able to understand their basic rights.[25]

Thus critics argue that the Carter proposal is not only too complicated to be dealt with effectively by the legislators who will debate it, and the administrators who may operate it, but also too complicated for the welfare recipients who may live under it. The complexities, some of which will be examined later, were minimized in discussions by the administration. HEW officials declare the president's program to be both administratively feasible and particularly efficient in its use of sophisticated and centralized data processing.

The Cost of Reform: Who Knows?

Substantial attention has been focused on the costs of the Carter program. If the overall costs are significantly different from those forecast by the administration, that would raise major questions about the feasibility of the program as a whole. The administration says the proposal would have a net new cost of $2.8 billion in federal dollars in its first year. But many question both the new program's costs and the way they were compared with existing expenditures.

Fersh of the APWA notes, "Many public welfare analysts are incredulous over the cost estimates provided."[26] And Rufus Miles concludes, "The cost estimates of both components of the program are unrealistically low."[27] Many complained that the administration's estimated cost for the jobs program was based on an assumed 1.4 million jobs; that figure assumes that 2.5 million people will move through these jobs in one year and that the unemployment rate will drop to 5.6 percent in 1981. Both assumptions are vigorously debated. Moreover, Miles argues that providing jobs is generally a costly operation, and could be expected to have large cost overruns.

The proposed cash assistance program makes many new groups eligible for aid, and some question if the proposed changes in the accountability period and eligibility would hold down outlays as indicated by the president. Even if a federal takeover of calculations and payments reduces the number of people needed to administer the system, overall costs might actually increase, Miles argues, because state employees will be replaced by federal employees, who are 30 to 50 percent more expensive.

Finally, the $600 million budgeted for emergency needs is widely thought to be a number pulled out of the air. Many estimate that actual expenditures will be much higher, noting that the emergency needs program assists all those who may lose benefits as a result of tighter eligibility standards.

In contrasting the proposal with existing programs, the estimated $2.8 billion in additional federal costs is, some critics charge, based on a comparison of new apples and old oranges, rather than on comparison of the new programs with appropriate old ones.

One expenditure to be replaced, as shown in Table 5.4, is the $5.9 billion stimulus portion of CETA and WIN; but this saving, like the size of the jobs program, depends on a drop in the unemployment rate, which might not occur. The anticipated wellhead tax revenue offset of $1.3 billion is contingent upon congressional enactment of the president's energy program. Including this offset ignores not only its uncertain fate but also the fact that its enactment and fiscal impact would occur quite independently of welfare reform. Can it, then, be considered a legitimate offset?

Welfare administrators question whether the administration can save $400 million by reducing fraud and error. So much has already been done by HEW in this area that some doubt such a large amount is left to be saved. Moreover, since the entire cost of AFDC and SSI—including overpayments and grants to ineligibles—is already included as an offset, the $400 million would seem to have been counted twice.

As for the anticipated saving of $700 million in extended unemployment insurance payments and $400 million in regular unemployment insurance expenditures as a result of the jobs program, the National Association of Counties's analysis of the proposal notes that these funds come from employer taxes paid into a trust fund. These earmarked funds could not be used to finance general revenue programs, and thus one could question their use as an offset.

Finally, the administration figures raise questions about the impact of the EITC, which would provide $3 billion to those not receiving income supplements. This means a $3 billion drop in federal tax revenues, but the figure is not listed as a cost of welfare reform.

Doubts about the administration's cost figures were fueled by the Congressional Budget Office. CBO estimates that the Carter proposal will cost the federal government nearly $10 billion more per year than the administration estimated—$13.9 billion more in fiscal 1982 under the proposed programs than under existing ones. It also estimates that state and local governments will save $4.26 billion instead of the $2.1 billion predicted by the administration.

The CBO and White House estimates are not directly comparable, since CBO figures are stated in 1982 dollars, while HEW used 1978 dollars. Moreover, CBO projections assume a 4.5 percent unemployment rate instead of the 5.6 percent used by HEW. But CBO did not assume an end of the unemployment insurance extended benefits program or of Title VI of CETA. Nor did CBO consider the wellhead tax or any new fraud and abuse savings as offsets.

While the figures are not directly comparable, if CBO's conclusions for 1982 were translated into 1978 dollars, a CBO staff member said, CBO projections would show a net new cost for the Carter welfare program of $12.4 billion, or more than four times the administration's estimate of $2.8 billion. These kinds of differences in cost estimates prompt some to conclude that the Carter program is too expensive to be enacted, and that many revisions will have to be made.

These questions and the skepticism they reflect will be the stuff of continuing debate over the president's program. The administration can be expected to support its own projections with further research.

JOBS PROGRAM ISSUES

The jobs component of the president's proposal sparks the greatest controversy. As James W. Singer wrote in the November 12, 1977 issue of the *National Journal*:

The Carter Administration's proposal to create 1.4 million public jobs for welfare recipients and other low-income persons seems to be creating 1.4 million questions and complaints.

The chorus of concern is not confined to a few special groups or persons but appears to be coming from almost everyone who has studied the welfare reform package.[28]

The Work Requirement

The proposal's heavy emphasis on getting welfare recipients to work incurred only limited opposition, in contrast with the situation a few years ago when the imposition of work requirements filled the air with talk of welfare slavery. Civil rights groups such as the National Urban League, and liberal economists like Robert Lekachman complained about the work emphasis, but this issue has clearly declined in controversy. As the New York *Times* editorialized on May 13, 1977, "It has been obvious for a decade that the only way to get the country to swallow the bitter pill of welfare is to sugar-coat it with work."[29]

More fundamentally, there have been significant changes in attitudes toward work in the last half-dozen years. After a period of flirting with ideas of superabundance and leisure during the 1960s, a kind of neo-Puritan work ethic has taken hold, in which work is seen as an important avenue toward self-realization and self-actualization. Increasingly, work is seen as offering real value, in contrast to the demeaning dependency of welfare, although many of the rewards of work are probably more accessible to the middle class than to those facing a life of low-wage work.

Changed attitudes are particularly important for women. The women's movement led more and more women into the labor force as it transformed ideas about women working. While a half-dozen years ago the idea of dragging a woman away from *kinder* and *kuche* was anathema to many, Senator Daniel P. Moynihan noted in an interview in *Time* magazine, "Work is no longer considered to be a form of punishment as applied to women. A liberal constituency no longer finds work unattractive."[30]

Although putting people to work has developed an appeal among liberals as well as conservatives, certainly there are differences in motives: Conservatives often see work as a punitive measure designed to cure slothful ways and extract something in return for aid, while liberals see it as a means of developing good habits, enhancing self-respect, and helping the community—the jobs provided were, after all, public service jobs. Differing value judgments converge in the feeling that life as a school aide, for example, is better than life on the dole; and the welfare debate no longer revolves around whether or not to put people to work, but rather, how to do it, and, above all, what to pay them.

Design and Feasibility of the Jobs Program

A variety of questions has been raised about virtually every element of the jobs program's design and scope.

The entry point for a needy family—the intensive job search—was criticized by Brown of the National Urban League because "the proposal does not offer any specific help for moving people into regular employment."[31] Instead, Elliott Currie wrote in *The Nation*, it offers only the "tired exhortation" to use existing placement channels in pursuit of jobs many believe are not there.[32]

As for the subsidized jobs, many shared Brown's concern that the "individual will not qualify for permanent employment by virtue of a PSE [public service employment] placement."[33] Although the administration said it would provide training in these jobs, nothing specific was proposed, and without skills training, critics warn, the program will provide little to equip the jobholder for finding work in the regular economy. Others faulted the program because the proposed jobs focus on tasks performed only by government agencies. Thus, the jobholders will not learn skills likely to be marketable in the private sector. Conservatives suggest involving the private sector more in providing the jobs.

The 12-month limit on holding a subsidized job was sharply criticized by Mitchell Ginsberg, dean of Columbia University's School of Social Work. He said the 12-month limit would simply create a revolving-door program, as many participants might find that there are no jobs in the inner-city areas where they live. Even with improved macroeconomic conditions, some people would simply not be placeable. For example, a 58-year-old former alcoholic with numerous minor ailments might be regarded as expected-to-work by the Department of Labor, Ginsberg noted, but such a person would be "an unlikely candidate for employment" by most private- or public-sector organizations and might end up going through several 12-month stints in subsidized jobs.[34]

Because of the numerous questions about the jobs program, several congressmen and others propose mounting a pilot project to demonstrate the feasibility of the program and provide some experience, before launching a full-scale effort.

The scale of the proposed effort is itself one of the issues raised. Some experts question the administration's 1.4 million figure; critics say it is simply the number of jobs Carter thinks the program can afford rather than the likely demand. Many question whether people would move through the jobs rapidly enough to enable the program to serve 2.5 million people a year, as predicted by the administration.

Some experts doubt the feasibility of creating the jobs proposed in the period suggested. In a paper prepared for the Joint Economic Committee of Congress in October 1977, Sheldon Danziger, Robert Haveman, and Eugene Smolensky, of the University of Wisconsin's Institute for Research on Poverty, wrote:

The mass creation of public service jobs for low wage-low skill workers is something with which this country has no previous experience. The effort is analogous to a private firm's promise to introduce a new product, the manufacture of which requires a technology which has not yet been developed. In all such cases, the effort is fraught with uncertainty, and the possibility of an ineffective and unproductive program must not be neglected.[35]

The administration argues that the CETA program has successfully moved from 50,000 jobs to 725,000 jobs in a relatively short period of time, and suggests the same kind of rapid buildup for its subsidized jobs program. But some insist that the CETA jobs are frequently make-work projects providing few benefits to either the community or the jobholder, and they warn that the new jobs program would be even less useful.

Wages and Treatment of Subsidized Workers

The issue that generates the most heat is clearly the administration's intention to pay subsidized workers the minimum wage. With the labor movement in the forefront, there is strong pressure to change the proposed wage level to the local prevailing wage. Leonard Lesser, general counsel for the Center for Community Change, notes that the prevailing rather than the minimum wage is specified in CETA Title VI, the Youth Employment Act, the Federal Unemployment Tax Act (which governs state unemployment compensation laws), and the 1969 Family Assistance Plan. He and others argue that the minumum wage is discriminatory and stigmatizing for the subsidized workers, as well as threatening to other workers.

Lesser notes that someone placed in a subsidized job might find himself working alongside regular workers being paid higher wages and fringe benefits. But the subsidized worker would have no fringe benefits, no vacation, no EITC, and no right to bargain collectively. As a result, the Carter proposal has a "retrogressive, stigmatizing effect" on the subsidized jobholders, Lesser argues.[36]

The administration's claim that these are new kinds of jobs for which there are no prevailing wages is generally considered nonsense. The claim that the jobs can be considered training opportunities, and therefore warrant lower wages, is dismissed because the training component has not been spelled out.

The administration argues that wages have to be low to hold down costs and avoid luring people away from regular jobs. But nearly a sixth of the jobs in the country pay less than the minimum wage, critics say; many think subsidized jobs would be relatively attractive to many low-wage workers.

The administration also argues that subsidized wages are not really all that low. With premiums to job-group leaders, state supplementation, and the legislated rise in the minimum wage, the average wage to be paid in 1981 will be $3.72 an hour. In a September 23, 1977 press release, Labor Secretary Marshall noted:

The wages of most workers would also be supplemented by cash assistance for family size so that total income will be equal to or greater than that currently provided by CETA. For example, a worker in a public service job would have his $5,512 base wage supplemented by a $1,444 cash assistance payment; thus he would be receiving a total income of almost $7,000. In a state supplementing the cash assistance by 10 percent, the wage would be $6,063, the cash assistance benefit would be $1,854 and the total income $8,000.

But precisely because additional funds would be going to these subsidized workers, it would clearly be possible to pay out more money in wages, the AFL-CIO said:

> We believe one of the primary goals of a jobs and income program should be to get those people who are working off the welfare rolls. Rather than using public funds in the form of welfare payments to subsidize inadequate wages, these funds should be used to insure that workers are getting fair compensation for their labor.[37]

By paying workers wages rather than welfare benefits, the welfare rolls would be limited solely to the aged, blind, and disabled. Advocates of the triple-track system (described earlier in this volume) say there would be less concern about shirkers and less opposition to raising welfare benefits if the welfare rolls were clearly composed only of those unable to work.

Impact on Other Workers and on City Services

The administration points out that subsidized jobs would not duplicate any current functions, nor would their creation affect the wages and benefits of other workers. However, leaders of the American Federation of State, County, and Municipal Employees, and other labor leaders are concerned about the impact of the subsidized jobs program on those who would hold the jobs and the effects on other workers. Bert Seidman, director of the social security department of the AFL-CIO, pointed out,

> There is no protection in H.R. 9030 against employers in both the public and private sectors lowering the wages of their present employees or firing them altogether. Indeed there is no assurance that the public service jobs under the proposal wouldn't simply replace jobs or workers now employed or who would otherwise be hired by state and local governments.[38]

There is particular concern over the fate of the 725,000 workers employed under Title VI of CETA. It is not altogether clear to some observers whether the administration's proposal assumes that the Title VI countercyclical-jobs program would disappear because of improvements in the economy or would be supplanted by the new program. Will Title VI workers, generally earning $7,800 a year, have their pay and fringe benefits reduced? Will they be terminated and forced into a five-week job search and then rehired for their old jobs at almost half the pay?

At issue is not only the fate of these workers but the financial health of many cities which have, despite the regulations, used CETA employees to deliver regular city services. CETA workers compose more than 20 percent of the city work force in St. Louis, Rochester, Buffalo, San Jose, Newark, and Hartford, among other cities. If Title VI workers are phased out, any fiscal relief from welfare reform will be eaten up in replacing them.

Conservatives are unhappy with the administraion's apparent redirection of the countercyclical-jobs money. They suspect the Carter proposal of seeking to capture the temporary countercyclical funds in CETA and transferring them to a permanent jobs program, thus achieving a kind of back-door Humphrey-Hawkins bill. The administration said many of the real and conjectured issues would be resolved as soon as it sent a CETA authorization bill to Congress, a measure scheduled for late 1978. Still, the impact of its welfare-reform jobs program on other workers became a major issue.

Issues Raised by Wage Supplementation

The requirement that states supplementing federal cash assistance payments also must supplement wages in the jobs program creates two potential inequities in the work incentive system.

Some states find that the cost of supplementing the wage by 10 percent will exceed the amount of cash assistance savings accruing to the state if the person is employed in a subsidized job; thus some states will find it cheaper to keep a family on welfare than to put a member to work.

Eligibility Requirements

Because there are no income or assets tests for the jobs program, the National Association of Counties warned, persons who are unemployed briefly and are eligible for unemployment insurance may seek a "welfare job" in states where the maximum unemployment insurance benefit is less than wages in the subsidized jobs programs.

Other observers are troubled by the program's varying eligibility standards. While any household is eligible for benefits if it meets income and assets tests, and any adult is eligible for the job search assistance program, the proposed jobs program is open only to parents. Single individuals and childless couples are not eligible for subsidized jobs, although their need might be no less than that of others. Critics say the different standards for different categories are unfair.

Some feminists criticized the administration for limiting access to the jobs program to the principal earner in two-parent families. Since women are less likely than men to have established work records and recent earnings, feminists contend that the proposed procedure will only perpetuate their spotty employment record.

THE CASH ASSISTANCE PROGRAM

The Benefit Levels

The administration's proposed benefit levels are a major issue in the debate over PBJI: many conservatives feel the proposed levels are too high; liberals think they are low. The debate is more muted than the controversy over benefit levels that was widely regarded as the undoing of FAP. Conservatives tend to focus more on the high cost of PBJI as a whole, and argue against broadening coverage to include nonparents and the working poor. They point out that the proposal raises benefit levels extensively in the South and provides jobs at wages higher than those paid in many private-sector jobs. The result, conservatives claim, is a threat to the economic base of southern states: low-wage workers will be lured away to subsidized jobs or welfare.

Liberals often agree with Currie, who wrote in the September 17, 1977 edition of *The Nation* that "for all the rhetoric about guaranteeing a dignified standard of living, the Carter plan is simply miserly."[39] Similarly, Seidman of the AFL–CIO said, "The proposed levels are inadequate by even the poorest of standards."[40] But many liberals are less vocal. Some have been chastened by the FAP fight and others by George McGovern's problems with welfare in the 1972 presidential campaign. Liberals are no longer being pushed by an organized welfare rights constituency to demand more; and, finally, many are pursuing a political strategy seeking to bring together enough support for a reasonably improved program.

The lower-tier benefits for those expected to work, however, is a focal point for liberal concern. The proposed $2,300 a year for a family of four would mean only $5 a week more than what is provided by the current food stamp program. This sum is not only insufficient to live on. But, as the California Health and Welfare Agency noted in its analysis of H.R. 9030: "Since aggressive job search activities usually involve additional expense, this provision may act more as a barrier to successful job search effort . . . and therefore could be counterproductive."[41]

Inequities

"In addition to the overall inadequacy of benefit levels," Seidman notes, "there is a wide range of payment differentials which raise a question of equity." Many of the apparent inequities are essentially transitional problems. Although states are required to grandfather in the program current SSI recipients, grandfathering may be applied only to 75 percent of the AFDC caseload. As a result of this and other omissions, Robert O. Reischauer, CBO's assistant director for human resources and community development, estimates that 1.8 million families below the poverty line, or nearly 26 percent of all current beneficiaries, will lose benefits under the Carter plan, Seidman told a Congressional committee.[42]

A major inequity in the eyes of many is the loss of indexing for SSI and food stamp recipients. While these programs have been indexed to changes in the cost of living, the proposed cash assistance program, like the existing AFDC program, would not be indexed, so recipients would have to depend on the largess of Congress rather than statutory provisions to ensure that their benefits keep pace with inflation. There are a variety of other perceived inequities. Many ask, for example, why a mother and child are to be given less to live on than an aged couple, or why needy individuals or couples under 65 should be expected to live on about half the benefits of those over 65. Some ask why the administration continues to permit the glaring disparities among benefit levels in various states, and others ask how one could justify offering an EITC to low-wage workers in regular jobs but not to those in subsidized jobs. Still others complained that the EITC is an efficient mechanism, aiding the middle class as well as the welfare population.

In its assessment of the proposed benefit structure, the Center for Social Welfare Policy and Law notes, "Clearly the only rationale for the different benefit levels was a basically political decision as to how to allocate funds from the total fixed pot among different categories of people."[43]

Elimination of Food Stamps

The president's proposal to end the food stamp program arouses great concern. The administration argues that the poor are capable of managing their income, but some observers favor continuing in-kind benefits as a guarantee that money will not be spent on frivolities. Advocates of the triple-track plan and others argue that food stamps are a useful way of aiding the working poor without burdening them with the stigma of welfare. Trade unionists support food stamps, because strikers may obtain them, but not welfare benefits—particularly under a six-month retrospective accountability period. Agricultural interests favor retaining food stamps, and powerful congressmen support them, as they want to preserve their bailiwick.

Many do not find the theoretical argument in favor of food stamps compelling, but the political support mustered by this program is impressive.

The Benefit-Reduction Rate

If welfare benefits are reduced too rapidly as earnings increase, there is little incentive to work; yet if the benefit-reduction rate is too gradual, work incentives remain strong but families remain eligible until they reach very high income levels. Therefore, the administration proposed a 50 percent benefit-reduction rate and put a limit on the reduction rates imposed by the states of 52 percent on the expected-to-work population and 70 percent on those not expected to work. The administration's efforts to maintain work incentives were welcomed, but both the level and the nature of the limits drew criticism.

High-benefit states dislike the benefit-reduction rates. If New York chooses to maintain its existing benefit levels, for example, the 52 percent rule would force it to continue cash aid to working families with incomes up to $11,923 a year. This would bring massive increases in the number of families eligible, and it could, for example, put 25 percent of the population of upstate Broome County on welfare. New York Governor Hugh L. Carey, chairman of the National Governors' Association Task Force on Welfare Reform, urged that the states be given "much greater flexibility in establishing benefit reduction levels."[44]

Others question the nature of the limits proposed. While AFDC recipients can deduct the first $30 of earnings plus one-third thereafter, California's Health and Welfare Agency said the proposed flat percentage system

> provides an inequitable advantage to higher income recipients whose fixed work-related expenses comprise a smaller percentage of their gross earnings than those of minimum wage earners. We believe that a flat work-related expense allowance with an appropriate benefit reduction ratio applied to the remaining income is a more equitable approach.[45]

The AFL-CIO also questions the 50 percent limit for the not-expected-to-work population. If people are properly categorized as not expected to work, they would be unlikely to have earned income, nor would there be much purpose in providing them with a work incentive; it only adds unnecessarily to the cost of the program, the AFL-CIO states.

Eligibility Criteria and the Emergency Needs Program

The president's plans for unifying and tightening eligibility standards are criticized for being unrealistic, difficult to administer, and unduly harsh in some respects. The administration contends that the regulations are designed to ensure that assistance goes only to those who are most in need.

The major bone of contention is the proposed retrospective accounting system to be used in measuring income to determine eligiblity and benefit payments. The California Health and Welfare Agency argues that under a retrospective system it "would be extremely difficult to ascertain and verify changes in income and other circumstances for members of a filing unit over a prior six month period."[46] While a middle-class professional might simply bring in the computerized stubs from his paychecks for the previous half a year, a low-skilled person who worked irregularly at several jobs might lack the records needed to verify his income. And checking the income for such a family may be difficult for a caseworker.

Retrospective accounting will be complex to administer and reduce the responsiveness of the welfare system. That is exactly what the administration is trying to do with its six-month accountability period: keep those with temporary needs off welfare. Critics say this procedure reflects limited understanding of the poor. A middle-class family suddenly deprived of income might live on savings while awaiting aid. But, Seidman argued, "It is both unrealistic and inappropriate to expect that the poor who are forced to live on less than they must have to meet their minimum needs can somehow budget money for an unforeseen period when they will have no income at all."[47] The lengthy waiting periods required for some families, as shown in Table 5.1, simply force the states to use emergency needs funds to aid those in immediate need but not yet eligible for regular aid, critics charge.

Another area of concern is the proposal to impute income from assets. As the California Health and Welfare Agency notes in its detailed analysis of H.R. 9030, this "would greatly increase administrative complexity while adding only a small amount to the available income of the recipient."[48] It will be difficult to establish the fair value of many assets, and while the concept may make sense for middle-class families whose portfolio of assets may be liquidated but by bit to generate income, the assets of the poor are unlikely to be easily marketed. The imputation of income will not only be a difficult calculation but one with little bearing on economic or financial reality. Rural America argues that the proposal is particularly harmful to rural people who own land that generates no income.

Under the Carter assets test, the most vexing problem remains untouched. The value of an owner-occupied house continues to be excluded from countable assets; this was considered reasonable and especially helpful to the elderly. But H.R. 9030 perpetuates the dilemma in which a person with a $30,000 house and $499 in the bank becomes eligible for welfare, while the family with no house and $600 in the bank remains ineligible until it spends some of its savings.

The new eligibility criteria, particularly the proposed retrospective accountable period, will exclude a number of people in immediate need from the regular cash assistance program. The administration points out that these people will be aided by the emergency needs program. But many argue that an emergency program should be reserved for those needing immediate aid in extraordinary circumstances, such as natural disasters, and should not become a safety net to catch large numbers falling between the standard eligibility criteria. People involved in the emergency needs program will have to rely on the discretion of administrators rather than legal entitlement in order to obtain aid.

The administration's proposed $630 million budget for emergency needs is widely regarded as inadequate. The National Association of Counties estimates that 28 major states are already spending $780 million a year for one-time payments.

THE ROLES OF EACH LEVEL OF GOVERNMENT

A number of issues center on the roles proposed for various levels of government in operating and financing welfare programs.

Administrative Issues

The Carter proposal rearranges the tasks performed by various levels of government in administering the nation's welfare system. Incrementalists warn that the proposed three-year transition period is too short to permit a smooth federal takeover of the computation and payment of benefits. They note that chaos ensued after the creation of SSI, with a caseload of 4 million, when the 14-month transition period proved insufficient for this program. The Carter proposal affects 11 million cases.

Many critics have administrative concerns that extend beyond the transition period. Miles said federal computation and payments will end up raising administrative costs because federal employees cost more than state employees, and the results will not necessarily be more efficient. A single, unified system is also susceptible to disaster, errors, and terrorism, Miles noted.

The states retain the option of performing intake and referral activities, but are obliged to maintain an administrative mechanism to run Medicaid, social services, and emergency needs programs. Thus, the network of federal cash assistance payments offices that will grow up alongside the state system may be seen as a duplication of effort. Since the state administrative apparatus must continue to exist anyway, why not capitalize on it, some ask. In a dual system, the federal government mails out checks while the states deal face to face with recipients. Thus, Fersh noted, "They will have direct contacts with clients and take the brunt of criticism for program failures. Yet they will lack final authority and tools to respond to people's problems."[49]

In addition to divided responsibilities in the cash assistance program, the National Association of Counties notes, "The proposal does not address the problem as to how the welfare system and the jobs program will coordinate service delivery."[50] The administration is unclear as to the role of the governor's office in planning the jobs program, although it seemed clear local CETA prime sponsors would run these programs. The National Association of Counties and the National League of Cities insist that the jobs program be run by locally controlled CETA prime sponsors in order to be responsive to local needs. But the governors and state legislatures note that since fiscal responsibility for cash assistance is theirs, and the jobs program is intimately related, they must exercise some control over both. They argue that statewide planning is an administrative necessity for the jobs program. The California Health and Welfare Agency warned:

H.R. 9030 proposes to fragment this authority by leaving the fiscal burden of the supplementary assistance program with the states, but delegating complete authority over the jobs component to a mix of jurisdictional and organizational entities that don't have statewide authority, uniform jurisdictional boundaries, nor even a uniform labor market area. For example, in the Los Angeles/Orange County areas, eight different prime sponsors and the State Employment Service provide employment and training services within a single labor market area.[51]

Much of the debate over the organization of the jobs program conceals a struggle for control over jobs and resources, but the administrative questions are still valid. Whatever the ultimate focus of control over the jobs program, Governor Richard Kneip of South Dakota told the Welfare Reform Subcommittee:

At this point, the Governors are not convinced that a program which provides for three types of administration to the same client group (essentially federal administration of the cash assistance portion, local administration of the jobs portion, and state administration for social services) will be more rational than the current system.[52]

The fragmentation of the overall system strikes some as an unintended consequence of HEW's efforts to divorce its cash payments mechanism from social services. While this may be appropriate in Washington, some welfare experts argue that mechanisms are needed for coordinating the various welfare activities at the local level. Definition of authority and responsibility for various decisions is required in order to avoid an utterly fragmented system.

Fragmentation will inevitably lead to poor service for welfare recipients. Miles warned:

Where should a bewildered client go if he doesn't know what he needs? No longer would there be a welfare office. There would be one office for regular cash assistance, one for emergency cash assistance, several for referrals to jobs and training, and none to aid the distraught, mentally handicapped or disturbed mother with multiple problems that she can hardly enumerate.[53]

The Carter proposal seems to create an administrative structure requiring special efforts to achieve coordination and to fix responsibility.

Fiscal Relief

For many state and local officials, fiscal relief has become the sine qua non of welfare reform. It was that part of the Carter proposal they scrutinized most carefully and cared about most deeply. Although initial reactions were favorable, three kinds of issues have been raised by state and local officials. Some say the date the Carter proposal becomes effective is too far off in the future; they need immediate fiscal relief. Others agree with Nicholas Carbone, City Council president of Hartford, who told the Welfare Reform Subcommittee, on behalf of the National League of Cities, that the proposed fiscal relief is fine as far as it goes but "it falls far short of total federal financing."[54]

The focal point for much debate on fiscal relief is whether the promised $2.1 billion in the first year and what Secretary Califano calls "an opportunity for additional relief in subsequent years"[55] is real or illusory. The problem is that projections of state expenditures and savings depend on assumptions about supplementation rates, benefit-reduction rates, welfare rolls, and other unpredictable factors. Different assumptions lead to sharply different results.

The administration said New York State would save $527 million, with $175 million passing through to New York City. Later Secretary Califano said the state would save $475 million and the city $156 million. But Governor Carey predicted the state would save only $335 million, and New York City officials said they expected to save only $110 million.

In California, the Carter administration said, the state's initial savings would total $432 million, but the state Health and Welfare Agency concluded that the proposal would actually cost the state money: "The additional non-federal cost of H.R. 9030 during the first year of operation will be substantially greater than under current welfare programs—approximately $348 million." The agency explained: "This increase is due to the addition of 1.5 million working poor, Emergency Assistance payments, the minimum wage supplement to Public Service Employment, Medi-Cal administrative costs, and the grandfathering of AFDC and SSI/SSP recipients." The difference between the California and HEW estimates resulted from differing assumptions. The California agency said:

It should be pointed out that this proposal could provide fiscal relief if California chose to select a higher benefit reduction rate or a lower supplementation rate than provided in these estimates. However, this would result in an adverse impact on some recipients.

Aside from the costs of welfare itself, the California analysis notes that HEW "did not reflect the additional potential cost of maintaining the current level of social services for the larger eligible population under H.R. 9030."[56] Even if there are significant state and local savings on public assistance costs, this may be erased by increased expenditures for related services.

In an analysis prepared for the Regional Plan Association, John P. Keith and Joseph M. Thomas noted that the proposal fails to adjust benefit levels in response to inflation. As the cost of living and the poverty threshold rise, state and local contributions to supplement basic benefits will rise. As they do, the federal contribution will drop from 90 percent to 75 percent to 25 percent. Thus, Keith and Thomas warned, "This could mean that states and localities would realize the most fiscal relief the initial year the proposed program becomes effective, with a gradual decline in fiscal relief during the following years."[57]

Lesser and others are concerned that the states will quickly perceive this and begin cutting back their supplementation programs after the maintenance of effort requirements end. But the administration is convinced that fiscal relief will continue well beyond the first year.

Whatever the actual fiscal relief that may result from the Carter administration's proposal for cost sharing, the reimbursement mechanism, which essentially accumulates liabilities on a case-by-case basis, arouses concern. Representative Fred Richmond says the cost-sharing formula is "so complicated that at this moment no major state has been able to adequately predict its fiscal impact";[58] and California's Health and Welfare Agency says, "We believe that such an intricate, case-by-case sharing mechanism is needlessly complex and may well prove unmanageable."[59]

AN OVERVIEW OF THE ISSUES

In shaping its welfare proposal the Carter administration sought to include something for everyone. Nathan said jocularly, "It seemed like the President was told at the outset, 'you have three alternatives—incremental change, the triple track, and the negative income tax,' and on May 1 [1977] he said, 'fine, I'll take one of each,' but no extra money for welfare."[60] The administration's ultimate proposal reflects no coherent, overriding philosophy. What it lacks in purity it hopes to make up for in breadth of appeal. But that is a two-edged sword. While many found much to like in the proposal, they also found much to oppose.

A few who felt their vital interests were endangered struck back. The AFL-CIO, bitter over the minimum wages proposed for the jobs program, stated, "The proposal in its present form is unacceptable."[61] But many others followed the path chosen by the National Association of Counties, which wrote that it "supports the broad outlines"[62] of the proposal and then went on to indicate the elements it liked and disliked. Vernon Jordan, executive director of the National Urban League, called the Carter proposal a "preshrunk" plan because, he said, all the compromises had already been made.[63]

While potential opponents are muted, potential allies are also subdued. The leader of one liberal public interest group said, "It's hard to be for the bill since it doesn't really do anything; it just moves people around."[64] This attitude helped lower the amplitude of the debate, Lenkowsky noted: "Since there was clearly no liberal consensus behind the bill, the conservatives did not need to do anything."[65]

While many find it hard to take issue with the broad aims of the bill, there is surprising resentment against much of the plan's underlying tone. "It represents economists run amok," one Washington public interest group executive said, adding: "It seems to have been written in the belief that if you got all the benefits and incentives and disregards structured right, you had solved the puzzle. There is no sense of any human needs in the bill. It's too complicated for the real world."[66]

The range of issues swirling around the Carter proposal reflects both the complexity of the proposal and the diversity of opinions on welfare. Many of the seemingly technical issues, such as retrospective accounting, often dissolve into moral and philosophical questions, for one's view of eligibility standards is often heavily colored by one's view of how generous a welfare system ought to be.

Moreover, the debate is shaped by the longstanding and strongly held belief of several well-defined schools of thought. The welfare reform debate hardly started de novo in 1977, and the Carter proposal is measured not only against dearly held values but also against carefully constructed alternative plans.

While some issues are open to settlement on the basis of objective evidence, much of the debate revolves around differences in values. Many fundamental questions about the Carter proposal cannot be settled by evidence, but rather depend on the ability of political leaders to put together a political consensus and a legislative majority.

THE POLITICS OF WELFARE REFORM

In assessing and analyzing prospects for the Carter proposal it is tempting to compare it with President Nixon's Family Assistance Plan. There are both important similarities and differences in the environment faced by FAP and that faced by the Carter program which followed it eight years later.

Many of the same old conflicts remain: there is the same split between those who think the answer is "more" welfare and those who favor "less"; and important differences as to what it is that needs reform. Some want changes in benefit levels, others are concerned primarily with fiscal relief, or administrative complexity, or national uniformity. Some think work is integral and others consider it irrelevant. Thus, the paradox remains: there is consensus on a need for change but no agreement on the nature of change.

There have been some important developments since Richard Nixon offered FAP. Above all, the passion that once enveloped welfare reform has ebbed. One soothing development was the passing of Richard Nixon from the issue, for he aroused liberal ire on a wide range of issues. In addition, the memories of civil disorders have largely faded, so the Carter proposal is not caught up in the symbolism that transformed FAP into a vote for or against rioting in the eyes of some. Liberal demands for higher benefits have become muted as no nationally recognized spokesman for welfare recipients emerged after the death of George Wiley of the National Welfare Rights Organization. Liberals have also become more receptive to work requirements.

Perhaps the most important calming force in welfare is the end of increases in welfare rolls. In retrospect it is clear that during the 1960s the nation's cities encountered major increases in welfare recipients because those who already had been eligible were beginning to seek benefits. By the early 1970s, that process had been completed, and welfare had slowed its growth. In New York City, the welfare rolls fell to an eight-year low in January 1978 after peaking in 1972. By the late 1970s, many state and local officials find their major concern is the dramatic rise in Medicaid costs, which exceed welfare costs in many local budgets. As a result of these changes, welfare reform does not summon as much thunder as it once did. Frank Raines of the White House staff says of the PBJI, "It's being dealt with as a normal legislative proposal—nothing more."[67]

For most congressmen there is no political mileage in welfare reform. "The people who receive welfare neither vote not contribute to campaigns," one congressional staff member noted.[68] But those who do vote and contribute are ambivalent about welfare, polls show. As Chester Finn of Senator Moynihan's staff says, "There is no reaction in the street, and not much editorial reaction."[69] There are not that many people on Capitol Hill who care very deeply if welfare is reformed or not, and most of the Congress prefers to stay clear of the issue.

"What this means is that welfare reform is something that wouldn't go through the House without a big Presidential push," notes Robert Harris, a vice president of the Urban Institute and former executive director of President Lyndon Johnson's Commission on Income Maintenance Programs.[70] A congressman is likely to take some initiative or go out on a limb for welfare reform only if offered a presidential stick or a carrot for doing so. Consequently, former Representative Glenn Beall wrote in early 1977 that the reform of welfare would depend on "the effectivness with which the Administration can bring the presently unaligned forces together in support of the President's plan."[71] What sort of leadership has the administration offered on welfare reform?

In developing its proposal, many complimented the administration for its openness in discussing alternatives. This openness meant there were few surprises when the proposal emerged, and few who felt they had not been consulted. However, this process also forced some people to state their positions before they knew the president's intentions; thus, if the president's plan didn't follow their suggestions, they felt constrained to oppose the White House. On August 2, 1977, for example, House Ways and Means Committee Chairman Al Ullman stated his objections to giving the working poor supplements based on family size; and when Carter came out with a plan that ignored that only four days later, Ullman went on to develop his own alternative reform proposal.

The openness of the process also provided fuel for the administration's critics when the White House was unable to meet it self-imposed deadline in completing the plan, and when earlier versions of the proposal were compared with what finally emerged. Most notably, the final proposal's benefit levels were lower than those contained in a semifinal version.

The major criticisms of the administration, however, were reserved for its handling of the proposal when it was made public. Many observers felt the administration did a poor job of explaining its proposal to the public, a prerequisite for mustering support and disarming potential critics. There were reports of problems in communications between the offices of the HEW assistant secretaries in charge of public affairs and of planning and evaluation. As a result, perhaps there was not enough simple explanatory material prepared on this terribly complicated proposal.

Moreover, those at HEW who had to explain this proposal to potential allies were often faulted for not making things clear. Largely drawn from academic or research organizations, they not only failed to simplify complicated programs; they also seemed to insinuate at some meetings that if the proposal seemed unclear the fault lay with the listener, not with HEW.

The same kinds of problems were raised in dealing with the Congress. The Carter administration has frequently been criticized for its handling of the Congress, and H.R. 9030 was seen as another instance of this weakness. Once again a major complaint was the failure to provide the kind of information needed to bolster support for the welfare proposal. "The style was all wrong," one congressional staff member noted: "Congressmen need to be given particular examples of how something affects their constituents, and all HEW talked about was norms and medians and national averages."[72]

While some faulted the administration for not bargaining more vigorously to line up support for H.R. 9030, others were concerned about failures on a symbolic level. Neither Secretaries Califano nor Marshall showed up at the first day of the House Welfare Reform Subcommittee's markup of the bill. And President Carter seemed to step back from his bill in a comment at a November 1977 press conference and in a year-end interview with James Reston.

It is clear the welfare reform bill faces a particularly arduous journey. It came at a time when the administration was sending Congress a number of other complex and controversial bills, including those on energy policy and social security financing. The welfare reform proposal not only affects 40 million Americans as potential recipients and everyone as taxpayers, it also contains provisions which require it to go before three committees in the House and two in the Senate. It faced scrutiny by Representative Ullman and Senator Long, each of whom has his own ideas about welfare.

Few bills could emerge from the arduous process facing H.R. 9030 without changes, particularly something as complex and controversial as welfare reform. The process Jimmy Carter set in motion with his speech in Plains, Georgia on August 6, 1977 is likely to evolve in a direction few would care to predict.

NOTES

1. The text of President Carter's welfare message to Congress may be found in the New York *Times*, August 7, 1977, p. 40.

2. Report of the 1977 Welfare Reform Study, (Washington, D.C.: Department of Health, Education, and Welfare, May 1977), p. 1.

3. "Carter Outlines Welfare-Overhaul Plan Needing No Added U.S. Spending at First," *Wall Street Journal*, May 3, 1977.

4. Interview with the author.

5. Interview with the author.

6. David E. Rosenbaum, "Carter Reaffirms Welfare Ceiling Despite Warnings, New York *Times*, May 27, 1977, p. A11.

7. Interview with the author.

8. Rufus E. Miles, Jr., "The Carter Welfare Reform Plan: An Administrative Critique," (Princeton, N.J., unpublished paper, December 1977), preface.

9. This sentence appears in Statement of Ray Marshall, Secretary of Labor, U.S. Department of Labor, before the Welfare Reform Subcommittee of the House Agriculture, Education and Labor, and Ways and Means Committees, September 19, 1977, p. 10; and Statement of Arnold H. Packer, Assistant Secretary for Policy, Evaluation and Research, U.S. Department of Labor, before the Intergovernmental Relations and Human Resources Subcommittee of the Committee on Government Operations, U.S. House of Representatives, September 27, 1977, p. 13.

10. Statement of Ray Marshall, September 19, 1977, op. cit., p. 7.

11. Statement of Arnold H. Packer, September 27, 1977, op. cit., p. 12.

12. Statement by Joseph A. Califano, Jr., Secretary of Health, Education, and Welfare before the Subcommittee on Welfare Reform, House of Representatives, September 19, 1977, p. 9.

13. Henry Aaron, "Reforming Welfare," New York *Times*, December 12, 1977, p. 35.

14. Richard P. Nathan, Testimony before the House Welfare Reform Subcommittee, October 12, 1977, p. 1; see also Richard P. Nathan, "For an Incremental Approach to the Problems of Welfare Reform," New York *Times*, November 4, 1977.

15. Richard P. Nathan, "The Case for Incrementalism," *City Almanac*, 2, no. 4 (December 1976).

16. Interview with the author.

17. "Comprehensive Reform vs Incrementalism, an exchange of views between Richard P. Nathan and John L. Palmer," *The Journal of the Institute for Socioeconomic Studies*, 2, no. 2 (Spring 1977), p. 6.

18. Interview with the author.

19. Testimony of Ronald H. Brown, Deputy Executive Director, National Urban League, Inc., before the Welfare Reform Subcommittee of the Committee on Agriculture, Committee on Education and Labor, Committee on Ways and Means on The Impact of Welfare Reform, October 31, 1977, p. 2.

20. Martin Hochbaum, "An Analysis of President Carter's Welfare Reform Proposals," Commission on Law, Social Action and Urban Affairs, American Jewish Congress, New York, October 1977, p. 10.

21. Testimony of Ronald H. Brown, October 31, 1977, op. cit., p. 12.

22. Robert J. Fersh, "Staff Analysis: Program for Better Jobs and Income," Washington, D.C.: American Public Welfare Association, November 10, 1977, p. 28.

23. Interviews with the author.

24. Fersh, op. cit., p. 1.

25. "Administration's Welfare Reform Plan," Center on Social Welfare Policy and Law (New York: August 23, 1977, revised September 2, 1977), p. 25.

26. Fersh, op. cit., p. 4.

27. Miles, op. cit., pp. 4, 59.

28. James W. Singer, "The Welfare Package—1.4 Million Jobs, 1.4 Million Questions," *National Journal* (November 12, 1977) p. 1764.

29. "Work, Welfare and the Sugar Coating," New York *Times*, May 13, 1977, p. A26.

30. "Working to Reform Welfare," *Time*, August 15, 1977, p. 9.

31. Testimony of Ronald H. Brown, October 31, 1977, op. cit., p. 2.

32. Elliott Currie, "A Piece of Complicated Gimmickry," *The Nation*, September 17, 1977, p. 232.

33. Testimony of Ronald H. Brown, op. cit., p. 8.

34. Interview with the author.

35. Quoted in James W. Singer, "The Welfare Package," op. cit., p. 1764.

36. Interview with the author.

37. Statement of Bert Seidman, Director, Department of Social Security, AFL–CIO, before the Welfare Reform Subcommittee of the House Committees on Agriculture, Education, and Labor, and Ways and Means, November 3, 1977, p. 9.

38. Ibid., p. 13.

39. Currie, op. cit., p. 13.

40. Statement of Bert Seidman, November 3, 1977, op. cit., p. 2.

41. "Better Jobs and Income Act: H.R. 9030," Sacramento, California Health and Welfare Agency, October 31, 1977, p. 16. Hereafter cited as California Health and Welfare Agency.

42. Statement of Bert Seidman, op. cit., p. 2.

43. "Administration's Welfare Reform Plan," Center on Social Welfare Policy and Law, op. cit., p. 13.

44. Testimony by Governor Hugh L. Carey before the House Welfare Reform Subcommittee, October 31, 1977, p. 6.

45. California Health and Welfare Agency, p. 4.

46. Ibid., p. 5.

47. Statement of Bert Seidman, op. cit., p. 2.

48. California Health and Welfare Agency, p. 5.

49. Fersh, op. cit., p. 22.

50. "NACo Comments on the Administration's August 6 Welfare Reform Proposal," Washington, D.C., National Association of Counties, September 6, 1977, p. 3.

51. California Health and Welfare Agency, p. 13.

52. Governor Richard F. Kneip, Chairman of the Committee on Human Resources, National Governors' Association, Testimony before the Special Subcommittee on Welfare Reform, U.S. House of Representatives, October 31, 1977, p. 4.

53. Miles, op. cit., p. 48.

54. Statement by the Honorable Nicholas Carbone, Council President, Hartford, Connecticut, on behalf of the U.S. Conference of Mayors and National League of Cities before the House Subcommittee on Public Assistance and Unemployment Compensation of the Ways and Means Committee, November 1, 1977, p. 2.

55. Statement by Joseph A. Califano, Jr., September 19, 1977, op. cit., p. 10.

56. California Health and Welfare Agency, p. 21.

57. John P. Keith and Joseph M. Thomas, "The Impact of the Carter Welfare Reform Proposal," *The Journal of the Institute for Socioeconomic Studies*, 2, no. 4 (Autumn 1977), p. 72.

58. Judith Cummings, "Carter's Welfare Plan Is Criticized," New York *Times*, November 10, 1977, p. B22.

59. California Health and Welfare Agency, p. 6.

60. Interview with the author.

61. Statement of Bert Seidman, op. cit., p. 15.

62. "An Open Letter to President Jimmy Carter," *County News* (September 19, 1977), p. 4A. (*County News* is a publication of the National Association of Counties, Washington, D.C.).

63. Vernan E. Jordan, Jr., "Welfare Reform Plan Can Be Improved," New York, National Urban League, August 10, 1977. This essay appeared across the country in Jordan's syndicated newspaper column, "To be equal."

64. Interview with the author.

65. Interview with the author.

66. Interview with the author.

67. Interview with the author.

68. Interview with the author.

69. Interview with the author.

70. Interview with the author.

71. J. Glenn Beall, Jr., "Comprehensive Welfare Reform-Congressional Prospects," *The Journal of the Institute for Socioeconomic Studies*, 2, no. 2 (Spring 1977), p. 27.

72. Interview with the author.

APPENDIX B

ATTITUDES TOWARD PUBLIC WELFARE PROGRAMS AND RECIPIENTS IN THE UNITED STATES

Natalie Jaffe

A REVIEW OF PUBLIC
OPINION SURVEYS, 1935-76

A review of the opinion-survey literature since the 1930s relating to welfare programs and recipients shows a small amount of polling on this subject and, to the extent that data are available, they confirm legislative assumptions about voter attitudes.

The list of surveys is brief: 37 Gallup poll welfare questions in 41 years; a few Harris surveys in the past decade; two studies published in professional journals; two demographic analyses of a 1964 Gallup poll; and one extensive eight-state survey of a wide range of welfare-related attitudes sampled between 1970 and 1973.

The data illustrate the complexities and inconsistencies of American attitudes toward poverty, its causes and systems for amelioration. Still, one conclusion emerges: Americans draw a sharp distinction between persons who are poor and persons who are on welfare.

When they refer to the poor, Americans apparently mean fellow citizens disabled by age or physical infirmity, hard-working but low-paid heads of families, the unemployed who are diligently looking for work and willing to take any job, and conscientious widows. Welfare recipients are viewed as unworthy. Several of the surveys shows, however, that efforts to correct myths about the welfare population can yield results in the form of more realistic attitudes. Everything depends on how an issue is presented or a question posed.

The policy implications of survey results show that the public is more likely to support programs that clearly distinguish between rehabilitation and maintenance, between employables and unemployables, between those considered capable of rehabilitation and the physically or socially disabled.

Favorable responses can be expected to program proposals to assist the potentially productive and responsible, but there is little evidence of potential support for assistance to those whose problems are viewed as irremediable or whose behavior can be defined as antisocial. Since both groups would be covered in any universal income support plan, acceptance of such a plan—according to the evidence of the polls—should not be expected.

GENERAL ATTITUDES TOWARD PUBLIC WELFARE

More than three-quarters of the respondents to a Harris survey of June 1976 felt that "the problem of welfare in this country is very serious" and should be a priority issue for the next president. Welfare ranked tenth on a list of 29 possible priorities, ahead of keeping military defenses strong, aid to education, controlling pollution and violence, federal gun control, and legalized abortion.

A Harris survey of July 1976 showed a majority of respondents feeling that welfare spending could be cut by one-third without serious consequences; two-thirds favored protecting social security from any erosion; and a majority opposed cuts in federal expenditures for jobs for the unemployed.

This theme, which has characterized most survey responses over the years, is highlighted in a Harris survey of January 1973, in which two-thirds of the respondents favored an increase in spending to "help the poor," while an equal number was opposed to an increase in spending for "people on welfare."

Similarly, an eight-state survey of 9,346 adults by the University of Southern California's (USC's) Regional Research Institute in Social Welfare ranked social security first among a list of possible federal funding priorities; welfare services had a ranking ranging from third in California to eighth in New York; and financial assistance to welfare recipients ranked even lower: fifth in California; seventh in Georgia and Washington; eighth in Nebraska, Ohio, New Mexico, and Florida; and ninth in New York.[1]

The most recent Gallup polling of general attitudes toward welfare was conducted in November 1964, when slightly less than half the respondents described their overall feelings as favorable, and an equal number as "mixed," while 6 percent recommended "doing away with" the welfare program altogether.

In the same survey, a question was asked about the amount of money being spent on welfare and relief programs in "your area." One-third felt the amount was "about right," 20 percent felt it was too much, and 18 percent not enough. Two sociologists from the University of Georgia, with access to the data on distribution of responses in this poll, found, not unexpectedly, that persons expressing negative attitudes toward welfare recipients in general tended to feel expenditures were too high.[2] Respondents with the least education were in the "about right" group, while young respondents were more likely to feel expenditures were too low.

Although the eight-state USC survey was the only poll to include a question on basic responsibility for the welfare system, the response was substantial enough to be definitive. Ninety-three percent of the respondents favored some form of tax-supported program: 54 percent felt it should be at a decent level of living for all with a clear need demonstrated by compliance with stringent requirements; 22 percent opted for higher benefits and more comprehensiveness than are offered by the present program; 17 percent wanted programs restricted to a bare maintenance level, and only for the aged and disabled. Only 5 percent favored a return to a "charity" approach that would rely entirely on voluntary contributions.

The three-quarters who favored the less restrictive approaches to public welfare were asked whether they favored mandatory employment-oriented rehabilitation for all welfare recipients "who might benefit" (this category was not defined). Eighty-five percent favored tax-supported mandatory training. Even the 329 respondents who disapproved of government funding of welfare grants favored tax-supported mandatory training at the response rate of 73 percent.

The question of availability of jobs for those who want to work was answered variously in the eight states, ranging from the 67 percent of Californians who believed there are plenty of jobs, to 40 percent who thought so in the state of Washington. No doubt this difference reflects local employment conditions. Half of all respondents polled in 1972 and 1973 believed there were jobs for all who want to work. Unfortunately, only the 44 percent who believed jobs were scarce were asked their opinion of a government program to create full employment, and three-quarters of these more bearish respondents favored such a program.

Welfare and Employment

The approval of government-supported employment and employment-oriented training demonstrated in the eight-state study is reflected in every poll covered by this review.

In a Harris survey of October 1969, while less than half the respondents favored President Nixon's Family Assistance Plan proposals, four out of five agreed with the provision requiring every recipient to take a job or enter job training.

Gallup poll results have been consistent since 1937, when nearly 80 percent of those surveyed disapproved of cash relief as a substitute for the WPA. The following year, the percentage favoring work relief over cash assistance rose to 90 percent.

In August 1961, and November 1974, Gallup polled response to the following propositions: "If men on relief who are physically able to work cannot find jobs, then they must work for the City on streets, parks and the like"; and "All men on relief who are physically able to work must take any job offered which pays the going wage." Both proposals, in both years, received 84 percent favorable responses. Given the questions, even a higher percentage would not have been surprising.

Gallup polls in September 1965, June 1968, and December 1968 sought opinions on guaranteeing families a minimum income. While a majority were against such a program, opposition to it dropped in poll responses from 67 percent in 1965 to 50 percent during the 1968 presidential campaign and rose again to 62 percent after the election. But an accompanying query on guaranteeing work in an amount worth $3,200 a year met with a nearly 80 percent favorable response in both election-year polls.

When interpreted in the light of other poll results, it seems clear that opposition to a guaranteed-income plan stems primarily from its lack of built-in requirements for monitoring of cases and rehabilitation of recipients.

Strong support for a supplementary income program for the working poor was demonstrated in the eight-state USC study. More than 85 percent approved financial assistance to the poor who work but cannot satisfy their basic needs, and a majority disapproved public welfare for the unemployed poor.

Respondents who opposed welfare for the chronically unemployed changed their view when they were told who these people were; upon being informed that most of them are "either blind, permanently disabled, mothers with very young children, or individuals unable to meet employment requirements for other, similar reasons," more than three out of four of the previously negative respondents changed their opinion. Even the 875 respondents opposed to assisting the employed poor changed their responses at a rate of 60 percent when informed that the poor in this category "are employed to the extent of their ability and work as hard as possible, but are still unable to satisfy their family's basic needs."

Attitudes toward Welfare Recipients and the Concept of the Deserving Poor

The eight-state survey mentioned earlier polled respondents in the least-weighted way possible, by presenting them with a list of 25 phrases to be ranked as attributes of poor people and welfare recipients. In analyzing the responses and their frequency, the USC researchers concluded that the emerging evaluations tended to be "no more negative than positive" in the case of welfare recipients, and "in a slightly more positive direction" in the case of the poor in general.

However, it is clear and significant that negative attitudes toward welfare recipients are much stronger. For example, the phrase "deserve to be helped" was the fourth most frequent comment on poor people, but failed to make the top ten attributes selected for welfare recipients. The comment "work whenever they can find employment" was chosen as an attribute of the poor but not of welfare recipients, while "often have skills and talent they are wasting" was on the welfare list only. "Unmarried mothers who have many children," not unexpectedly, appeared exlusively on the list of attributes of welfare recipients.

All the surveys illustrate the tenacity with which the public believes that women continue to have illegitimate children in large numbers while they are on welfare. In addition to the USC survey, evidence related to this exists in two

Gallup polls, done in August 1961 and November 1974. In answer to a question about what should be done with women who continue to have illegitimate children and get additional funds for each new child, only 10 percent in both surveys favored continuing aid. Other options included terminating aid, forcing the mother to work as a condition for continuing aid, institutionalization of the mother, and sterilization. The question itself was worded so as to imply that the phenomenon was a well-known fact.

Another revealing group of responses to USC survey questions related to different categories and circumstances under which financial assistance and welfare services should be provided. Four out of five respondents would spend "however much is necessary" to help welfare children become productive adults. But in response to the question, "Would you continue to agree if you were told that providing support for children often meant providing support for their unproductive parents?" only half would approve continuing support.

The point is dramatized by responses to a question about whether or not AFDC would be a "good use of public funds" in the case of assistance to a conscientious widow with three young children. Four out of five approved this use of public funds. However, approval declined to half the respondents when the mother was defined as "not working" and the father as "not present," and to 15 percent when the mother was described in terms implying that she was lazy.

The overwhelming support for financial aid and services for children exists, then, as an ideal in a vacuum, vulnerable to opinions about whether the parents or guardians are deserving.

Public perceptions of the honesty of welfare recipients was the subject of only one Gallup poll, in November 1964, when about two-thirds of the respondents were of the opinion that either most or some recipients are on welfare for dishonest reasons. The University of Georgia researchers mentioned previously found that this opinion was held by two-thirds of those who were relatively more positive about welfare recipients.

Perceptions of the responsibility for poverty are mixed, as documented in another Gallup poll of November 1964. When asked to place the blame for a person's poverty on his own lack of effort, on circumstances beyond his control, or on both, the responses were evenly divided into a third for each position.

Among the negative respondents, the Georgia study found a preponderance of better-educated persons, lower-status white-collar workers, and farmers. Among the more positive were younger respondents, persons over the age of 50, skilled and blue-collar workers, and professionals. Those with negative responses to this question also tended to feel that too much money is being spent on welfare and that some or most welfare recipients are dishonest.

A demographic analysis of the same Gallup poll by Ernest H. Wohlenberg of Indiana University disclosed that the most positive responses came from New England and the West North Central region; the most negative from South Central and Western states.[3] Viewing existing welfare policies in relation to the distribution of responses, Wohlenberg concluded that "the higher the proportion of respondents in a given region who express negative feelings about the poor, the more restrictive are the welfare eligibility standards; the more the 'deserving poor' are favored; the lower the grants in relation to cost of living; and the lower the composite poverty index."

The complex of attitudes toward persons on welfare is digested in the results of two surveys posing similar questions. The first, by Joe R. Feagin of the University of Texas at Austin, was conducted in 1969 under a grant from the National Institute of Mental Health.[4] In his nationwide sample of 1,107 persons, a plurality of respondents took a negative position toward persons on welfare on six out of seven characterizing phrases. On four items, a majority were anti-welfare.

The majority agreed that too many people receiving welfare should be working, that many people on welfare are not honest about their need, that many women on welfare are having illegitimate babies to increase the money they get, and that we are spending too much money on welfare in this country.

In addition, a plurality disagreed that most welfare recipients seek work for self-support, and agreed that "a lot" of people move their residence in order to increase their welfare grants. As for whether welfare allowances are adequate, the responses were about evenly divided, with an unusually large 18 percent of respondents uncertain on this issue.

The second study—of attitudes toward welfare among a sample of 300 black women and 300 white women in Baltimore in 1971—yielded similar responses to a similar group of questions.[5] The black and white groups agreed in their negative perceptions, with several exceptions: three-quarters of the black women agreed that too many welfare recipients spend their grants on liquor, while only slightly more than half the white women agreed with this charge. Only one-third of the white women believed that most welfare clients try to find jobs, while nearly half the black women believed this about people on welfare.

The Baltimore study included an additional question about women with illegitimate children, with interesting results: 80 percent of the respondents agreed that welfare should be given to a mother with illegitimate children, but when asked whether welfare mothers "are having illegitimate kids to increase the money they get," half the respondents agreed.

Attitudes toward Welfare Services

Respondents in the eight-state USC survey overwhelmingly preferred to emphasize welfare services over financial assistance to welfare recipients. When given a choice between increasing grants or services, each at the expense of the other, three-quarters of the respondents preferred increasing services even if it meant reducing grants. In every state, services were favored over cash support by at least four to one.

A majority of respondents in six of the eight states supported the universal availability of services on a sliding-fee scale, and two-thirds disapproved of delivery of services by private rather than governmental agencies.

The USC study also found overwhelming support for most of the major public social services now being provided. In rank order of priority, these are medical care, foster-home care, protective services, adoption service, emergency assistance, day care, employment assistance, home care, mental health and family planning—all of which were defined as a good use of public funds by more than 60 percent of the respondents.

Services receiving priority votes by fewer than half the respondents were (in descending order) family preservation, money management, information and referral, suicide prevention, and abortion counseling (the only service perceived as a poor use of public funds).

The picture is consistent with other survey results, demonstrating public support for medical care and services to children even before employment assistance, as well as the failure to perceive that services to families are related to the protection and nurture of children.

When each of the services was described to a respondent with examples, support varied only slightly in response to the perceived merit of the recipient's claim, with the exception of the AFDC example discussed above, an emergency-assistance example, and a mental-health service case. When the causes of difficulty are attributed to individual or family-management deficiencies, or when the cause appears hopeless, respondents were less favorably inclined toward providing services.

CONCLUSION

Although this reviewer takes a less sanguine view of attitudes measured by the USC study than do the authors of the interpretive material, their conclusion from months of studying results of the most extensive survey of welfare attitudes ever undertaken is convincing:

> Public opinions about welfare in this nationwide sample follow a broad distribution. The continuum may begin with 'let each take care of himself and get the federal government out of the picture' to the other end of the continuum which reflects a desire to equalize opportunities for all and facilitate the pathway for each to realize her own potential. If there were a way to distribute respondents' values about welfare as an overlay on a national distribution of political values, the two distributions would probably make a good fit at a similar point in time.

> The policy implication which stems from the distribution of responses on welfare issues follows other patterns of value expressions in this country. When the majority 50-60% fall into a middle range with mixed opinions, there is unlikely acceptance (for any length of time) of welfare policy which falls at either extreme.

The mixed 60 percent middle range of values, attitudes and opinions about welfare issues may not dominate the formulation of policy but in the longer run will most likely determine its acceptance.[6]

NOTES

1. Regional Research Institute in Social Welfare, *Welfare Concepts and Welfare Services: Results of an Opinion Poll of Public Attitudes* (Los Angeles: School of Social Work, University of Southern California, December 1973).

2. Jon P. Alston and K. Imogene Dean, "Sociological Factors Associated with Attitudes Toward Welfare Recipients and the Causes of Poverty," *Social Service Review* 46, no. 1 (March 1972).

3. Ernest H. Wohlenberg, "A Regional Approach to Public Attitudes and Public Assistance," *Social Service Review* 50, no. 3 (September 1976).

4. Joe R. Feagin, "America's Welfare Stereotypes," *Social Science Quarterly* 42, no. 4 (March 1972).

5. David J. Kallen and Dorothy Miller, "Public Attitudes Toward Welfare," *Social Work* 16, no. 3 (July 1971).

6. Regional Research Institute in Social Welfare, op. cit.

APPENDIX C

SUMMARIES OF A SERIES OF WELFARE POLICY PAPERS

WHOSE OX WOULD BE HEALED? THE FINANCIAL EFFECTS OF FEDERALIZATION OF WELFARE

Edward Hamilton
Francine Rabinowitz

SUMMARY

There is a tendency today to view welfare federalization as primarily an instrument of general fiscal relief for states and cities. This tendency is nourished by trends in intergovernmental finance. Welfare has been one of the three fastest-growing categories of state and local spending since 1955. It has also been a model of cost sharing among state, local, and national governments. This paper seeks to determine what states and localities would benefit most, and what ones the least, from the direct financial effects of federalization. It also speculates about the probable patterns of utilization of state and local resources freed by federalization and compares the effects of welfare federalization with that of other instruments of general fiscal relief, particularly general revenue sharing.

The definition of welfare used here includes Aid to Families with Dependent Children (AFDC), medical services for the poor and medically indigent (Medicaid), food stamps, Supplemental Security Income for the aged, the blind, and the disabled (SSI), and general assistance to those who have little income but are not eligible for aid under other programs. It was estimated that in 1977 combined federal, state, and local expenditures for these five programs would total some $43.5 billion, of which about $17.4 billion would come from state and local contributions. The paper assumes that federalization means that the national government would simply substitute its own resources for all nonfederal welfare funds now being supplied. This form of takeover, while unlikely to occur in fact, is a useful reference point for thinking about the effects of more likely but less simple variations such as an expanded share of financial support for existing programs short of 100 percent support, takeover of a single type of welfare activity, or establishment of uniform minimum federal benefit levels across the country.

JURISDICTIONS THAT WOULD BENEFIT DIRECTLY

The federal government spent some $33 billion in 1975 to support jointly financed welfare programs. Federal spending already accounts for about 60 percent of total expenditures in these programs. About 80 percent of all nonfederal welfare costs are now financed at the state level. Most of the remaining 20 percent is raised from county tax bases. Only where cities also serve as counties do municipalities make any substantial contribution.

Full federalization would have provided some $12 billion in fiscal relief in 1975 to all states and localities. The bulk of this relief would have been highly concentrated. Six state governments would have received almost $7.6 billion (California, Illinois, Massachusetts, Michigan, New York, and Pennsylvania). Localities within the six would receive another $2.26 billion. Consequently, these states would receive some 75 percent of total relief on the 1975 base. But these figures do not tell the full story. There are differences between the absolute dollar effects and the per capita effects. Such smaller states as Hawaii, Oklahoma, and Rhode Island would receive per capita relief of the same order as the larger states that receive the bulk of the dollars. The state-by-state pattern would deliver more dollar help to states with high per capita incomes and more percentage relief to lower-income states.

The key to these effects is which programs are federalized. Changes occur in the rank order of beneficiaries because the programs have grown at different rates and are applied in different proportions by different states. The key dollar question is what happens to Medicaid, the fastest-growing program. The partial action that would yield a pattern most different from simple federalization would be takeover of general assistance. The largest per capita spenders on general assistance include such states as Oklahoma, Ohio, and Vermont, which are not in the top ten for other programs.

If the 33 states that now require a local contribution to some aspect of welfare finance were to permit the local contributor to realize the full effects of simple federalization, more than $2.6 billion in fiscal relief would be granted to counties and cities. A major issue in the use of welfare as fiscal relief is the degree to which it would assist urban areas suffering from severe and long-term fiscal malaise. Relief to big cities and to counties that are cities would amount to some $1.3 billion. Aid to big cities would be heavily concentrated in six large urban cores (Baltimore, Denver, New York, Philadelphia, San Francisco, and Washington) which also serve as counties. They would receive some 80 percent of all relief given to big cities. Still, federalization would be of major fiscal help to these cities only on the assumption that the state governments permitted the cities to benefit fully from the relief. This is not a simple issue, for in each case the state has granted the city special taxing authority to correspond with the added obligation of welfare. There would be a case for removing this revenue source should the obligation disappear.

Federalization would also result in some $47 million in relief to 28 other large cities. Only in two would this amount to more than 5 percent of the municipal budget.

Urban counties other than those that consist of one city would receive $1.1 billion in relief. Twelve of the 20 largest recipients would be located in California and New York. Beneficiaries in other states would include the counties which contain all or parts of the cities of Minneapolis, Milwaukee, and Cleveland. Although each of the beneficiary cities except Denver is in serious fiscal trouble, the list would not give proportionate relief to such troubled city governments as Boston, St. Louis, or Detroit. Indeed, the pattern of relief would not show any strong correlations with per capita income or degree of fiscal/economic difficulties.

The Indirect Effects

Indirect effects involve projections on the basis of past history of what states might do with fiscal relief brought by federalization. At the outset it is not clear whether there would actually be any relief to distribute, at least in the early years. The pattern that followed the establishment of the fully federal SSI program to supplant federal/state benefits to the disabled, aged, and blind in 1974 may be suggestive. In this program, federalization produced increased federal spending of more than $2.3 billion per year and also an increase in state spending of more than $225 million. Thus, if welfare were federalized, much of the fiscal relief it is designed to bring to the states with high welfare benefits might well be taken up by state supplements to federal payments. Discounting the likelihood of state supplements, fiscal relief would probably accrue to states in inverse proportion to their propensity to spend their own resources on all public services, on welfare, and on aid to localities.

To the extent that federalization does generate relief, there will be many claimants. The relief that would accur to high-benefit states would likely be translated into aid to localities, and these states contain most of the big cities currently in fiscal distress. Yet these are also the states most likely to offset all relief through supplementation.

WELFARE FEDERALIZATION COMPARED WITH GENERAL REVENUE SHARING AS A VEHICLE FOR FISCAL RELIEF

The desire to use federalization as a fiscal device is in part related to the view that revenue sharing has produced distributive inequities. Revenue-sharing payments are allocated according to a formula emphasizing population, and take into account relative poverty and state and local tax effort. This formula results in a distribution quite different from what would emerge from simple federalization. Of the top ten states benefiting from federalization, only New York is among the top ten in per capita receipts from revenue sharing. Four states that would receive the least from federalization are, conversely, among the largest per capita beneficiaries of revenue sharing. Direct effects on the cities are also quite different. Revenue sharing delivers much-needed funds to cities in fiscal trouble and also subsidies to suburbs that are in substantially better fiscal shape, while welfare federalization would be very useful mainly to the six city/counties, but provide small direct benefits to the rest of the cities.

The Tests of Federalization as Fiscal Relief

To the degree that welfare federalization seeks to provide fiscal relief, it must be designed to yield benefits that will extend over time to recipients likely to be in fiscal straits. There is debate currently about whether the severe state/ local fiscal distress experienced during the last five years represents a short-term aberration or a chronic imbalance. Even if the prevailing optimistic projections for the fiscal health of the state/local sector are accurate, there is little doubt that some states, localities, and regions will not be able to balance revenues and responsibilities. Since simple federalization—federal takeover of current state/ local obligations with no controls on subsequent state actions—will not by itself bring substantial relief to most places, any federalization proposal should consider mechanisms that provide a high enough level of federally financed benefits so that the high-benefit states will actually realize substantial relief; contain inducements for the states to pass through, to their fiscally afflicted cities who do not get direct benefits, part or all of the relief the states receive; prevent states from reducing existing state subventions to afflicted cities helped by federalization; ensure that the fiscal effect of welfare federalization will not be nullified by cuts in existing subsidies; and discourage the use of fiscal relief for new services or salary increases. Once these mechanisms are in place, a hard look will need to be taken at whether this federalization plan is the most efficient transfer mechanism to move resources to the fiscally strapped cities, or a feasible competing approach exists without so many possible points of slippage. Given the complexities of designing, enacting, and implementing a welfare federalization scheme as a device to effect fiscal relief, our preference would be to see federalization enacted as a matter of social justice, with adjustments in revenue sharing, block grants, and categorical grants, and with whatever additional devices might be appropriate to deal with the prevailing fiscal problem of the cities.

WORK AND WELFARE IN THE 1970s

Sar Levitan

SUMMARY

The public's changing views of AFDC recipients over the past 15 years have spurred a series of federal work and training programs aimed at relieving AFDC caseloads. These efforts have included working off relief, rehabilitation through social services, comprehensive training, job creation, and strict work requirements. The frequent changes in emphasis have reflected the frustration of dealing with ill-defined issues. Inevitably, there has been an evolution from early optimism to skepticism about the government's ability to effect reform.

Seeking a scapegoat for the limited success of workfare programs in solving welfare problems, the blame has been placed on the alleged laziness of recipients and bureaucratic bungling. In fact, a more critical determinant appears to be the limited extent to which the welfare population can find a niche in the labor market. This perspective has been ignored all too often by policymakers and evaluators.

Employability is a complex balance of economic, social, and psychological factors, and attempts at precise measurement must be inconclusive. However, it is clear that welfare recpients' employability hinges not only on their motivation, but on the state of the labor market and the characteristics of the welfare population. Although the weight of the evidence suggests that welfare recipients' commitment to the work ethic is no less strong than that of nonrecipients, an examination of recipients' characteristics suggests that, for many public assistance clients, achieving full independence is an unrealistic goal. With suitable training, supportive services, job opportunities, and work incentives, many more welfare recipients could work and earn money. But these earnings could in most cases only supplement, and perhaps partially substitute for, public assistance— not completely replace it.

On the supply side, employability is usually associated with work experience, education, race, and skills, and with the absence of health problems, child-care responsibilities and other barriers. In these areas, AFDC mothers and fathers are disadvantaged in comparison with the rest of the population.

On the demand side is the fact that even in the best of times the labor market does not provide jobs with adequate incomes to millions who work diligently, not to mention those who remain unemployed. More than one-fourth of the 63 million wage-and-salary workers in May 1976 earned less than $3 an hour and about one-tenth earned less than $2.25 an hour. The usual jobs that AFDC recipients fill stand them in poor stead because they compete for work with millions to whom low wages and intermittent employment are a way of life. Moreover, the future growth prospects of these jobs—nationwide—are not good, and many AFDC recipients live in areas where the economy may be declining. What these extra dimensions of the problem imply, then, is that there is a great deal of middle ground between complete welfare dependency and a full-time job that returns an adequate income.

Against this backdrop of circumstances more complex than some officials seem to recognize, policymakers have advocated workfare measure perversely at odds with what conditions demand. Many workfare efforts are premised on the view that the public assistance population is a stagnant mass which can be chipped away, little by little, until its great bulk is reduced. In fact, turnover is considerable. Of the 3.4 million cases on the rolls in January 1975, 1.5 million were closed in that year. About one-fifth of these families were able to get off public assistance because of employment or increased earnings.

This would indicate that, for many at the margin of economic self-sufficiency, small changes can spell the difference between work and public assistance. Yet, in spite of the fact that for many the choice is not simply between work and welfare, the Work Incentive Program (WIN)—the federal government's main vehicle for increasing the economic self-sufficiency of welfare recipients—has been conducted with the single-minded purpose of getting recipients off public assistance completely.

The WIN program has been an expensive attempt to fit the problem to the solution. It has changed through the years ostensibly to improve its performance, but in fact to reflect public sentiment toward those on the dole. Throughout its frequent reformulations, the WIN program has carried a total price tag of more than $1.5 billion, including $300 million for 1976. When it started, WIN was labeled an "all-out effort to direct manpower and social welfare services to a common goal"—reducing welfare rolls through employment. But the administration soon grew disenchanted with expensive efforts to train or retrain welfare recipients. Instead of offering a rich diet of training, job placement, child care, and social and followup services for the few, WIN has moved increasingly to provide a meager portion for the many.

Although WIN officials parade impressive statistics on placements and welfare savings, the proper focus must be on what WIN accomplishes that would not otherwise occur. For example, the Labor Department claimed that more than 2 million persons participated in WIN during fiscal 1976, 675,000 received services to improve their employability, 211,000 found full-time unsubsidized jobs, and 20,000 more found part-time jobs; however, based on past experience, probably not more than one-third of these persons were able to leave the welfare rolls. Most evaluators have found that WIN's net benefits are small and that claims of welfare savings are highly optimistic.

Impatient with WIN's slow progress, the federal government and some states and localities have approached workfare from different angles, and with varying success. The federal government has moved to integrate WIN with other employment and training efforts and has also funded modest job creation programs. States have tried two additional, coercive methods: making welfare recipients work off their assistance, along the lines tried unsuccessfully in the early 1960s; and requiring AFDC recipients to search for jobs, a measure similar to work requirements for food stamp and unemployment insurance recipients.

Some basic conclusions to guide future policy emerge from an assessment of recent efforts to replace welfare with work and training programs:

1. Despite the multiple problems faced by AFDC recipients, they are not a distinctive, homogeneous population. There is considerable turnover within the welfare population, and recipients are no less committed to the work ethic than the rest of society.

2. Carrots are preferable to sticks in bringing about change. Limited employability brought most AFDC recipients to the public dole in the first place, and strict work requirements have only limited effect, especially when many other persons are unemployed. On the other hand, job creation, skill training, and real work incentives offer substantive help to recipients.

3. Real improvements will be costly. Job creation, skill training, and child care are effective, but expensive. Providing such services to a significant proportion of AFDC recipients will require a substantial commitment of resources. On a more limited scale are proposals to use public assistance funds to create jobs for welfare recipients. Simple arithmetic shows that additional funds will be needed to provide decent jobs (at $7,000 or so a year, plus perhaps another $1,000 for child care and other expenses) for persons currently receiving welfare (at $3,500 or so a year). Such jobs must provide enough after-tax earnings to increase recipients' spendable income—not just to allow them to work off their relief checks. There would be no shortage of willing takers for good jobs. And, although higher outlays are required, there is considerable public appeal in getting a year's worth of public service in return for $8,000 in wages instead of getting nothing in return for $3,500 in welfare.

4. Goals for public policy should be realistic. Because of high costs, it is not likely that society will commit billions upon billions of dollars for job creation and other programs. Accordingly, there is no escaping the conclusion that many AFDC recipients' earnings will do no more than supplement their welfare checks.

5. Stronger local ties between WIN, local employment service offices, and sponsors of employment and training programs could produce more efficient administration and operations. However, integration can accomplish little if adequate funding is not forthcoming. Going a step further, consolidating job search efforts under AFDC, food stamps, and unemployment compensation would also improve administrative efficiency.

Proposals to replace welfare with work may make appealing campaign slogans, but unrealistic expectations continue to breed a sense of futility. A realistic program would view workfare as complementing welfare—not focus on either work or welfare! Such a program would realize that in the foreseeable future millions of Americans will be among the working poor—even if they can find and keep steady jobs. For these people the work alternative will not magically pull them up over the poverty threshold.

Samuel Johnson enunciated the criterion that "a decent provision for the poor is the true test of civilization." To meet Johnson's test, public policy must recognize that for millions of needy Americans work and welfare go together.

THE DYNAMICS OF
WELFARE DEPENDENCY

David W. Lyon

SUMMARY

The objective of this paper is to draw upon available research in welfare dynamics to answer a set of specific questions regarding the use of public assistance—questions that are central to the design of alternative income maintenance systems. We take stock here of what we know and, by exclusion, what we don't know about the use of welfare.

First we look at length and pattern of dependency and answer the question, How is the caseload distributed between short-term and chronic users of welfare? Second, we describe the welfare decision and answer the following questions: What are the major factors that bring a family to turn to public assistance? What are the reasons a family leaves the rolls? What impact do program features have on the welfare decision? Third, we investigate levels and sources of income for welfare families and answer the question, How much income from nonwelfare sources do welfare recipients have over time? We assess the impact of job training and employment programs on the welfare decision and attempt to answer the question, What effect would work programs have on improving chances for nonsubsidized employment and reducing the welfare rolls? Finally, we look at the long-term effect of dependency on family behavior and discuss the implications of research on caseload dynamics for welfare reform.

Research on the dynamics of welfare dependency includes caseload forecasting for federal, state, and local government welfare agencies, experimental studies of work incentives and income guarantees, and studies of welfare families over time, identifying length of dependency, income sources, and impact of government programs on the welfare decision.

This review emphasizes research on the AFDC and general assistance programs, drawing upon analysis of caseload behavior at the local, state, and federal levels.

LENGTH OF DEPENDENCY

A key factor in length of welfare dependency is that the existing welfare system provides cash and in-kind benefits that greatly exceed incomes available from full-time employment in minimum wage jobs. At the same time, getting public assistance is not a permanent condition for a majority of families on the rolls; most cases stay on the rolls for less than three years and the average stay is between two and three years in duration.

Three types of caseload samples have been used to measure length of dependency: numbers on the rolls at a certain point in time; all cases ever on welfare; and first-time recipients (opening cohorts). Each gives a different profile of the duration of stay and has a different purpose for policy analysts: over 60 percent of cases on the rolls at a point in time are cases of long-term continuous dependency (three years or more); less than 10 percent over a six-year span will be long-term cases; and a third of all cases in an opening cohort will be long-term dependents. Therefore, before conclusions are drawm from studies of welfare dynamics, the characteristics of the caseload sample must be known.

In addition, patterns of welfare dependency suggest high levels of caseload turnover. Over half of the nearly one million cases on welfare in New York City from 1967 to 1972 were replacing cases that had been on the rolls but had moved out of welfare.

THE WELFARE DECISION

Following are some of the factors involved in the movement of families onto and off the welfare rolls.

Benefit Levels versus Wages. Findings support the alternative-income hypothesis: as benefit levels or benefit/wage ratios rise, case openings, applications, and welfare participation increase and employment rates decrease.

Benefit-Loss Rates. Higher benefit-loss rates result in less work effort; lower loss rates result in more work effort. Lower benefit-loss rates tend to result in more mothers (on AFDC) working rather than an increase in hours worked.

Policy variables like the benefit-loss rate are not likely to have much effect in moving families off the rolls. The mean employment rate—18 percent— is so low that large percentage changes in work effort do not change the fact that most AFDC mothers do not work.

Work incentives are likely to increase welfare costs because of higher administrative costs or higher benefits for mothers who already work. Lag in reporting income and caseworkers' discretion in counting deductible income result in lower benefit-loss rates.

Multiple Benefits. The AFDC grant is only 55 percent of the total income (welfare and nonwelfare) received by dependent families in New York City, Michigan, and California. Eighty-three percent of all AFDC cases in New York

City receive cash and in-kind benefits at a value higher than the poverty line, and 95 percent have multiple-benefit incomes (food stamps, Medicaid, shelter allowances, child care, nonwelfare income, and the basic AFDC grant) higher than that yielded by a full-time minimum wage job without government supplements.

Short-term cases have much higher levels of Medicaid-paid health care than long-term cases. Much of the movement onto welfare is caused by demand for health care not covered by private insurance plans. Welfare may mask a large number of families that are in need of low-cost health insurance rather than cash assistance.

Employment Opportunities. The job market has a measurable effect on the welfare decision in spite of widespread concern that public assistance is a system quite apart from the ups and downs of the national economy.

The explosion of the AFDC caseload during the 1960s, when the national economy was healthy, was related primarily to factors other than changes in employment opportunities.

Migration. Rather than being a direct reason for interregional migration, the welfare system enhances the attractiveness of regions with high wage levels, because it represents insurance in case a job is not available. But the primary factor in deciding where to migrate seems to be labor market conditions; differences in state AFDC benefit levels have only a minor influence on the relocation decision of poor families.

Family Composition and Desertion. Reform of the welfare system is not likely to reduce the trend toward nonwhite female-headed families, a trend that has far more complex origins than the availability of public assistance.

Attitudes Toward Dependency. Growth of the AFDC rolls during the 1960s was primarily the result of more people moving on the rolls and secondarily, of increased grant levels. More people were enrolled because more people found out about welfare's availability and because it was increasingly acceptable to be on welfare—both changes having been fostered by the welfare rights movement.

A similar change in attitude might greatly increase participation and caseload size for the AFDC–unemployed fathers program. Currently, in part because of sensitivities to income origin in this group, participation rates are low for this program.

Administrative Factors. Administrative discretion is an important factor in the constantly changing patterns of the AFDC caseload. The short-run forecasting of caseloads is confounded by sudden shifts in case openings and closings related to changing administrative procedures. However, it does not offset the evidence that welfare dependency is essentially an economic decision.

EMPLOYABILITY AND INCOME

What is the role of earnings from nonwelfare sources in the employability of welfare families?

• Employability is an elusive concept because objective measures do not fully reflect either the potential for or the motivation of welfare families for finding work.

• Far more families on the welfare rolls are employable and receive earnings from employment over periods of one or two years or more than is reflected in point-in-time samples of the caseload.

• The public cost of day care and related work expenses is so high for many welfare mothers that they may actually earn less than it takes to keep them employed.

• Earnings play a major role in the long-term income package of families who are on welfare at various times, even though earnings are less important in those times when welfare is received.

• There is little difference between the income package of female-headed families who have been on welfare and the package of those who have never been on welfare.

• The income and behavior of welfare families must be tracked over time to understand how welfare fits into an overall package of family income.

Employment and Training Programs

There is little evidence that job training and employment programs have been the source of the dynamic patterns uncovered in studies of the welfare population. Employment programs may, at best, decrease the level of public assistance payments while the duration of stay is unaffected.

Case Behavior and Length of Dependency

Welfare recipients may become used to dependency and more resistant to leaving the rolls, the longer they are on them. This phenomenon has been called the settling-in effect. If settling-in occurs, it could result in the need for a continuation of stringent work and income eligibility tests under any welfare reform option—from an incremental to a full guaranteed-income approach. However, there is no clear evidence on whether settling-in actually occurs and what, if any, policies are necessary to offset its effects.

Implications for Welfare Policy

It cannot be accurately predicted whether labor force withdrawal and/or work disincentives would be greater under a guaranteed-income plan than under AFDC. The impact of a guaranteed income can be only partially estimated from existing research on welfare dynamics.

In spite of the many inefficiencies and inequities in the current income support program, most families use the welfare system as intended—as a temporary source of income during periods of unemployment or other loss of normal income.

ADMINISTRATION OF PUBLIC WELFARE IN THE CASE OF AID TO FAMILIES WITH DEPENDENT CHILDREN

Abe Lavine

SUMMARY

Aid to Families with Dependent Children (AFDC), which in 1978 distributed nearly $10 billion in federal, state, and local funds to more than 11 million individuals—one in 20 Americans—was conceived in 1935 as something of a stepchild of the social security program.

Designed only to help children whose fathers were deceased or disabled, AFDC was thought by Depression-era planners to be effectively self-limiting, and even self-terminating in the wake of the 1939 expansion of social security to provide survivor benefits.

Since then, a variety of social and economic forces at work on the structure of society in general, and on the American family in particular, has created the burgeoning, costly AFDC program of today along with a dozen related—but not integrated—programs intended to meet needs not covered by AFDC: food stamps, medical assistance, social services, public housing, and the like. Each of these add-ons has its own eligibility criteria and administrative procedures, few of which mesh smoothly with the administration of AFDC.

Despite sporadically intense national debate on the need for reform, restructuring and/or replacement of the program throughout its four-decade history, AFDC remains an unwieldy hodgepodge of 54 individual state and territorial programs remarkably dissimilar in benefits and administration. Indeed, virtually the sole common denominator among the states in their administration of this ostensibly national program is the presence of federal reimbursement: about $5.5 billion of the $9.9 billion in benefits in 1978 flowed from the federal treasury to those 54 jurisdictions through the Department of Health, Education, and Welfare (HEW).

THE FEDERAL ROLE

Although federal law and regulations permit the states to take a laissez faire approach to determining benefit levels, earned income disregards, and other pivotal program features, Washington does insert itself strongly in the administrative trappings of the state-operated AFDC programs. With a massive array of statutory and regulatory language—no little of which has resulted from court actions—the federal government dictates the minutiae of the various state program practices: for example, the contents of the state plan of operation, the promptness of hearings for aggrieved AFDC recipients, the thoroughness of reports, and claims for federal reimbursement. Inevitably, many of the hundreds of federal statutory and regulatory prescriptions can appear, from the states' point of view, contradictory, unproductive, impractical, or disruptive of good administration.

Indicative of the federal bureaucracy's own view of its limited role in the AFDC system is that the bulk of HEW's central and regional office manpower is devoted to activities other than clear-cut assistance to the states in the management of the program.

HEW has at its disposal a number of oft-threatened, but seldom-deployed fiscal sanctions designed by the Congress to punish inadequate or illicit state program practices. These penalty mechanisms range from wholesale cutoff of federal AFDC reimbursement for wholesale violation of law or rules, to one-shot penalties of relatively small amounts for lesser infractions.

Attempts to Tighten Up

Short of substantive reform of the federal-state AFDC system, Congress and HEW have both sought material improvements in the program. Among these initiatives the following have been the principal ones.

The Workfare Approach. Enacted in various forms in 1962, 1964, 1967, and 1971—and now called the Work Incentive Program (WIN)—the workfare approach has effectively foundered on the hard realities of AFDC caseload characteristics and economic conditions. There are simply too few able-bodied AFDC recipients and too few jobs for placement to make much of an impact on caseload or expenditures. Moreover, the administrative cost of the WIN program and its predecessors has consistently exceeded demonstrable savings on the AFDC side of the ledger.

Find the Father. The find-the-father approach, enacted with singular lack of success in amendments adopted in 1950, 1965, and 1967, has been given new life in a 1974 statute embodying strong fiscal penalties for states failing to make every effort to track down absent parents and extract support payments to supplement or supplant AFDC benefits for the families they left behind. While four out of every five AFDC families have a living parent residing outside the home, it is too early to tell how many of these can be made to contribute to their families' support. An early indication: HEW believes only about $150 million in net AFDC savings might be expected annually by 1980.

Quality Control. First imposed on states via regulation in 1964—but never enforced until 1973—the concept of quality control (QC) is now high on HEW's agenda and has had a salutary effect on caseload error rates throughout the nation. Although temporarily enjoined by the courts from eliminating federal reimbursement of AFDC payments to ineligibles or overpayments exceeding arbitrary tolerance levels, the HEW QC initiative has caused states to decrease caseload error rates through tightened eligibility and recertification processes and through strengthened capability to monitor and upgrade caseworker performance. Withal, HEW estimates that errors are still costing the system as much as $1 billion yearly, indicating the scope of the problem the QC approach is intended to resolve.

Automated Data Processing. Since AFDC is essentially a disparate amalgam of individual state programs, state use of automated data processing (ADP) has developed unevenly and with wide variance in effectiveness. Compounding the confusion is the fact that most other income and service programs impacting on AFDC recipients have their own eligibility criteria, making it onerous, if not impossible, for states to integrate computerization within their own borders, let alone with that of neighboring states or the federal government. While HEW has established a technical assistance capacity to help states capitalize on the obvious advantages of ADP, Congress has yet to provide a fiscal incentive to prod states into energetic development of automated AFDC systems. Congress has, however, created such an incentive for the Medicaid program through 1972 legislation offering 90 percent reimbursement for startup costs and 75 percent matching of funds for operations of ADP systems.

THE STATE ROLE

Because states are free not only to set AFDC benefit levels but also to decide what kinds of families they will help (intact versus single-parent only), when they will help (in emergencies and/or for long-term need), and under what conditions (for example, what kind of work-related expenses might be disregarded, how much in assets an AFDC family can retain, at what point a deserting father is to be so deemed), the states' laws, regulations, and procedures are as varied as their geographies.

If any one characteristic can be seen as common to large numbers of state AFDC programs, it is the locus of front-line administrative responsibility. In 32 states, three territories, and the District of Columbia, with approximately half the national AFDC caseload, the program is operated at the state level. All other states supervise their counties—and in some cases, cities—as they operate the program.

Options

The foregoing observations lead to inevitable conclusions: AFDC isn't really a system, is far too complex from anyone's point of view, and is without a sense of direction.

Notwithstanding the pessimistic tone of these conclusions, it is more than probable that the time is opportune for a substantive change in the federal-state AFDC system. The enormously complex administrative problems of the AFDC program exist independently of what has come to be called welfare reform and should be treated as such.

The impetus for action on both programmatic and administrative reform may lie in the mounting fiscal crisis affecting state and local governments everywhere. If Washington opts to cope with that crisis via federal fiscal relief—which many states and localities are increasingly demanding of the Congress—a most obvious and available funnel for any new federal dollars will be human services programs, particularly welfare and health care, two salient components of most state budgets.

With any new federal AFDC dollars would come a commensurate tightening of federal strings and, inevitably, a reappraisal of the federal-state relationship, depending upon how greatly such funding is increased.

For example, there are many who demand immediate, full federal funding of the program, with federal administration to be phased in—a takeover that would offer maximum fiscal relief and relieve states of an enormous administrative burden. It is more likely that any move toward federalization of the AFDC program will take one of two courses, or a combination of them: a gradual increase in federal funding with increasing federal emphasis on bringing disparate state programs into closer harmony; a phasing in of federal administration (for example, starting with regional caseload data banks), giving the new program breathing room and time to make its inevitable mistakes here and there, rather than everywhere at once, as happened with the federal assumption of responsibility for the adults' assistance caseload in SSI.

All of this is not to say that the sole potential means of improvement in AFDC management lies in federalization of its costs and/or its operation. A variety of initiatives might be undertaken as prelude to, or in concert with, movement toward increased federal financial and management roles in the program.

Program Standards

The many variations on the AFDC theme could not exist if the Congress and HEW had, in the past, viewed the program to some coherent degree as national in its purposes, if not in its administration. Were Washington to move now to refocus its view of the program—as it must if any movement is made to increase federal AFDC financing—here are some incremental changes that might be made:

1. A uniform methodology—with regional minimums—could be enforced for use by states in arriving at needs and payment standards. Under this approach, which could be phased in over time, states could be led gradually toward payment standards more truly reflective of recipient needs rather than of political and fiscal pressures.
2. A standardization of earned and other income disregards could be achieved. Few aspects of the AFDC eligibility process are responsible for as much inequity or as many administrative problems and payment errors as is the question of how to treat and compute income and work-related expenses. Only Congress can ultimately settle this issue, but HEW could do much more, even without legislation, to regulate state practices in this critical area.
3. A standardization, again with regional variations, could be given to the treatment of assets and resources. Inequities and administrative complexities are inherent in the present system. Again, Congress must ultimately act—but HEW does have authority to make some sense of this issue.
4. Benefits for intact families with unemployed fathers (AFDC-U) and emergency assistance could be mandated in all states. The failure of 26 states to provide AFDC-U, and of 27 to offer even minimal emergency assistance benefits, amply illustrates one of the basic faults of the program—its failure to ensure that all state administrators have the same tools to cope with the same problems.
5. Other national program standards could be adopted for such critical matters as eligibility and payment determination, the definition of "continued absence" in assessing the responsibility of relatives, work obligations, and provision for consolidated grants.

State or Local Administration

Relevant to any discussion of federalization is the advisability of state administration of the AFDC program in those 18 states (with about half of the nation's caseload) wherein counties administer the program under state supervision.

State administration offers some obvious advantages over state supervision of county management of the program. Buckpassing, prevalent as it is in the federal-state relationship, is only compunded when local government is deeply in the picture. Mechanically, such improvements as development of effective computer systems are made much more difficult when the eligibility and recertification functions are handled locally rather than on a statewide level. In a fragmented system it is difficult for clients and taxpayers to know where to place the blame when services fall apart or taxes rise. And, if the direction is toward federalization, it will be easier to convert one state system than 50 county systems.

Management Improvement

Other critical aspects of AFDC administration concern procedural requirements, for example, the application process, eligibility determination and redetermination; relationships between income maintenance and social services; personnel standards, expecially qualifications of the data-intake worker; and data processing.

Should Congress and the administration decide to increase the federal share of AFDC costs toward a wholly federal program, steps toward developing national standards in these managerial areas would become more pressing.

Should that not occur, federal intrusion into these areas will be strongly resisted in most states. Given that circumstance, the federal role would most liikely be a combination of encouraging and helping states improve their management through consultation and dissemination of information; and using some form of quality control as a means of measuring administrative performance and inducing corrective action: possibly applying penalties, if legal issues are resolved, and/or incentives.

By and large, incentives for better state performance are punitive in nature—threatened withholding of all or a portion of federal funds for a state's failure to do one thing or another.

The states and the program would be far better served were Washington to develop many more positive goads to good performance such as upfront monies for AFDC automated data processing systems, bonus reimbursement for states coming in below the national norm for eligibility error rates, other bonus funds for installation of management improvements that have been proven effective in other states, technical assistance by HEW to those in the states actually running the AFDC program, and HEW funding of research and demonstration projects.

Until and unless Washington so reorients its thinking, federal-state programmatic relationships will ever be something of a catch-as-catch-can audit game which neither side can win.

Implicit in the foregoing options is the willingness of the states to make the most of a bad situation as they go about the job of running the AFDC program. Whether under federal, state, or local administration—pending more fundamental reform—a worker in Detroit (Wayne County), or in Essex County, New Jersey, will still be expected to consult a three-inch pile of regulations to help decide whether the applicant across the desk meets all the conditions for eligibility and none of the exceptions, and then to figure out whether the applicant is telling the truth.

MICROSIMULATION: A TECHNIQUE FOR MEASURING THE IMPACT OF FEDERAL INCOME ASSISTANCE PROGRAMS

Herman P. Miller
Roger A. Herriot

SUMMARY

There is a growing demand for information about the projected costs and distributional impact of both current and alternative federal income assistance programs.

Existing data—for the most part based on administrative records—tell us a good deal about those who receive payments under individual existing programs. With more comprehensive surveys of the population, we could even find out more about those who receive benefits from more than one program. But even the best data would tell us little about how the costs and distribution of benefits would change if new programs were added or existing ones modified.

The preparation of this information requires the use of an analytical technique such as microsimulation. Although this technique is still in the developmental stage, it is increasingly being used by the federal government to analyze tax and welfare programs. HEW and the Congressional Budget Office (CBO) are now actively involved in the development and use of microsimulation models for measuring the impact of economic and demographic changes on welfare caseloads and costs, and for simulating the impact of proposed changes in welfare programs on the poverty-prone population. While the microsimulation approach to estimating program costs and benefit distribution is basically sound and reasonable, administrators as well as policy analysts should be aware both of the problems inherent in the process and the steps necessary to increase its accuracy.

Microsimulation refers to a process whereby data collected from administrative records or from household surveys are adjusted to make up for response errors and other known deficiencies. These adjustments are often made by modifying the information reported by households so that in the aggregate it agrees with such preestablished control totals as current estimates of the population, of each type of aggregate income, of demographic characteristics, and of participants in and payments by various transfer programs. In the process, each individual record (the microrecord) may be changed and augmented with new information such as the value of nonmoney transfer payments.

By means of this technique it is possible to estimate the number and characteristics of families that currently receive benefits from various types of programs, the amount of benefits they receive from each program, and how those benefits would change if the programs were changed. The impact of program changes can be simulated by retabulating the information according to revised eligibility rules. At the aggregate level, this procedure permits us to analyze how the program costs would change under alternative assumptions about population growth, family formation, inflation, productivity, and other factors that affect overall expenditures for income maintenance programs.

Microsimulation is unique in trying to combine in a single model information about the demographic and economic characteristics of households, together with the impact of federal tax and income maintenance programs on those households under existing law. The model does this by first creating a data file which purports to show as realistically as possible how much each family would get—given its composition, place of residence, income, and other characteristics—from each program under existing rules. The model also makes it possible to estimate how much each family would receive if the rules were changed. This simulated information is combined with actual information (sometimes substantially different from what the families actually reported) about the amount of income the family actually received from earnings, property, and other nontransfer payments. The structure of the model also makes it possible to forecast what the income of families will be in the future, given assumptions about changing levels of unemployment, productivity, inflation, and other relevant economic variables. Given this information and these assumptions about the eligibility rules for each income maintenance program, it is possible to make estimates about the cost and distributional impact of alternative programs in the future. Although microsimulation deals with individual (micro) records, the objective is not to produce correct estimates for each person or family, but rather to produce more accurate estimates for various groups.

A microsimulation model called MATH, developed by the Mathematica Policy Research Group, is being used extensively by several government agencies, principally CBO, to analyze income maintenance programs. The MATH model, as employed by CBO, uses as its basic data file the Current Population Survey (CPS), in which individual records are first adjusted for underreporting of employment and income, and other known deficiencies, and are augmented with estimates of nonmoney transfer payments to which the individuals would be entitled under existing legislation. Three major operations are thus performed on the adjusted basic data file:

1. Sample weights for each person (indicating the number of persons in the total population represented by this CPS sample person) are modified to reflect

expected changes in the size and demographic characteristics of the population in future years. This adjustment makes it possible to measure the impact of demographic changes on the cost of income maintenance programs in the future.

2. Income data reported in the household survey are adjusted for under-reporting. This makes it possible to obtain a more realistic estimate of the number and characteristics of families eligible to participate in the various income maintenance programs.

3. The value of nonmoney transfer payments is imputed to individual households, based on the eligibility rules of each program and on the characteristics of the individual families. This adjustment makes it possible to prepare more complete estimates of the distributional impact of the income maintenance programs.

After the revised basic data file is created, new tabulations are made showing how the number and characteristics of recipients and the amounts paid would change if the programs were changed.

While the utility of the information briefly described above is obvious, it is not without serious limitations, including the following:

1. Any such model is only as good as the underlying assumptions and the underlying data. If the assumptions about the future are unrealistic—and past experience with other projection techniques shows that they often are—the results based on the model will differ sharply from reality. If large segments of the population are inadequately represented, if nonresponse rates are unreasonably high, and if income adjustments are excessive, the entire procedure, with all its sophistication, can produce misleading results.

2. In adjusting individual records to meet control totals, there is room for a good deal of error. For example, nearly all reports of nontransfer income are adjusted upward to meet control totals. Means-tested transfer payments actually reported by the individual household are discarded and, instead, payments are simulated on the basis of the characteristics of the household, and the eligibility rules of the state in which the household resides. In this process, there is danger that reasonably accurate information in many individual cases is being replaced with inaccurate information, partly because of errors in simulation, and partly because no computer program, however sophisticated, can accurately approximate the intricacies of the eligibility rules for welfare programs and how they are actually applied. In short, there is a danger that in attempting to correct some of the known deficiencies in the raw data, new and perhaps equally serious deficiencies are being created.

3. Even the relatively simple task of establishing control totals to which all other estimates are linked appears on close inspection to involve major complexities and to leave substantial room for error.

4. Some of the procedures for adjusting the survey data to the control

totals appear to be rather simplistic in light of the heavy burden they are expected to bear.

5. The assumptions underlying the imputation of nonmoney transfers to individual households is also questionable in some cases.

6. While the model is ingenious in its overall conception and the individual components have been developed with great care, it has not been systematically tested. This is a defect which can and should be remedied in the near future. All it takes is money. Some of the components of the model, such as the demographic-aging procedure and the employment and income adjustment procedures, should be applied to an early CPS file to see how well the current actual demographic profile of the population can be simulated. Such a test would provide one basis for appraising the overall soundness of the model.

7. The CPS, which now provides the basic data-file information used in MATH, was designed primarily for the collection of labor-force rather than income information. A new income survey, now being planned by HEW and the Census Bureau, would provide more timely, more detailed, and more accurate income data geared to the data needs of welfare programs. Moreover, in designing the new survey, active consideration is being given to the incorporation of information from administrative records. Such information, regularly collected, would do much to improve the reliability of the simulation model. It would reduce the need for adjusting survey responses and would improve the basis for doing so when required.

To conclude, our criticisms of some aspects of the basic procedures of microsimulation and of their application to the CBO project should not obscure our judgment that this approach to the measurement of the distributional impact of welfare programs and to the estimation of the cost of alternative welfare proposals is reasonable and basically sound.

Microsimulation can be a powerful tool for policy analysis, but only when we understand exactly how it works and are prepared to reject results when the procedures are farfetched, or to accept them—with the usual reservations that statistics are no substitute for judgment—when the procedures and assumptions are reasonable and have been subjected to adequate efforts at validation.

There is no escape from the use of microsimulation as an analytic technique today. It is not something to be for or against; rather, it is a process that must be understood in its operational details, buttressed by more reliable data, continuously improved as a technique, and accepted or rejected on the basis of the procedures and assumptions used by a particular model at a particular point in its evolution.

WELFARE AND VALUES IN AMERICA

William Lee Miller

Americans' disdain for welfare programs is caused by the clash between welfare policy and such cherished national values as self-reliance, competitive individualism, and the importance of work as a measure of one's worth.

These and other values that stress individualism are rooted in the American past, when there was a frontier, when daily experience gave strength to the notion of the survival of the fittest, when the family was a self-supporting economic unit and was perceived as an extension of the individual personality.

Despite vastly different conditions today, the traditional values have endured, largely because of the economic and political successes of the nation. Indeed, Americans feel generally that these values have been a major reason for the nation's successes in building a new society.

While the premium on self-help and self-reliance is validated by past experience, it has in more recent times tended to thwart collective measures, especially governmental efforts, for the general good or for distributive justice. Charity and generosity are important elements of the national value system, but mainly in the form of voluntary acts for needy people. Governmental intervention on behalf of the needy is often seen as coercive and as violating individual freedom.

Government welfare programs thus evolved piecemeal and often haphazardly. Aid for Families with Dependent Children (AFDC), for instance, began as a minor section of the original Social Security Act, which, in turn, was based on state programs providing help to widows with small children. Popular support for additional forms of governmental aid seemed conditioned on the general public's ability to identify or sympathize with the recipients, that is, widowed mothers, the blind, the disabled and, of course, the large numbers of families hurt by the Great Depression. In this last example, public assistance was seen as temporary relief.

The welfare program, designed over 40 years ago to serve one clientele, has since been stretched to cover another, with whom the general public has great difficulties identifying. There is the image of the welfare mother who has given birth to many illegitimate children and who seems thereby to make herself a permanent welfare recipient. Other critical factors are that the poor are a minority, and that a large segment of welfare recipients are nonwhite. The majority of Americans are not poor and are white. They have difficulty sympathizing with those who are poor and black. What is more, the identity problem works both ways: Many people on welfare find that some of the tenets of the dominant value system, such as planning ahead, frugality, or even cleanliness, are irrelevant to their condition.

The impact of these attitudes and value clashes may be seen in the public attitudes toward two distinct welfare programs: those for veterans and those for the AFDC poor. Americans support generous veterans' benefits because they represent justice for those who have risked their lives in defense of the nation, when, in fact, not all veterans took such risks. Welfare benefits, on the other hand, are usually seen as handouts, in many instances to chiselers, when, in fact, only a relatively small number of recipients may be taking unfair advantage of the system.

Changes in welfare policy still occur incrementally, and they result in programs that are often more efficiently run than the public believes. Nonetheless, fundamental changes to produce a more rational and humane welfare system await a change in values. Americans must become more accepting of the variety of cultures in the nation, more appreciative of the interdependence of people, and more understanding of the element of chance and of the impersonal collective forces that affect all of us.

ABOUT THE CONTRIBUTORS

LESTER M. SALAMON is deputy associate director for organization studies, Office of Management and Budget, President's Reorganization Project. While he was working on the project, Dr. Salamon served as Professor of Political Science and Policy Studies, and director of the Institute of Policy Sciences and Public Affairs at Duke University. He has acted as consultant to a number of government agencies and private institutions and is the author of numerous articles and books dealing with congressional policymaking, urban policy, economic development, and public administration.

HARVEY D. SHAPIRO is a writer and consultant living in New York City. He has been associated with the President's Commission on Income Maintenance Programs, the New York City Rand Institute, and the Ford Foundation. He has frequently written on social issues for the *New York Times Magazine* and other publications.

EDWARD K. HAMILTON is president, Hamilton-Rabinovitz, Inc., and Adjunct Professor of Public Management, Graduate School of Management, University of California at Los Angeles. Mr. Hamilton has been recognized for his professional achievements in local and national government, as well as for his articles and reports dealing with policy analysis and research on public issues and financial systems. He is former deputy mayor of the City of New York.

ROGER A. HERRIOT is an economic statistician with nine years' experience in the collection and analysis of income data from household surveys. He has authored publications on income statistics in various professional journals.

NATALIE JAFFE is a former newspaper reporter and director of public affairs, New York City Human Resources Administration. Ms. Jaffe has brought to the project many years of experience as a writer and consultant in the field of public welfare.

ABE LAVINE is executive vice president, Jewish Child Care Association of New York, and former commissioner of social services for the State of New York. Mr. Lavine has brought to the project 28 years of experience in senior management positions, which include key leadership roles in national organizations and responsibilities in the areas of policy planning, program management, labor relations, organization and systems analysis, and financial administration.

SAR A. LEVITAN has been Research Professor of Economics, and director of the Center for Social Policy Studies, at George Washington University since 1967. His career has combined research and teaching with government service centered in the fields of labor economics and social policy. Dr. Levitan is also chairman of the National Commission on Employment and Unemployment Statistics.

DAVID W. LYON is deputy vice president, Domestic Programs Division, The Rand Corporation. He was senior economist at Rand at the time of the project. Dr. Lyon's responsibilities over the years have included research activities in the areas of criminal justice, economic development, urban policy, housing, education, and population. His findings have resulted in many articles and books in the field of urban dynamics and welfare reform.

HERMAN P. MILLER, president, H. P. Miller, Inc., is an economic consultant with expertise in the area of population and income. A former high official with the Bureau of the Census and Adjunct Professor of Economics at Temple University, Dr. Miller has authored several books dealing with income distribution in America, as well as numerous technical articles in scientific journals.

WILLIAM LEE MILLER is director, Poynter Center, Indiana University, where he is also Professor of Political Science and Religious Studies. Author of the current book, *Yankee From Georgia: The Emergence of Jimmy Carter*, Dr. Miller has published many books and articles in the area of social ethics and political values.

FRANCINE RABINOVITZ is vice president of Hamilton-Rabinovitz, Inc., and Professor, Schools of Public Administration and Urban and Regional Planning, University of Southern California. Dr. Rabinovitz has conducted research and evaluations for organizations in the public and private sectors and for foreign governments. She is the author of over 25 articles and publications in the area of national and international urban policy.

WELFARE POLICY PROJECT
ADVISORY COMMITTEE

The identification of each member of the Advisory Committee relates to their affiliation at the time of their work on the Welfare Policy Project. Where changes have occurred, they are provided in parentheses.

JOHN T. DEMPSEY, Director, Michigan Department of Social Services, Lansing, Michigan.

MITCHELL I. GINSBERG, Dean, Columbia University School of Social Work, New York, New York.

TOM JOE, Consultant, Lewin & Associates, Inc., Washington, D.C.

SANFORD KRAVITZ, Dean, School of Social Welfare, State University of New York at Stoneybrook, Stoneybrook, New York.

JUANITA M. KREPS, Vice Chancellor, Duke University, Durham, North Carolina (now Secretary of Commerce, U.S. Department of Commerce, Washington, D.C.)

JOAN LEIMAN, Doctoral Candidate, Columbia University, New York, New York (now Project Manager, WIN Research Laboratories, Manpower Demonstration Research Corporation, New York, New York).

LEONARD LESSER, General Counsel, Center for Community Change, Washington, D.C.

STEVEN MINTER, Program Officer, The Cleveland Foundation, Cleveland, Ohio.

RICHARD P. NATHAN, Senior Fellow, The Brookings Institution, Washington, D.C.

BERT SEIDMAN, Director, Department of Social Security, AFL-CIO, Washington, D.C.

JULE SUGARMAN, Administrator, City of Atlanta, Atlanta, Georgia (now Vice Chariman, U.S. Civil Service Commission, Washington, D.C.)

ALAIR TOWNSEND, Senior Analyst for Human Resources Program, House Budget Committee, U.S. Congress, Washington, D.C.)

RELATED TITLES

Published by
Praeger Special Studies

*PUBLIC LAW AND PUBLIC POLICY

        John A. Gardiner

WELFARE POLICY MAKING AND CITY POLITICS

        Sharon Perlman Krefetz

EMPLOYMENT, INCOME, AND WELFARE IN THE RURAL
SOUTH

        Brian Rungeling, Lewis H. Smith,
        Vernon M. Briggs, Jr., and
        John F. Adams

INCOME INEQUALITY IN THE UNITED STATES:
Public Attitudes Towards Distributional Justice

        Richard T. Curtin

MINORITY ACCESS TO FEDERAL GRANTS-IN-AID:
The Gap Between Policy and Performance

        John Hope II

*Also available in paperback.

DATE DUE

MAY 2 '80			
OCT 28 '80			
NOV 1 5 1984			
APR 20 1987			
FEB 09 1988			
FEB 2 4 1988			
MAR 0 4 1988			